CAMBRIDGE STUDIES IN RUSSIAN LITERATURE

Bulgakov's last decade

CAMBRIDGE STUDIES IN RUSSIAN LITERATURE

General editor MALCOLM JONES

Bulgakov's last decade

The writer as hero

J. A. E. CURTIS

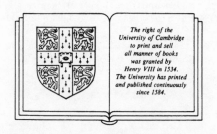

The right of the
University of Cambridge
to print and sell
all manner of books
was granted by
Henry VIII in 1534.
The University has printed
and published continuously
since 1584.

CAMBRIDGE UNIVERSITY PRESS

CAMBRIDGE

LONDON   NEW YORK   NEW ROCHELLE

MELBOURNE   SYDNEY

CAMBRIDGE UNIVERSITY PRESS
Cambridge, New York, Melbourne, Madrid, Cape Town, Singapore, São Paulo, Delhi

Cambridge University Press
The Edinburgh Building, Cambridge CB2 8RU, UK

Published in the United States of America by Cambridge University Press, New York

www.cambridge.org
Information on this title: www.cambridge.org/9780521106528

First published 1987
This digitally printed version 2009

A catalogue record for this publication is available from the British Library

Library of Congress Cataloguing in Publication data
Curtis, Julie.
Bulgakov's last decade: the writer as hero.
(Cambridge studies in Russian literature)
Bibliography.
Includes index.
1. Bulgakov, Mikhail Afanas´evich, 1891–1940 – Criticism
and interpretation. I. Title. II. Series.
PG3476.B78Z63   1987   891.78´4209   86-23323

ISBN 978-0-521-32671-1 hardback
ISBN 978-0-521-10652-8 paperback

To R. C. O.,
with love and with gratitude for
his deft midwifery and
unstinting support

Contents

Preface

The biography of Mikhail Bulgakov has been the object of a number of studies in the West as well as in the Soviet Union, and the present study assumes that the availability of these monographs renders it unnecessary to rehearse the story of his childhood and of the first part of his career as a writer. My purpose here is to draw attention to a distinct period in Bulgakov's writing, his last decade, and to suggest the many ways in which his intellectual preoccupation with the fate of literature spilled over into his fiction and even came to dominate it during the 1930s. Within the chronological limits set for this study, I have traced a pattern of gradual retreat in Bulgakov's treatment of the major theme of his writing throughout the period of the composition of *The Master and Margarita*, that of the writer and his relations with society. Official rejection of his biographical works on Molière and on Pushkin, and the frustration of his attempts to introduce Gogol as the lyrical narrator of his own literary creations, obliged Bulgakov increasingly to concentrate his views about the destiny of the writer in the purely fictional character of the Master, hero of a novel that looked unlikely to be published. In the last years of his life Bulgakov's concern at the constraints imposed on creative endeavour gave way to bitterness at the realization of his own defeat. None the less, within his last novel Bulgakov insists on the special status of the writer and of his creation; fulfilment is denied to the artist in the dimension of reality which *The Master and Margarita* presents, but on another plane, in an unorthodox after-life, their value is assured.

In adopting an interpretative rather than a biographical stance I am seeking to sketch a literary profile of the writer. The opportunities I have had to work in Soviet archives, and especially in Pushkinsky Dom and in the MKhAT Museum, have made it possible to draw on documentary materials to illuminate Bulgakov's working methods. Much of my study, therefore, is taken up with textual analysis on the basis of drafts, variants and other archival materials, and this is complemented by a survey of Bulgakov's handling of the sources he used for his works throughout this period.

The separate endeavours of Ellendea Proffer, Lesley Milne, Colin Wright, Peter Doyle and Lydia Yanovskaya have brought together a vast amount of information about Bulgakov's life and work. I am particularly happy to acknowledge also the importance for my study of the wide-ranging archival work of Marietta Chudakova, whose interest in Bulgakov's reading opened up many of the paths that I wanted to explore in order to show how the ways in which Bulgakov worked on his materials fitted in with the views he put forward about the functions of art and the role of the writer. The idea of approaching Bulgakov as an artist who can be related to the European Romantic tradition has been broached before, in the work of T. R. N. Edwards, although I have developed it in a rather different direction in my concluding chapter.

I should like to record my gratitude to the following for their help, advice and support: many friends and scholars in Moscow and Leningrad, including Bulgakov's second wife Lyubov' Yevgen'yevna Bulgakova-Belozerskaya; the staff of the Taylor Institution Slavonic Annexe, the Bodleian Library and St Antony's College, Oxford; staff at the Lenin Library, the MKhAT Museum and the Vserossiyskoye Teatral'noye Obshchestvo in Moscow, and at Pushkinsky Dom in Leningrad; Michael Shotton, Michael Nicholson, Lesley Milne, Peter Doyle and Colin Wright for help and suggestions provided at various stages of my research; the British Council, to whom I am indebted for supporting me on several research visits to the Soviet Union; my colleagues at the Department of Russian Studies at the University of Leeds for their generosity in allowing me enough time to complete this book; and my patient family, especially Mike Randall, who was just in time to help with the final version.

Leeds, 1986

Notes on the text

Translations

All the translations in the text are my own. I have given the original Russian alongside my prose translations for verse passages only; Russian and English titles have been given together for first references to works of fiction, but English titles have been used thereafter; titles of newspapers and journals have been transliterated but not translated.

Transliterations

The transliteration scheme used is based on that adopted for the *Slavonic and East European Review*. Where names have an accepted equivalent in English this has been used, except when there is a deliberate strangeness in the original; so 'Iyeshua' – but 'Pilate', 'Caiaphas', 'Eva', 'Kiev', etc.

Abbreviations

AN	Akademiya Nauk (Academy of Sciences)
ed. khr.	edinitsa khraneniya (archival item number)
F.	Fond (archive number)
NEP	Novaya Ekonomicheskaya Politika (New Economic Policy)
MKhAT	Moskovsky Khudozhestvenny Akademichesky Teatr (Moscow Arts Theatre)
RAPP	Rossiyskaya Assotsiyatsiya Proletarskikh Pisateley (Russian Association of Proletarian Writers)

1

The tempering of the steel

Drafts can never be destroyed. In poetry, in the plastic arts, and in art as a whole there is no such thing as a ready-made work.[1] Osip Mandel'shtam

We shall shortly be celebrating the twentieth anniversary of the arrival of a new master on the literary scene, an author whose reputation is still gathering momentum in the West, while today in the USSR he is frequently spoken of as the greatest prose writer of the Soviet era. The publication of the first complete text of *Master i Margarita* (*The Master and Margarita*) in 1973 after an earlier, partial publication in 1966–7 marked not so much the rehabilitation of Mikhail Bulgakov as his resurrection.[2] For his fate was not that of Mandel'shtam or Babel'; he was never accused of any crime, and he survived the Terror of the late 1930s to die in his bed of a hereditary disease in March 1940. This is not to say that his path had been an easy one, and the integrity of his writings has indeed quelled any doubts in the minds of those who initially wondered how he came to escape the fate of so many of his colleagues. He can now be ranked alongside Akhmatova and Pasternak as one of those writers who earned the dubious privilege of Stalin's respect, and whose tactical concessions to the ruler's vanity weigh as nothing when measured against their ardent championing of freedom and of art.

In Bulgakov's case, recognition of his full stature has been much delayed; for it was only some twenty-five years after his death that his widow Yelena Sergeyevna succeeded in fulfilling her vow to publish *The Master and Margarita*. She had until then kept the existence of the manuscript a close secret, and it was only a narrow circle of friends who were allowed to know of the novel's existence, let alone read it. For a long time it had looked as though Bulgakov, whose work as a playwright had surrounded his name with controversy throughout the 1920s, was destined to remain in the relative obscurity into which he lapsed during the 1930s. The publication of *The Master and Margarita* has reminded us just how important a place Bulgakov occupied in the literary and theatrical world of the 1920s before he was banished from the limelight; and it has caused us therefore to reassess the rest of his works, the majority of which were also not published in his lifetime. Equally, now that it has been established that Bulgakov was secretly engaged in the composition of *The Master and Margarita* throughout the last twelve years of his life, from 1928 to 1940, his other works dating from the same period begin to appear to us in a new light. Although virtually every work by Bulgakov written after 1929 met with official hostility and, more often than not, rejection, he never seems to have abandoned his attempts to be read or to be performed on stage. Perhaps his faith in the potential of his art was kept alive by the knowledge that he was, if only surreptitiously, engaged in other labour of major import.

The interest which the publication of *The Master and Margarita* aroused in Bulgakov's work has borne fruit over the last twenty years in a wide range of critical investigations of many aspects of his writing; and despite the restrictions which have been placed on access to his archives in the Soviet Union, a number of substantial studies have been published over the last ten years as documentary material has become available. The story of Bulgakov's life and a comprehensive account of the fate of his works has been provided in four biographical studies;[3] and we now await only further archival and documentary publications to fill some remaining gaps. Apart from this, there have also appeared a number of studies focussing exclusively on *The Master and Margarita*.[4] The aim of the present study is to continue the work of previous scholars both in illuminating aspects of Bulgakov's biography, and also in offering a new interpretation of *The Master and Margarita*; but to achieve this by adopting a different approach, which is at once less broadly biographical and at the same time less narrowly focussed on the one work. In considering the entire period during which *The Master and Margarita* was being composed, I shall hope to show how the majority of his other works of the same period are bound up with the central theme of *The Master and Margarita*, that of the creator and his art. It is clear, moreover, that this is no coincidence; from 1928–9 onwards Bulgakov seeks in a variety of ways to express his increasing preoccupation with the destiny of the artist. There are particular reasons why this concern should have arisen in 1929, the year which marks a turning-point in his writing away from the themes and forms of the 1920s towards a more single-minded purpose in the 1930s. The reader will therefore not find in this book much discussion of Bulgakov's feuilletons, of his Moscow satires of the NEP (New Economic Policy) period, of his science fiction, or even of his works on Civil War themes, *Belaya gvardiya* (*The White Guard*), *Dni Turbinykh* (*The Days of the Turbins*), or *Beg* (*Flight*). This is no reflection on the merits of these works, which in the case of *The White Guard* and *Flight* have been by and large underestimated hitherto. But Bulgakov in the 1930s is a different man and a different writer from his earlier self, and the corresponding transformation which can be traced in his works demands independent study of the last decade of his life.

To identify 1929 as a watershed in Bulgakov's writing career is not to suggest that there was no concern whatsoever with the problems of art in his previous writing. Indeed, one of his earliest sustained pieces of prose writing, *Zapiski na manzhetakh* (*Cuffnotes*) (1920–1), takes as its central theme the experiences of a novice writer in the Caucasus and in Moscow during the turbulent years immediately after the Revolution. This clearly autobiographical story is dedicated 'to the writers of Russia in their sufferings and in their journeyings by land and sea', a tribute which indicates Bulgakov's anxiety about the continuity and survival of Russia's literary culture.[5] The work is topical, and does not yet ascribe special importance to the artistic vision of the writer–narrator. But already here Bulgakov confronts a fundamental truth which, as we shall see, was to prove central to his understanding of the nature of artistic creation as portrayed in *The Master and Margarita*. His narrator writes a play on local themes in collaboration with a native of the Caucasus, but when he comes to read it over he is so ashamed of its quality that he starts to tear it up. Then he stops short:

Because suddenly, with extraordinary, miraculous lucidity, I realized that people are right to say that you can't destroy something once you've written it. You can tear it up or burn it ... or conceal it from people. But from yourself, never! That's that! It's irrevocable![6]

Already in this story, where he mockingly reveals the prosaic and absurd circumstances in which literature was being created in the early years of Soviet rule, he is aware of the higher value with which all artistic endeavour is invested; humdrum or even unsuccessful art nevertheless proclaims the author's identity in Bulgakov's vision of a world where 'manuscripts don't burn'.

In the mid-1920s Bulgakov's work deals principally with contemporary or recent historical topics: the Revolution and the Civil War in *The White Guard*, *The Days of the Turbins* and *Flight*; the problems raised by the Marxist attempt to reform man along scientific principles in *Rokovye yaytsa* (*The Fateful Eggs*) and *Sobach'ye serdtse* (*The Heart of a Dog*); and the grotesque realities of Moscow and of Russia as a whole during the NEP period, at a time when the uneducated and as yet inarticulate workers were coming to grips with their newly won power. The first indication of Bulgakov's renewed interest in the writer after *Cuffnotes* comes in his 1927 farce *Bagrovy ostrov* (*The Crimson Island*), based on the April 1924 story of the same name.[7] The original prose version had been little more than an allegory of the Revolution, using characters from the novels of Jules Verne to represent the Western-European interventionists anxious to preserve their financial interests at the expense of the recently liberated natives of the 'crimson' island. The 1927 stage version is elaborated in an entirely new direction. The allegory of the Revolution is framed here as a play within a play. The revolutionary play's author is one Dymogatsky, whose failure to deliver the work to the theatre by an agreed deadline means that the play has to be given an instant dress rehearsal by the resourceful cast, for the play can be put on only if it is approved by the censor Savva Lukich before he goes away on holiday. The censor initially bans it because the crew of the English ship sail away from the island at the end of the play rather than joining in the world revolution. When this faux pas has been remedied, however, Savva Lukich relents, and *The Crimson Island* ends with instructions to the box office to start selling tickets for Dymogatsky's play.

This play-within-a-play structure is a stratagem Bulgakov favours; in several of his works he sets the main story within an external framework, creating novels within novels as well as plays within plays. The effect of this is always to emphasize the subjective nature of the hero's vision, either by making him an author, as in this case and in *The Master and Margarita* and *Teatral'ny roman* (*A Theatrical Novel*), or by presenting the inner story as a dream. In *The Crimson Island* the device affords Bulgakov an opportunity to elaborate his satirical survey of the forces engaged in the battles of the 1917 Revolution, and to incorporate into the same text a satire on censorship in the 1920s. A direct stimulus for the latter theme was undoubtedly provided by Bulgakov's experiences at MKhAT (The Moscow Arts Theatre) with his play *The Days of the Turbins*, which suffered from the opposition of the cultural bureaucrats and censors who sat in judgement over it. Savva Lukich's refusal to pass the play is above all absurd. Dymogatsky's account of the Revolution is certainly mocking, with the Kerensky figure Kiri-Kuki an out-and-out opportunist, the White Guard literally changing the colour of their feathers at the switch of a lamp, and the native heirs of the Revolution emphatically naive. But Savva Lukich entirely fails to grasp the true satirical implications of the work and focusses instead on a trivial formality. The text of *The Crimson Island* contains a number of quotations from nineteenth-century classics of the Russian stage; Dymogatsky, paraphrasing a famous speech from Griboyedov's *Gore ot uma* (*Woe from Wit*), throws up his hands in despair:

And who are the judges? They're so ancient that their hostility to freedom is implacable. They cull their opinions from forgotten newspapers of the Kolchak era and the time of the subjugation of the Crimea! (184)

The Soviet determination to muzzle free speech as though the country were still on a war footing is, as Bulgakov was to argue in a notorious letter to the government in 1930, threatening to destroy drama altogether.[8]

At the very beginning of Bulgakov's professional career as a writer, while he was still living in Vladikavkaz, he submitted his play *Parizhskiye kommunary* (*The Paris Communards*) to a competition in Moscow, the terms of which required that he should identify himself and his entry with a motto. The one he chose on that occasion might have served as a slogan for the rest of his career: 'To the free god of art'.[9] It is certainly in the ebullient humour of *The Crimson Island* that his concern for the writer's right to freedom from censorship is first given expression. Just how controversial the issue was is indicated by the wave of criticism the play provoked when it was staged in 1928. The critic Turkel'taub was outraged at the insult offered by Bulgakov to the literary establishment:

Bulgakov's specific aim is unambiguous: he has to demonstrate to the audience that Soviet theatrical censorship is in the hands of idiots.[10]

The producer of the play, A. Tairov, even endeavoured to evade attacks in a 1928 interview by seeking to suggest – most unconvincingly – that the action of *The Crimson Island* took place not in Moscow, and not in MKhAT in particular, but in some distant and backward provincial town.[11] Bachelis, writing in 1929, went further still than Turkel'taub in affirming the subversive intent of Bulgakov's play:

The Crimson Island is, in its form, a parody on the theatre; but in its essence it is a pasquinade on the Revolution.[12]

Only one commentator, Pavel Novitsky, was prepared to make out a general case in defence of satire; as for Bulgakov's play, he noted that it would certainly need to be handled with tact, but summed it up as 'an interesting and witty parody'.[13] In his letter to the government of 28 March 1930, Bulgakov takes up Novitsky's point that the play was at least witty, and continues:

I cannot undertake to judge how witty my play is, but I confess that an ominous shadow does indeed loom over it, and that is the shadow of the Chief Repertory Committee. For it is they who nurture helots, panegyrists and cowed 'lackeys'. It is they who are murdering creative thought, they who are destroying Soviet drama; and they will destroy it.

I have not been expressing these ideas in whispers in some corner. I put them into a dramatic pamphlet and staged that pamphlet . . .

. . . When the German press writes that *The Crimson Island* 'is the first call in the USSR for freedom of the press' (*Molodaya gvardiya*, no. 1, 1929), it is writing the truth. I admit it. The struggle against censorship, whatever its nature, and whatever the power under which it exists, is my duty as a writer, as are calls for freedom of the press. I am a passionate supporter of that freedom, and I consider that if any writer were to imagine that he could prove he didn't need that freedom, then he would be like a fish affirming in public that it didn't need water.[14]

As Bulgakov reminds the authorities, all these points had been made quite openly in the play. But by the time this letter came to be written, *The Crimson Island* had already been banned a year previously, and Bulgakov's fighting words have to be set against the reality of his comprehensive defeat at the censors' hands. Nevertheless, the problem of censorship and the importance of a flourishing satirical genre to Soviet literature were two questions that continued to stir him during the 1930s. In *Zhizn' gospodina de Mol'yera* (*The Life of Monsieur de Molière*, 1932–3) he describes the extreme solutions Molière resorted to in his attempts to have the ban on *Les Précieuses ridicules* lifted, at the same time cocking a snook at censorship's attempts to neutralise the effects of satirical writing:

This device has long been known to dramatists, and consists in the writer resorting under pressure to a deliberate disfiguring of his work. What an extreme method! It's how lizards behave when, having been seized by the tail, they let it be torn off and take to their heels. Because every lizard understands that it's better to live without a tail than to do without life altogether.

Molière's reasoning was sound: the King's censors didn't realize that no alteration was going to change the basic meaning of a work one jot, nor in any way diminish its undesirable influence on the spectator.[15]

There is certainly a degree of wishful thinking here, but Bulgakov was to return to his point that the one redeeming feature of censorship is the gullibility of those entrusted with the task. In *A Theatrical Novel* (1936–7) the unsuspecting Maksudov encounters unforeseen difficulties with his recently finished novel when his friends explain that it will not be passed by the censors. Despairing of his literary career, he is about to commit suicide when he is interrupted by the arrival of the Mephistophelean publisher Rudol'fi, who is quite confident that the censors are easily hoodwinked:

You will have to cross out three words: on page one, page seventy-one, and page three hundred and two.
I cast a glance at the notebooks and saw that the first word was 'Apocalypse', the second 'archangels', and the third 'devil'. I meekly crossed them out: true, I wanted to say that this crossing-out was naive, but then I looked at Rudol'fi and kept quiet.[16]

Needless to say, Rudol'fi's confidence proves justified, and Maksudov's novel is soon published.

The Crimson Island can be seen, therefore, as the first in a series of works in which the subject of censorship is raised. It is an indication of the fact that Bulgakov was, even in the 1920s, concerned about the difficulties of his profession. But although the writer–hero Dymogatsky makes certain plaintively lyrical speeches as he bemoans the fate of his (as he thinks) rejected work, there is not yet here the depth of sympathy and understanding that Bulgakov was to display in his subsequent, more profound studies of the writer. The play is plainly more comic than tragic, a relative proportion that is not often found in Bulgakov's later works. His concern in *The Crimson Island* is with problems of theatrical censorship shared by author, actors and director alike. Not until 1929, in Bulgakov's play about Molière, does the writer come forward to occupy the centre of the stage, a position he was scarcely to relinquish for the remainder of Bulgakov's writing career.

If it is possible to identify ways in which the theme of the writer was adumbrated in Bulgakov's writing during the 1920s, the question naturally arises as to what it was that made his work of 1929 and beyond palpably different from what had come before, and why his focus on the figure of the artist becomes so unwavering in the 1930s. In considering Bulgakov at the threshold of a new phase in his life, we will have to take into account not only the circumstances which made 1929 a year of crisis for him, but also the cultural baggage which he brought with him into the new decade; this will later require some consideration of what we know about his reading and his literary tastes.

The crisis of 1929 came about as a number of factors combined together to thrust the problem of the destiny of the writer into the forefront of Bulgakov's attention, and their particular character proved crucial in shaping his subsequent literary explorations of the topic. Firstly, 1929 was the year which brought the pluralism and relative freedoms of the NEP period to an end, in the field of culture as well as in political and economic terms. Stalin, by allowing the aggressive proletarian group RAPP to establish dictatorial control of literary affairs from December 1929, was in fact just giving formal recognition to a situation which had been allowed to develop over the previous year or so. The main targets of the hyper-orthodox RAPP ideologues were the 'poputchiki' or 'fellow-travellers', to which broad liberal grouping Bulgakov patently belonged. RAPP questioned whether the uncommitted 'poputchiki' could still be allowed to coexist with the Soviet régime. One wonders whether it is just a coincidence that Pasternak has his idealistic poet–hero Yury Zhivago perish in the summer of 1929, just as it began to become clear how stringent were to be the restrictions placed on creative enterprise. Over the next three years the RAPP group carried out what was effectively to be a purge of the literary world, and it seems only to have been the shock of Mayakovsky's suicide in April 1930 which, together with Gor'ky's increasing concern about RAPP's ravages, may eventually have persuaded Stalin to check their excesses and finally disband the group in 1932. Meanwhile, however, Bulgakov and others were being given their first real taste of political oppression.

Having more or less abandoned prose in 1925 and spent the next few years concentrating on drama, Bulgakov returned to the prose genre towards the end of 1928 with the first phase of work on what was eventually to become the novel *The Master and Margarita*. At this stage, however, the projected work was planned as a satirical study of contemporary Moscow which, while it was to include a devil figure with his retinue and a retelling of the Gospels, had not yet acquired its writer–hero. The Master would only enter the novel some time later. This first draft of the novel was broken off in the spring of 1929, however, as a series of events obliged Bulgakov to devote his energies to more urgent and practical problems. For after a period when, despite the furore of criticism and controversy aroused by his plays, he had been continually lionized in theatrical circles, he was now to discover that the hostility of the Establishment could have potent consequences. In February 1929 it became known that Stalin considered the play *Flight*, currently in rehearsal at MKhAT, to be essentially anti-Soviet in the form in which it stood; and the production was promptly abandoned.[17] This expression of disapproval, qualified though it was, had a snowball effect as the various theatres rushed to act before they could be implicated in Bulgakov's fall from favour. *The Days of the Turbins*, which had run for more than 250 performances since 1926, was, like *Flight*, swiftly removed from the MKhAT repertoire; *Zoykina kvartira* (*Zoyka's Apartment*), which had been playing at the Vakhtangov theatre, was also taken off; and *The Crimson Island* at the Kamerny theatre was banned as well. On 6 March 1929 the newspaper *Vechernyaya Moskva* proclaimed triumphantly that 'the theatres are freeing themselves of Bulgakov's plays'.[18] And Mayakovsky joined in with relish to predict in *Klop* (*The Bedbug*, 1928–9) that in his vision of the future Bulgakov's name would be relegated to a dictionary of obsolete words.[19] For Bulgakov, suddenly ostracized, in debt, and with no immediately obvious ways of earning a living, the prophecy must have sounded all too accurate. And, as if his professional life was not sufficiently in turmoil, a further crisis began to take shape in his personal life during the spring of 1929. For in February 1929 Bulgakov made the acquaintance of Yelena Sergeyevna Shilovskaya, and by May 1929 he found himself involved in a relationship which was increasingly to divide his emotional loyalties between his new love and his wife of five years, Lyubov' Yevgen'yevna Belozerskaya. The 1928–9 draft of *The Master and Margarita* differs from the final version not only in that it lacks the figure of the Master, but also in the absence of Margarita from its pages. Only after the crises of 1929–31 would the writer and his lover come to occupy their central roles in Bulgakov's masterpiece.

In the spring of 1929, therefore, Bulgakov seemed to be facing a bleak future. Nothing changed as the summer wore on, and he came to the conclusion that his only hope lay in an appeal to the highest authorities to release him from his plight. In July he duly composed a letter to Stalin. The text describes the hostility with which his works had been greeted by Soviet critics, and speaks of the apparent hopelessness of his position. Referring to an earlier request simply to travel abroad, which had been turned down, he now asks to be exiled from the Soviet Union altogether.[20] In a further letter on 3 September to Yenukidze, the Secretary of the Central Executive Committee, he explained the reasons for his desperation:

In view of the fact that my works are evidently quite unacceptable to Soviet public opinion; in view of the fact that the complete ban which has been imposed on my works in the USSR condemns me to perish; and in view of the fact that the destruction of me as a writer has already resulted in disaster for me in material terms (I can provide documents to prove that I have no savings, that it is impossible for me to pay tax or indeed to live, starting from next month); and given my utter exhaustion and the fruitlessness of all my endeavours, I appeal to the supreme body in the Soviet Union, the Central Executive Committee of the USSR, to allow me to go abroad with my wife Lyubov' Yevgen'yevna Bulgakova for whatever period the Soviet government deems necessary.[21]

On the same day Bulgakov also turned to Gor'ky for assistance:

I appeal to you, Aleksey Maksimovich, to support my application. I wanted to set out to you in a detailed letter all the things that have been happening to me, but my exhaustion and my sense of hopelessness are beyond measure. I cannot write a thing.

Everything has been banned, and I have been ruined, I feel persecuted and completely isolated.

Why keep a writer in a country where his works are not allowed to exist? I appeal for a humane decision – to let me go.[22]

Gor'ky evidently received the letter and passed it on to some higher
authority, for he then sent a message through the writer Yevgeny
Zamyatin asking for a copy of the original. Bulgakov replied that
he had not kept a copy, but sent a rough version of what he had
previously written, adding this conclusion:

All my plays have been banned, not a line of mine is being printed
anywhere, I have no finished work ready, and not a kopeck of royalties is
coming in from any source. Not a single institution or official replies to any
of my applications. In other words, everything that I have written during
the course of 10 years' work in the USSR has been destroyed. It only
remains for one last thing to be destroyed – me.[23]

Bulgakov's chances of receiving a sympathetic hearing were,
however, remote. This was underlined in an article in *Izvestiya* on
15 September, in which R. Pikel' commented with pleasure on the
prospect of a season without any plays by Bulgakov. He made it
clear that what was now expected of him was that he should see the
error of his ways and make a serious attempt to become a loyal
Soviet writer:

This season audiences will see none of Bulgakov's plays ... We do not
thereby mean to say that Bulgakov's name has been struck off the list of
Soviet dramatists. His talent is as evident as is the socially reactionary
nature of his writing. We are talking only of his past plays. *That* Bulgakov is
not needed in the Soviet theatre ... The taking-off of his plays heralds a
return to healthy themes in the repertoire.[24]

The new Bulgakov who emerged from these trials was not,
however, the one that Pikel' and his like were apparently
expecting.

1929 was proving a difficult year for Bulgakov, but he was by no
means the only writer to have run into such problems. The most
notorious example of RAPP persecution was the campaign which it
waged in the summer of 1929 against the two recognized leaders of
the 'poputchiki', Zamyatin and Pil'nyak. Zamyatin was virulently
attacked for having allowed the publication abroad of his novel *My*
(*We*) some years earlier, and despite his protestations of innocence
in the matter, he continued to be denounced as an internal émigré.
In 1931 he was finally allowed to leave the Soviet Union, after
obtaining the reluctant support of Gor'ky for his application.
Pil'nyak, on the other hand, who had been reproached with the

Berlin publication of his *Krasnoye derevo* (*Mahogany*), recanted
and sought to redeem himself by rewriting the work in 1930 under
the title *Volga vpadayet v kaspiyskoye more* (*The Volga Flows into
the Caspian Sea*). It is the persecution of Zamyatin, however, which
is of particular interest to us here; for while it has been established
that Bulgakov had little liking for Pil'nyak and his writings,[25] the
quite different extent and closeness of Bulgakov's friendship with
Zamyatin has gone unnoticed.

Zamyatin's attention was first drawn to Bulgakov in 1924, when
the latter's story *D'yavoliada* (*Diaboliad*) was published in the
journal *Nedra*,[26] and he wrote a review of the issue singling out
Bulgakov's story as having particular merit:

With Bulgakov *Nedra* has, it seems, for the first time lost its classical (and
pseudo-classical) innocence and, as is often the case, the seducer of the
provincial old maid turns out to be the first lively young man who turns up
from the city. The absolute value of this piece by Bulgakov – which all in all
is very unconsidered – is not so great, but evidently we can expect much
good work from this author.[27]

The two men became friendly, and the relationship between the
Moscow writer and Zamyatin, his younger, if longer-established,
Leningrad colleague, had become particularly close by the end of
the 1920s. Zamyatin wrote to Bulgakov in an affectionately teasing
tone in 1928 about his failure to produce an article for an almanac
that Zamyatin was editing with A. Kugel', an article initially due to
be entitled 'The Dramatist and the Critic' and later referred to as
'The Première'.[28] Zamyatin addresses him with a familiarity
unusual among Bulgakov's correspondents; as 'dear old man'
('starichok'), and subsequently as 'comrade instructor', 'respected
producer', and 'master of drama'.[29] A letter of July 1929 confirms
that beyond this mock veneration lay genuine respect as well, for
Zamyatin turns to him for advice about which Moscow theatre he
should approach with his project to translate Hecht and
MacArthur's play *The Front Page*.[30]

The fact that Bulgakov and Zamyatin saw a great deal of one
another from 1928 to 1931, the period when Zamyatin was having
to fight back against continuous attacks on him, is confirmed in a
number of letters from Zamyatin to his wife of which extracts have
been published.[31] Bulgakov's second wife, Lyubov' Yevgen'yevna,
recalls that Zamyatin was a frequent visitor to the household at the
time,[32] and a number of private sources have suggested that

Zamyatin was indeed Bulgakov's closest friend during these crucial years. Bulgakov would have shared in Zamyatin's struggle to obtain permission to emigrate, and they presumably consulted one another about the best ways of approaching the authorities, since Bulgakov was attempting precisely the same thing at the time. It is worth bearing in mind that Bulgakov's letter to Yenukidze and his first letter to Gor'ky were both written on 3 September 1929, the day after the attacks on Zamyatin had reached their climax: the 2 September issue of *Literaturnaya gazeta* had devoted its whole front page to the Pil'nyak/Zamyatin affair, in an article which included an ominous dictum to the effect that 'the concept "Soviet writer" is not a geographical but a social concept'.[33] On the same day, 2 September, RAPP had passed a resolution demanding that all writers and literary groups should 'determine their attitude towards the actions of Ye. Zamyatin and B. Pil'nyak'.[34] Clearly, Bulgakov's own appeals must at least in part have been dictated by the awareness that if the situation was becoming critical for Zamyatin, then the prospects for himself could be no more promising.

Zamyatin was, however, eventually successful in his application to emigrate, while Bulgakov failed. They remained close friends, and two years later, in October 1931, a letter from Zamyatin promises that they will see one another shortly before he and his wife leave the country in November. The letter also congratulates Bulgakov on the fact that his Molière play had at last been approved by the Repertory Committee, thanks to support from Maksim Gor'ky:

And so: hurrah for the three M's: Mikhail, Maksim, and Molière! This wonderful combination of three M's will work out very profitably for you, and I'm delighted. And consequently you will join the ranks of the dramatists, while I join those of the Wandering Jews.[35]

Bulgakov and Zamyatin continued to correspond after his emigration, and letters dating from 1928 to 1936 have been preserved in the archive, although not all have been made available to researchers.[36] One letter from Bulgakov is notable for the fact that it was begun on 5 October 1932, the very next day after his marriage to Yelena Sergeyevna. Although this indicates how precious Zamyatin's friendship was to Bulgakov, since he was one of the first people he wanted to inform about this sudden change in his circumstances, the letter was not completed that day and was in fact started several times more over the next six months; it may never have been posted in the form in which it has survived in the archive. But the warmth of feeling between them is again confirmed by the familiarity – very untypical of Bulgakov – of his manner of addressing Zamyatin: 'dear wanderer', 'Ahasuerus' ('Agasfer'), and even simply 'Zhenya'.[37]

This all suggests that Bulgakov was intimately acquainted with Zamyatin's writings, with his views on literature, and with his anxiety about the strait-jacket into which he believed it was being forced by authorities terrified by the possible consequences of artistic 'heresy'. Bulgakov's own views on art would take the shape of a preoccupation with the continued preservation of eternal values, rather than a revolutionary hostility to cultural monuments, but he and Zamyatin shared an immediate revulsion against the rigid regimentation of literature. Bulgakov's alarm at the worsening situation would have been intensified by his personal knowledge of the pressures to which his friend was being subjected; and we can infer that Zamyatin's experiences contributed significantly to a major theme in Bulgakov's work, as he began to reflect in a new and urgent way on the writer's position in society. Their friendship was to prove a formative influence in Bulgakov's life.

September 1929 seems to have marked the culmination of Bulgakov's crisis, as it became clear that the authorities were neither going to allow him to be published and performed as before, nor offer him the opportunity of emigrating. But at the time of his greatest isolation and pessimism his new love for Yelena Sergeyevna, who was away on holiday at that particular moment, enabled him to rediscover his inspiration, and this provided him with an outlet for his feelings as well as demonstrating that the creative spark had by no means been quenched. For in September 1929 he embarked on a piece of autobiographical writing dedicated to Yelena Sergeyevna and entitled *Taynomu drugu* (*For my Secret Friend*), obviously a reference to their clandestine relationship. The manuscript, which was eventually to be reworked into *A Theatrical Novel*, also includes moments which relate it to his earlier *The White Guard*, and to what would become *The Master and Margarita*. The work is unfinished, but was evidently intended as a bitter review of the events of the previous few years, and it opens with a weary question to the work's addressee: 'And so, you insist that I should tell you in this year of catastrophe how it was that I became a dramatist?'[38] By now the message had been brought home to Bulgakov that the writer is a figure especially vulnerable to arbitrary control, and he became increasingly determined to defend and justify his own stance against the constraints which seemed to threaten his future. The autobiographical *For my Secret Friend* comprises his first comment on his struggles, and I would concur with Chudakova that it is this work of September 1929 which really marks a new departure for him:

With the story we have just been discussing a new theme enters Bulgakov's work; the destiny of the artist. More than once he had come quite close to it with his favourite heroes, but only starting with this story does it become the object of the author's unremitting attention, manifesting itself in his works in ever new variations.[39]

During the summer of 1929 Bulgakov had been largely preoccupied with the past; but as the autumn progressed and he began to regain confidence in himself, he also started to look ahead. This had an unexpected consequence for which future researchers would have reason to be grateful: for, perhaps because of his now heightened awareness of the ephemerality of success, Bulgakov seems at this point to have acquired a greater faith in his own importance and in the value of his vocation. This new attitude is reflected in the care with which he now preserves his papers, evidently with the ultimate intention of building up a literary archive:

Only towards the beginning of the 1930s did Bulgakov begin to display a methodical attitude towards his papers. From approximately 1929 onwards, he began to preserve not just his manuscripts, including drafts, and not just copies of his letters, but also folders of documents, neatly arranged, which illustrate the stages of the author's work on a manuscript, and then its publishing or stage history.[40]

It is as though he now defies the circumstances which seem to be joining together to deny him freedom of expression by establishing the basis for a collection of documents which will trace the course of his struggle against that oppression.

Bulgakov presented *For my Secret Friend* to Yelena Sergeyevna in its unfinished form as soon as she returned from her holiday in the autumn. But although this meant that the autobiographical novel was now abandoned, Bulgakov had by no means turned his back on his new theme. Realizing perhaps that he could not safely express his feelings about the position of the writer in an explicitly autobiographical genre, he began work in October on an entirely new project, a play which was to be based on the life of Molière. It would be wrong to suggest that the Molière work has an exclusively autobiographical significance; but it would also be difficult to deny that the anger Bulgakov had accumulated over the previous few months provided the primary inspiration for the work.

Bulgakov took about three months to write the play which, together with his other works inspired by Molière, will be considered separately below. But his work was still not acceptable to the Establishment: just a year after the disaster with his four earlier plays, Bulgakov learned in March 1930 that his Molière play had not been accepted for production either. He addressed a last desperate appeal to the government in the controversial letter of 28 March 1930, commenting on the storm aroused by *The Crimson Island* and again requesting to be allowed to emigrate, or that he should be found a job. He also acknowledged the title of satirist with which he had been labelled, and went on to comment on what this means in the world of Soviet literature:

Only once, at the beginning of my period of renown, was the comment made with a tinge of, as it were, haughty surprise that 'Bulgakov wishes to become the satirist of our epoch' (*Knigonosha*, 6, 1925).
    Alas, the verb 'wishes' is mistakenly given in the present tense here. It should be turned into a pluperfect: Bulgakov *had become a satirist* precisely at a time when true satire (that which penetrates into forbidden areas) became unthinkable in the USSR. It did not fall to me to have the honour of expressing this criminal thought in print. It is expressed perfectly clearly in an article by V. Blyum ... and the purport of this article can be brilliantly and precisely condensed into a single formula: anyone who writes satire in the USSR is questioning the Soviet system.
    Am I thinkable in the USSR?[41]

Bulgakov had as passionate a belief in the importance of satire as he did in the right to freedom of expression, and he was to continue campaigning on its behalf, especially when the move towards a prescriptive policy of socialist realism became apparent. The insistence on positive heroes and RAPP's hostility towards anything that smacked of defeatism seemed to toll the knell of satire. For Bulgakov too, it was by no means just a question of art:

He was convinced of the necessity of pitilessly satirical depictions of life. This was not just the play of a mocking mind, but the author's civic stance.[42]

Bulgakov's response to the socialist–realist view that truth must be depicted 'in its revolutionary development' is summed up in the line from Horace which he selects as the epigraph for his prose biography of Molière:

And what is to hinder me from telling the truth with laughter?[43]

The problem, as he suggests, is not the satirical laughter in which criticism may be dressed, but the uncomfortable truth that satire is liable to reveal. This would become an important theme of the Molière biography, where Bulgakov argues that it is in the very nature of the relationship between the satirist and the State that that they cannot be – and should not seek to be – reconciled:

As every literate person knows, satire can be truly honourable, but one would be hard put to find a single man in the whole world who would be able to offer the authorities a sample of permissible satire. (110)

In the autumn of 1933 Bulgakov returned to the topic of satire in his answers to a questionnaire sent out by the publishers of the series *Literaturnoye nasledstvo* (*Literary Heritage*) concerning the relevance of Saltykov-Shchedrin to the writers of the day. Bulgakov wrote two drafts of a reply: the first, following the points on the questionnaire fairly closely, was dated 19 September 1933, while the second was a briefer, continuous piece of writing which dealt with all the questions at once, written on 11 October the same year. The replies to the questionnaire were not published until 1976, when the editors decided to use Bulgakov's second draft as the basis for his entry. There is, however, one interesting discrepancy. One of the questions asked of the contributors concerned Saltykov-Shchedrin's usefulness as a model for present-day writers: 'Your assessment of Shchedrin as a classic of satire in relation to the task of creating Soviet satire.'[44] The end of the published version of Bulgakov's reply reads as follows:

I am convinced that all attempts to create satire are doomed to utter failure. Satire is impossible to create. It creates itself, all of a sudden. But I consider that all Soviet satirists should be recommended to make an earnest study of Shchedrin.[45]

It turns out that the 1976 editors have softened the force of
Bulgakov's reply here by replacing the end of the second draft with
the somewhat milder conclusion to the first draft. The closing lines
of Bulgakov's final draft should actually read like this:

(It creates itself, all of a sudden.) And it will create itself when a writer
appears who considers that modern life is not perfect, and who will
indignantly undertake an artistic denunciation of it. I imagine that the path
of such a writer will be extremely hard.[46]

It seems extraordinary that, even in 1976, Bulgakov's suggestion
that Soviet satirists tend to have political difficulties was too
controversial to be published.

In March 1930, too, Bulgakov's comments on satire were
scarcely likely to find favour with the authorities or persuade them
to revise their attitude towards him. But here external circumstances intervened, for Bulgakov's letter actually reached Stalin
much at the same time as the news of Mayakovsky's suicide on 14
April 1930. Stalin telephoned Bulgakov shortly afterwards, on 18
April, apparently offering him the opportunity to emigrate; but by
now Bulgakov had either decided that it would not be politic to
accept such an offer, or that he preferred in any case to stay.[47]
Stalin then undertook to find him the job he wanted, and his
influence ensured that Bulgakov was taken on by MKhAT as a
producer by the summer of 1930. It appeared that his difficulties
were over. The lessons of 1929–30, however, were never forgotten,
and the crisis marks a clear boundary between the first and second
decades of his writing career. Henceforth Bulgakov would return
again and again in his fiction to the problems that beset the creative
artist.

Having established the immediate political, professional and
personal circumstances which moved Bulgakov to address a new
theme, another question still remains to be considered. If Bulgakov's concern is now with literature and the position of the writer,
we need to know more about what sort of literature interested him
and what sort of a writer he was. For he naturally brings to the
problem a wealth of intellectual and cultural experience drawn
from his national traditions as well as from his personal history. All
Bulgakov's writings, whether fictional or not, are notably pervaded
by the author's sense of the literary traditions which he inherits and
to which he belongs. My purpose here is not just to explore his

tastes in literature, nor only to establish what place he occupies within the literary tradition, but also to examine the ways in which Bulgakov's awareness of his literary heritage becomes itself a central element in his work, with important repercussions for the way in which he would present the writer as the hero of his fictional creations. By providing a context for Bulgakov's studies of the writer, we will not only elucidate his interpretations, but also confirm the ultimate coherence of his vision.

No account of Bulgakov's reading and literary tastes can hope to be comprehensive, since we are inevitably dependent on incidental documentary evidence for all our information.[48] But perhaps the best general description of the overall shape of Bulgakov's library, and one which is confirmed by all available sources, is that provided by his friend Sergey Yermolinsky:

Russian literature of the nineteenth century was well represented in his library; there were few books by foreign authors, whereas there were a great many by second-ranking writers whose names we have now forgotten, but which reflect, as is always the case, the literary taste and attainments of an era, as well as a mass of details about day-to-day life.

He loved (and knew very well) Gogol, Saltykov-Shchedrin, Sukhovo-Kobylin. He was indifferent to Chekhov ...

However, he never took any interest in problems of literary criticism. Books using scholarly language to explain literary devices, genres, and influences, or analysing those devices and genres, only aroused boredom and astonishment in him. He was always interested in biographical materials. He loved to dig about in old magazines, especially historical and archival ones. He used to collect dictionaries, lexicons, and reference works.[49]

The richness and variety of Bulgakov's use of literary reference certainly allow us to confirm Yermolinsky's point that he had a detailed knowledge of the canon of nineteenth-century Russian literature. Yermolinsky mentions here his particular fondness for Gogol, Saltykov-Shchedrin and Sukhovo-Kobylin, to whom we may add Griboyedov and Leskov as significant representatives of the Russian satirical tradition, and also perhaps Ostrovsky, even if he does seem to figure in a notably negative light in *A Theatrical Novel*, where his bust provokes the envy and irritation of the narrator Maksudov.[50] Bulgakov seems to have favoured the writers of the earlier part of the century, with Pushkin and Gogol reigning supreme in his pantheon; whereas the works of Goncharov, Dostoyevsky, Bunin and Gor'ky, while naturally figuring as the everyday currency of his literary discourse, do not appear to have fired his imagination to anything like the same extent. Some exception may be made here for Tolstoy who, for various reasons, remained a far from remote figure for Bulgakov throughout his career. In 1923 Bulgakov wrote a story called *Kiev-gorod* (*The City of Kiev*), in which he prophesied the coming of a chronicler worthy of describing the city's recent experiences:

When a bolt from heaven (for there are limits even to heavenly patience) exterminates every single modern writer, and there appears in about fifty years' time a new, real Lev Tolstoy, an astounding book will be written about the great battles in Kiev.[51]

It would seem that he then went on to try to fulfil his own prophecy much more immediately in writing *The White Guard*, where the scope and subject of a domestic drama set against a turbulent historical setting are clearly redolent of *Voyna i mir* (*War and Peace*), even if the style draws more on modernist, ornamentalist practices. Bulgakov retained an active interest in Tolstoy through his close friendship in the late 1920s and 1930s with the literary historian Pavel Sergeyevich Popov, whose wife Anna Il'yinichna was one of Tolstoy's granddaughters. When Bulgakov embarked on his eventually unsuccessful stage adaptation of *War and Peace* in 1931, he was readily given access to the draft materials for the novel, which Anna Il'yinichna had been working on at home.[52] But any sort of direct influence from Tolstoy, as from any of the other major mid- to late nineteenth-century novelists, including Dostoyevsky, can be said to have diminished as Bulgakov came to establish his own distinctive literary style from the mid-1920s onwards.

Yermolinsky makes a particular point of Bulgakov's relative lack of enthusiasm for Chekhov, which is confirmed by Lyubov' Yevgen'yevna in her memoirs:

Bulgakov liked Chekhov, but not with a fanatical love, as with certain Chekhov specialists, but rather with an affectionate love, such as one might have for a good and clever older brother. He particularly enjoyed his notebooks.[53]

Chekhov did in one sense represent an older-brother figure for Bulgakov, as was recognized by the Assistant Director of MKhAT, V. G. Sakhnovsky, in a letter of June 1934 where he commented to Bulgakov that for the younger generation at the theatre *The Days of the Turbins* had been 'a new *Chayka (Seagull)*'.[54] While Bulgakov would have appreciated Sakhnovsky's intended compliment regarding his play's importance for the development of the theatre, he may have had reservations about any parallels between himself and Chekhov as a personality. There is no evidence to suggest that Bulgakov prized any of Chekhov's stories or plays especially highly, and in 1935 he wrote to Popov to tax him with his enthusiastic evaluation of an edition of Chekhov's correspondence:

You've distressed me with your opinion of the Chekhov correspondence. The letters from the widow and from the deceased made an abominable impression on me. It's a nasty little book. But the fact that we have different views of the same thing will do nothing to hinder our friendship.[55]

Another, more striking lack of enthusiasm on Bulgakov's part was his general coolness towards poetry, as described by his second wife:

M. A. had no avid inclination for poetry, although he knew perfectly well what was good and what was bad, and was capable on occasion of resorting to verse form himself.[56]

His own verse composition on the whole takes the form of songs for his plays or for the libretti he wrote in the 1930s for the Bol'shoy theatre; or else he would occasionally compose comic verse for his friends and relatives. But only one example has survived of an attempt by Bulgakov at serious verse, namely the rough sketches towards a poem called 'Funérailles', written in December 1930, which explores familiar Bulgakovian themes of remorse and death.[57]

When talking about poetry, Bulgakov used to make an exception for Pushkin: in April 1932 he confessed to Popov that 'since childhood I've found poetry unbearable (I'm not talking about Pushkin, Pushkin isn't poetry!), and if I have ever composed any, then it has always been satirical'.[58] It may have been the unaffectedness of Pushkin's diction which made his works more appealing to Bulgakov. For when it comes to the poetry of his contemporaries, it becomes clear that, for all Bulgakov's interest in 'the poet' in the Romantic sense of the word (the character who was to become the Master was at one time described as such in Bulgakov's notes),[59] he found trying the pretensions and mannerisms of those who displayed too self-conscious a sense of their own vocation.

Bulgakov was, for instance, rather put off by his first encounter
with Mandel'shtam's poetry:

In Tiflis he made the acquaintance of Osip Mandel'shtam, who was living
in poverty, proudly and with poetic unconcern ... Until then he had not
known Mandel'shtam's poems, neither the collection *Kamen'* (*Stone*) nor
Tristia ... But the somewhat bombastic and meaningful manner in which
the poet read his verse was not to Bulgakov's taste. He would always
ridicule this sort of manner, and listened to it with embarrassment.[60]

Ardov in turn describes how Akhmatova and Bulgakov became
friends, with Akhmatova expressing great admiration for his work
while recognizing that there was no point in reading him any of her
own.[61] Lyubov' Yevgen'yevna recalls that Bulgakov always kept
well out of the way when Voloshin settled down to read his verses
during their visits to Koktebel', and records also their first meeting
with Pasternak, whose recitation created an unfavourable impression on the playwright.[62] There is, then, an element of paradox in
Bulgakov's difficult relationship with lyric poetry, combined as it is
with his explicit concern to defend the writer's individual voice; and it
seems that the sobriety and clarity of a Pushkin were necessary ingre-
dients to reconcile him with the self-absorption of the poetic form.

Bulgakov seems to have had a less than burning interest in the
writing of his contemporaries. We can assume that he was familiar
with the major works of the satirical writers with whom he had
worked as a journalist in the early 1920s on the newspapers *Gudok*
and *Nakanune*: Olesha, Katayev, Il'f and Petrov, possibly Lunts,
Zoshchenko and Babel'. He would naturally also have read all the
works of his close friends Zamyatin and Erdman. But the information about his book-purchasing habits which is provided by
Chudakova on the basis of the diary of E. F. Tsippel'zon, a
bookseller whose shop Bulgakov frequented, and on the basis of
entries recording his purchases made by Yelena Sergeyevna in her
diary, suggests that Bulgakov rarely bought works of the post-
Revolutionary period.[63]

This view seems to receive confirmation in a passage in his
semi-autobiographical *A Theatrical Novel*, where the aspiring
novelist Maksudov attempts to gain inspiration for his second novel
by reading the best of modern literature:

I set off to the bookshops and purchased books by my contemporaries. I
wished to find out what they wrote about, how they wrote, what the magic
secret was of this craft.   (305)

Maksudov is disappointed by the dreary obscurity of Agapyonov, a figure apparently modelled on Pil'nyak. He is also horrified to find himself caricatured and traduced in the latest story by his supposed friend Likospastov – a reference to Bulgakov's reaction on reading a novel by Yury Slyozkin called *Devushka s gor* (*The Girl from the Mountains*), in which he is portrayed by this friend from his Vladikavkaz days in an extremely malicious manner.[64] Altogether, Maksudov's excursion into modern literature proves unproductive:

My grief and my reflections on the subject of my own imperfections were as nothing, actually, in comparison with the horrifying realization that I had derived nothing from the books of the very best writers, that I had not, so to speak, uncovered any tracks or seen any light up ahead; and it all began to seem hateful to me. And, like a worm, the dreadful thought began to eat away at my heart that I wasn't in fact going to turn out to be any kind of a writer at all. And then I was struck by the even more horrifying thought that ... well, supposing I were to turn out like Likospastov? And, to be bold, I will go even further: what if I were to turn out like Agapyonov? (306–7)

In many ways this is a reflection of the development of Bulgakov's own attitude to modern literature. At the beginning of his career, as he established himself in the early 1920s in the literary circles of Moscow, we find him, for example, planning to compile a biographical dictionary of modern writers spanning the years 1917–22;[65] he also appears to have taken part in a scheme to write a collective novel, which evidently never materialized.[66] But even such modest participation in the literary world of his own time diminished as Bulgakov's career progressed and he determined his own literary identity. Gradually he acquired the confidence to disregard the debates and the writings of a literary world increasingly uncongenial to his own concerns. This withdrawal into a private world is a characteristic aspect of his attitude towards the artist and his art.

A distinction needs to be drawn here between Bulgakov's view of the world of literature and his rather different relationship with the theatrical world. In *A Theatrical Novel*, one evening spent in the company of writers and their hangers-on suffices to dispel all Maksudov's illusions:

Yesterday I saw a new world, and I found that new world repellent. I won't join it. It's an alien world. A loathsome world! (302–3)

When Maksudov first enters the theatre, however, he is entranced
by it, and this enthusiasm survives even his ill-treatment at the
theatre's hands. As with Maksudov, Bulgakov's sense of belonging
in the theatrical world – like his heroes Dymogatsky, Molière, and
to some extent Gogol too – survived all the disasters which befell
his plays, and lasted even beyond the virtual cessation of his career
as a dramatist in 1936. At his death, more theatrical people
attended his funeral than writers.[67]

One point made by Yermolinsky in his description of Bulgakov's
library is perhaps misleading: this is the comment to the effect that
there were few foreign books in his library. We should not conclude
from this that Bulgakov was in any way ignorant of the literature of
Western Europe and America. His education at the Kiev gymna-
sium had given him a thorough grounding in the classics; and while
it is probably fair to say that he was not a gifted linguist, he was at
least familiar with Greek and Latin:

He valued Latin highly for its laconic concision, its rhythm and sonorous-
ness. He was fond of Lucian and had of course read Tacitus, Ovid and
Cornelius Nepos. His favourite Greek dramatist was Sophocles.[68]

Bulgakov also knew some French, and had smatterings of English,
German and Spanish. He did not, admittedly, own many works
written in foreign languages, although these did include a New
Testament in English, *Don Quixote* in the original, and a Hebrew
edition of the Gospels (it is not known that he could actually read
Hebrew). But if we are to judge by the extensive use of references
in his fiction and his correspondence, his reading of foreign authors
was wide-ranging. Lyubov' Yevgen'yevna mentions the names of
Molière, Anatole France, Zola, Stendhal, Goethe and Schiller,[69]
who together with Shakespeare, Dickens, Maupassant, Cervantes,
and Hoffmann certainly formed part of his cultural world, which
was by no means oriented exclusively towards the Russian tradition. He also had a wide knowledge of the popular classics of the
European and American tradition of detective stories, tales of
adventure, and early science fiction through his reading of Defoe,
Dumas, Fenimore Cooper, Conan Doyle, Jack London, Jules
Verne, Mark Twain, H. G. Wells, O. Henry and Mayne Reid.

Yermolinsky goes on to refer to Bulgakov's fondness for little-
known works; not in the sense of neglected gems of Russian
literature, but rather curiosities and specialist works on non-

literary topics. Typical of these is an item such as N. Reutt's *Psovaya okhota* (*Hunting with Hounds*, 2 vols., St Petersburg, 1846), a detailed introduction to the art of hunting with borzoi hounds, which also explains all about their training and upkeep; this was said to have been one of his very favourite books.[70] Yermolinsky also mentions his fondness for old historical and archival journals, which is borne out by a letter from Yelena Sergeyevna saying that her husband was frequently to be found with encyclopaedias and dictionaries, especially his beloved Dal', in his hands.[71] Information of this kind all helps to build up our impression of Bulgakov as a man fascinated by the detail, rather than the broad outlines of history; an appreciative reader of the best of nineteenth-century scholarship in a variety of fields and an author who possessed an eclectic range of learning.

One other detail picked out by Yermolinsky is relevant to our concern in this book with Bulgakov's portrayals of the writer; this is his bafflement at the industry of literary criticism. When he works on a particular writer, Bulgakov's interest is always in historical or archival materials about the artist himself, not in the analysis of the poet's creation or in its literary context. Bulgakov himself saw and experienced composition as a spontaneous act following on inspiration; Chudakova has commented on the unusual neatness of his drafts, which sometimes go virtually unchanged from the first version through to publication.[72] In all his studies of the writer, Bulgakov scarcely ever describes the creative process. When he does so in *A Theatrical Novel*, he again emphasizes the spontaneity of the experience:

At night, sometimes until the first light of dawn, I sat in my attic writing a novel.

It first came into being one night when I had woken up after a sad dream. I had dreamed of my native city, of the snow, of the winter, and of the Civil War . . . And so I began to write a novel. I described the snowstorm of my dream. (277–8)

In this case, Maksudov does have to labour at the task of writing, and spends a great deal of time on corrections. But when the novel is finished Maksudov, like Bulgakov with *The White Guard*, discovers that the work still has a will of its own. The characters of his book return to him in his dreams, and he is eventually obliged to get the book out again. As he reads, he finds that a curious structure seems to take shape on the page, a box, like a puppet-theatre, in

which his fictional characters move about and speak. Maksudov
goes on to describe the writing of the play based on his novel – a
reflection of Bulgakov's own transformation of *The White Guard*
into the play *The Days of the Turbins* – as an almost mechanical
process of taking down what his characters say and describing what
he sees happening (307–8). Bulgakov is here presenting composition as an entirely subjective, visionary experience; and we shall
see that his sense of the irrelevance of the study of literary
techniques or schools to the creative process is a significant aspect
of the presentation of the artist in his works, always in isolation
from any literary movements or organizations.

We shall have occasion to return to this emphasis in Bulgakov's
outlook on the individuality and subjectivity of the artist. It
contributes to what one could call the 'literariness' of his writing,
the way in which he continually reminds the reader not so much of
the formal conventions and artifice of the work of art as of the
presence of the creator behind it. His use of literary reference is
extensive; but these references are almost always to writers rather
than to their works. It is as though he were wanting to invoke their
personae, their presence, in his work, to establish a community of
feeling between himself and his predecessors, in a way which
sometimes bears little relevance to the immediate concerns of the
work in which the reference is encountered. As for stylistic manifestations of the same phenomenon, it is characteristic that he
should assert his own authorial persona in his writing through
structural devices, narrative perspectives, lyrical stage directions,
and voiced epigraphs. It is a topic which still awaits thorough
investigation, but which may emerge as crucial to our understanding of the self-consciously poetic nature of much of Bulgakov's
work.

Bulgakov's narrator is an exhibitionist, always seeking to draw
attention to himself. Hence the frequent use of multiple structures,
the plays within plays and so on, which serve, among other things,
to introduce a narrator to the body of the text; in his prose works,
Bulgakov is particularly skilful at introducing a narrator, sometimes literally, as in *The Life of Monsieur de Molière*, or in a more
complex fashion in *The Master and Margarita*. He enjoys disrupting
narrative illusions by suddenly inserting genuine autobiographical
details into his fictions, as when his own *The Days of the Turbins* is
abruptly referred to in *The Crimson Island* (185), or when Maksu-

dov in *A Theatrical Novel* describes the plot of a new work he is planning (395–6), which the reader cannot fail to recognize as *Zoyka's Apartment*. Bulgakov then further teases the reader – thereby again drawing attention to himself – by having Maksudov announce that the work in question was never actually written: 'But I didn't ever write down what I'd thought up' (396).

A further assertion of authorial presence is to be found in the effects Bulgakov achieves, for the readers rather than the theatre audiences of his plays, by means of his lyrical stage directions. These can represent a great deal more than simple instructions to the actors or the producer: in *The Crimson Island*, for instance, the direction 'Murmuring gloomily, the ocean descends' (97) is rather an attempt to amuse the reader by the unexpectedness of its poetry than a baffling challenge to the theatre-director's ingenuity. In *Adam i Eva* (*Adam and Eve*) the opening stage direction whimsically evokes a hypothetical situation wholly unrelated to the action of the play:

The most notable feature of the furnishings is a lamp hanging over the table, with a thick shade. It would be nice to lay out a game of patience beneath it, but all thoughts of patience vanish as soon as Efrosimov's face appears near the lamp.[73]

This narrative stage direction introduces an exclusively authorial perspective, which the reader is invited to share behind the audience's back, as it were; but then the author withdraws again into the fiction of narratorial dispassion, and allows the play to proceed on its course. These examples of the insistence of the authorial voice in Bulgakov's writing demonstrate again his disregard for the aim of achieving 'objectivity'.

All these features lend further weight to the argument that Bulgakov perceives art primarily through the person of the artist, rather than through his work, the greatness of which is assumed and not discussed. Both biographical and autobiographical perspectives are deployed in his work: he writes about historical figures in some instances, and about himself in other, more or less autobiographical works such as *Cuffnotes*, *For my Secret Friend*, and *A Theatrical Novel*. In his work of the 1920s his interest in the person of the creator had assumed another guise, that of the inventor (a theme possibly inspired by his own brief career as a man of science). In *The Fateful Eggs*, *The Heart of a Dog*, *Adam and Eve* and *Ivan*

Vasil'yevich (Blazhenstvo) (Ivan Vasil'yevich (Bliss)), the genius professors are all involved in endeavours to transcend the limitations of time, of space, or of mortality; never, as it turns out, with complete success. But while their achievements are impressive, they do not compare with those of the writer. Never in Bulgakov's works of science fiction is the inventor invested with the aura of immortality which belongs to his portrayals of Pushkin, Molière, or the Master. From 1929 onwards, Bulgakov's sense of literature as a sacred vocation will dominate his writing until it finds its most elaborate expression in *The Master and Margarita*: the author becomes the hero of Bulgakov's fiction, inspired, but always tragically athwart his own time.

2

Bulgakov and Molière

As for foreign writers, Bulgakov didn't just love Molière, that's not the right word; he was in love with Molière.[1]

Bulgakov's fascination with the figure of Molière dates from September 1929 and the beginning of his work on the play *Kabala svyatosh (Mol'yer)* (*The Cabal of Hypocrites* (*Molière*)); and over the next six and a half years this interest was to engender four separate works differing greatly in form and purpose. Bulgakov had naturally been long familiar with Molière's plays from his reading and from his theatre-going, but what particularly captivate his attention now are the details of the playwright's biography. This emphasis may have arisen directly out of the anguish of Bulgakov's own experiences in the late 1920s. But by now the political situation was such that he could not risk expressing his views in an explicitly autobiographical piece; and the next work he wrote must, for financial reasons if no other, be accepted by the authorities for publication or performance. The story of Molière's life offered enough historically authenticated material to justify a work whose main theme was to be the pressures to which the writer is exposed, particularly since the socio-political setting was a suitably deplorable absolute monarchy at a remove of nearly three centuries.

This is not to suggest, however, that Bulgakov's sole aim in writing about Molière was to express in disguised form his opinion of the Stalinist régime, as has been argued by Tatiana Chambers, one of the few Western critics to have written about Bulgakov's 'Molieriana':

From whatever angle Bulgakov chose to depict the French court and courtiers, the King, the dignitaries of the Church, the actors, Molière himself, both his biographical novel and the play (and indeed many of his other works) belong to the genre of cryptographical literature which was growing in strength in those years.[2]

The evidence provided by the texts themselves suggests that Bulgakov's purpose was far from being so unsubtle; and that while there

29

can be no doubt that he would expect his audiences and his readers
to draw analogies appropriate to the current situation, these works
on Molière nevertheless fulfil their manifest purpose as studies of a
historical figure.

The four Molière works provide an opportunity for us to explore
aspects of Bulgakov's use and adaptation of historical and literary
materials. The biographical play *The Cabal of Hypocrites (Molière)*
(1929–31) underwent a number of changes as a result of difficulties
it encountered during rehearsals at MKhAT. These help both to
bring out the central issues of the play and to underline the
idiosyncrasy of Bulgakov's rendering of Molière's story; at the
same time, the play's textual history reveals the difficulty of
establishing an authentic text. Bulgakov's prose biography *The Life
of Monsieur de Molière* (1932–3) was criticized on the grounds that
it was unhistorical; and an examination of his use of sources for this
particular work will throw light on larger questions about his
approach to historical writing and to the art of biography. *Poloumny Zhurden (The Follies of Jourdain)*, Bulgakov's 1932 adaptation of *Le Bourgeois gentilhomme*, has widely been described as
an exercise in stylistic parody; but it is questionable whether this
can really be understood as the main purpose, or indeed a true
purpose of a work which has suffered undue neglect. A brief look at
Bulgakov's much later translation of *L'Avare* (1935–6) also reveals
textual problems, which in this case shed doubt on the authenticity
of the published versions. All four works remind us that when
Bulgakov responds to Molière, it is through the story of his creative
life, rather than through the impact of his works or the influence of
his style. This is a pattern which will be repeated in his treatment of
his other literary heroes.

The Cabal of Hypocrites (Molière) (1929–31)

A good account of the writing of this play is to be found in
Chudakova's article on the Bulgakov holdings in the Lenin Library,
although this naturally disregards archival holdings elsewhere,
particularly in the MKhAT Museum.[3] The history of the play's
production is a long tale, however, even though the first full draft of
the work was written very quickly, between October and
December 1929. Bulgakov submitted it to MKhAT for consideration early in 1930; but on 18 March came the news that the Chief

Repertory Committee had refused to allow it to be staged, and
Bulgakov returned the work to his drawer. Then in the autumn of
1931 he made some additions and alterations to it in line with
suggestions made by the Repertory Committee, and the work was
finally approved on 3 October 1931. The play was immediately
taken on at MKhAT: preliminary meetings about it were held in
the spring of 1932, and a cast-list was drawn up for the 1932/3
season. But progress on the production soon got bogged down, and
rehearsals were held only intermittently.[4] At the end of 1934
MKhAT's director, Stanislavsky, attended the 115th rehearsal of
the play, and subsequently decided to superintend the work of the
producer Gorchakov, with the consequence that a number of
rehearsals were held at Stanislavsky's home at 6, Leont'yev Street
during the spring of 1935.[5] Anxieties about the play led the theatre
to insist on a number of emendations being made to the text during
1935; and, after four years of rehearsals, the play finally received its
première on 15 January 1936. But after just seven official performances, it was withdrawn and cancelled.

The story which underlies this brief account of the play's history
up to its first performance is a complex one, and we are fortunate
that a certain amount of documentation has survived to reveal the
true nature of the disagreements and apprehensions which accompanied the work through its unhappy and short-lived career. The
response from MKhAT when Bulgakov first submitted the play in
1930 was a favourable one, their principal reservation being that
their repertoire was seriously lacking in plays on contemporary
themes, and that *The Cabal of Hypocrites*, as it was known at that
stage, would not help to solve their problem.[6] The Repertory
Committee, however, was hostile; we do not know the specific
grounds for their rejection of the play in 1930, but their comments
evidently suggested that they were worried about what they considered to be mystical overtones in the work.[7] When Bulgakov
returned to the text a year later, in the autumn of 1931, he removed
from the stage directions certain details stressing the mysterious
atmosphere; he altered a passage suggesting that Archbishop
Charron was a demonic figure; omitted from the last act a sinister
nun who comes to collect all Molière's costumes from his dressing-
room as he lies dying on stage; changed the title of the play from
The Cabal of Hypocrites to *Molière*; and cut out the last line of the
play, where Lagrange suggests that ultimately the responsibility for

the tragedy lies in the hands of fate.[8] Bulgakov then sent the corrected version of the text to Gor'ky, and apparently with his assistance succeeded this time in winning the Repertory Committee over.[9] In October the work was passed, and Bulgakov wrote to Gor'ky in December to express his appreciation of his support.[10] Gor'ky responded by writing a further enthusiastic report on Bulgakov's behalf for Fischer Verlag, who were to handle the play abroad:

As for M. Bulgakov's play *Molière*, I can tell you that in my opinion it is a very good, skilfully wrought piece, in which each part provides the actor with solid material. The author has pulled off a great success, and this once again confirms the generally-held view of his talent and of his capacities as a dramatist.

He has drawn a brilliant portrait of Molière in his decline. A Molière exhausted by the disorders of his private life and by the burden of fame. Equally good, bold, and I would say beautiful, is the portrait of the Sun-King, and indeed all the parts are good. I am absolutely convinced that the play will be a success at the Moscow Arts Theatre, and I am very glad that it is being put on. It is an excellent play.[11]

The play's future seemed to be assured; but then a blow fell from an unexpected quarter. The play had not only been taken on at MKhAT, but also at the Bol'shoy Dramatichesky theatre in Leningrad. The first Bulgakov knew of the trouble was when the theatre, having already committed itself to the production and even paid him an advance of 1200 roubles, suddenly abandoned its plans to stage the play.[12] Eventually his friend Popov, who was staying in Leningrad at the time, was able to discover what had gone wrong; this was that the influential critic Vsevolod Vishnevsky had published such an attack on the theatre that it had taken fright and decided to dissociate itself from Bulgakov. Vishnevsky's article was a general critique of the theatre's reactionary stance, which he felt was epitomized in the choice of Bulgakov's play for the repertoire:

Bulgakov's ideological position in art is familiar to us from *The Days of the Turbins* and *Diaboliad*. Maybe in *Molière* Bulgakov has taken a step in the direction of 'reconstruction'? No, this is a play about the tragic fate of a French court dramatist (1622–73). Very relevant for 1932! One can understand and approve the idea of those who put *Tartuffe* on: let's show the classics. But why waste energy and time on a drama about Molière when you've got genuine Molière at your disposal?[13]

These comments proved sufficient to foreclose on the possibility of the production being staged in Leningrad; and perhaps they go some way towards explaining why MKhAT, who kept it on, were so peculiarly dilatory in working on the play between 1932 and 1934. No doubt the administration at MKhAT, sensitive to the fact that the theatre was always vulnerable to attack for its old-fashioned outlook, was rather regretting that it had committed itself to a play so blatantly beyond the pale of socialist realism.

Rehearsals dragged miserably on until the point when Stanislavsky involved himself in the production in October 1934, and even then continued only intermittently. But in the spring of 1935 he decided to take the production seriously in hand. Stenographic records of the rehearsals trace the course of the growing disagreements between Stanislavsky and Bulgakov, who had an official post as assistant director on the production, and reveal that Stanislavsky hoped to introduce fundamental changes to the content and the spirit of the play before it reached the stage.[14] Bulgakov himself only attended a small proportion of these rehearsals, and his attendance diminished as the hostility towards his work was made more and more explicit.[15] This meant that Stanislavsky could feel even more at liberty to pursue his policy of encouraging the actors to improvise the text in certain predetermined directions, in the hope that Bulgakov would be won over to Stanislavsky's view of the play and would agree to alter his text accordingly. It is indeed occasionally difficult to identify in these records just whose text is being rehearsed, especially on those days when Bulgakov was absent.

The first record that we have dates from 5 March 1935 and covers a discussion which took place after a run-through of the whole play except for the scene of Molière's death – a scene which, if we are to believe Gorchakov, Stanislavsky considered sentimental, complaining that it failed to convey to the audience anything of Molière's significance for posterity.[16] Stanislavsky and Bulgakov talked about how much work remained to be done on the text, with Stanislavsky concerned that the character of Molière was too mundane. He was anxious to bring out the socio-political issues raised by the biography:

A great deal of preparatory work has been done. But there is too much intimacy, too much bourgeois life, and there are no strokes of genius . . . The court, the Cabal, and the world of the artist need to be approached correctly from the theatrical point of view. It seems to me that the play needs to be taken up again now and all three lines need to be gone over ... You can make a whole scene out of a simple exchange. Just open it up a little, and the actor will do the rest.   (94–5)

Bulgakov, understandably, protested that five years had elapsed since the play was first written, and that it was impossible for him to start elaborating his interpretation now. But it is clear that he had in fact already made certain concessions – Stanislavsky mentions that he has insisted that the Cabal scene should take place in a cellar rather than in a cemetery – and that unless he did go on rewriting the work, Stanislavsky would not allow the production to go ahead. In an angry letter to Popov on 14 March 1935, Bulgakov gave vent to his exacerbation with Stanislavsky:

Now Stanislavsky has taken command. They ran through Molière for him (except for the last scene, which wasn't ready), and he, instead of giving his opinion of the production and the acting, started to give his opinion of the play.

In the presence of the actors (five years on!) he began to tell me all about the fact that Molière was a genius, and how this genius ought to be pictured in the play.

The actors licked their lips in glee and began to ask that their parts should be made larger.

I was overcome with fury. For a heady moment I wanted to fling the notebook down and say to them: you write about geniuses and ungeniuses if you like, but don't teach me how to do it, I won't be able to do it anyway. I'd be better acting instead of you.

But you can't, you can't do it. So I stifled it all and began to defend myself.

Three days later the same. He patted my hand and said that I needed to be rubbed up the right way, and then it was the whole business all over again.

In other words I've got to write in something about Molière's significance for the theatre, and somehow I've got to demonstrate that Molière was a genius, and so on.

This is all primitive, feeble and unnecessary. And now I'm sitting in front of my copy of the text, and I can't lift my hand to work on it. I can't not write it in: declaring war would mean wrecking all that work, stirring up a proper commotion, and harming the play itself; but writing green patches into the trousers of a black tail-coat! ... The devil knows what I should do?![17]

At first Bulgakov gave in to the unremitting pressure from Stanislavsky, and made further alterations to the text over the following weeks. On 17 April 1935 there was a rehearsal of the Cabal scene, which Bulgakov did not attend because he was too busy rewriting the love scene between Armande and Moirron. Stanislavsky treated the text as though it were just a rough outline:

There's material here for a strong scene . . . We will have to finish off what Bulgakov has left undone.[18]

He was particularly concerned to shift the emphasis in the scene away from the personal vendetta between Molière and the Archbishop, Charron, and to bring out the larger issues involved in this unholy alliance between a clergy which felt threatened by the scandalous innuendos of *Tartuffe* and an aristocracy jealous of the King's patronage of Molière. He therefore wanted to see a major denunciatory speech about *Tartuffe* introduced into the scene, to offset the Cabal's rather sordid interest in Moirron's allegations about Molière's supposedly incestuous relationship to his wife. Stanislavsky was also worried about the ending of the play, which he considered unacceptably pessimistic, and he even toyed with Gorchakov's suggestion that a heartening slogan might be more suitable:

Perhaps we really should finish off with an announcement: 'He is dead, but his glory and his creations live on. Tomorrow the show continues.' I think that's not bad.
    If we generally keep going along the lines we've sketched out, then we'll end up with a good play. Bulgakov sells himself short at times. If he were to agree to what has been proposed, then it would be a good play. He funks depths, he's afraid of philosophy.[19]

The extraordinary condescension with which Bulgakov – the author of *The Days of the Turbins*, MKhAT's most successful play since 1917 – was treated by the theatre's director finally exasperated him. When he saw the stenographic record of the rehearsal and realized how much more writing he was going to be asked to do, he sent Stanislavsky an ultimatum:

Today I received an excerpt from the record of the rehearsal of *Molière* on 17 April 1935, sent to me by the theatre.
    Now that I have acquainted myself with it, I find myself obliged to refuse categorically to make any alterations to my play *Molière*, since the changes to the Cabal scene outlined in the record, like the textual changes to other scenes proposed previously, would, as I have concluded, utterly destroy my artistic conception, and would lead to the composition of a new play,

which I am incapable of writing since I am fundamentally in disagreement
with it.

If *Molière* does not suit the Arts theatre as it stands, even though the
theatre took it on precisely as it is and has rehearsed it for a number of
years, then I would ask you to withdraw *Molière* and return it to me.[20]

Gorchakov reports that Stanislavsky, stung by this letter, declared
that he would now refuse to assume responsibility for the production; Gorchakov was told that he would simply have to go ahead
and see it through on his own, which he did.[21] Bulgakov would
never forgive Stanislavsky for the way he was treated over these
rehearsals; and when we come to read *A Theatrical Novel*, we find
that his fictional retelling of his experiences is not perhaps as
far-fetched as the satirical tone in which it is couched might mislead
us into assuming. In the end, Stanislavsky did not perhaps succeed
in altering the text to an enormous extent, and certainly not as
much as he would have liked. It would also be fair to point out that
some of his suggestions may have been governed by an all-too-
realistic awareness of the impact the theatre would make with such
an uncompromisingly old-fashioned psychological drama. But
what is certain is that in withdrawing his protection from the
production he was consciously exposing it to the disastrous reception which it then suffered.

The first months of 1936 were scarcely auspicious: in January and
February two articles in *Pravda* marked the inauguration of a new
period of repression in the cultural world, and the beginning of a
fierce campaign against Shostakovich in particular.[22] The official
première of *Molière* was due on 15 February, but a number of
performances took place earlier. Bulgakov's wife, Yelena Sergeyevna, recorded in her diary that the first performances were all a
sensational success, with up to twenty curtain-calls.[23] But Bulgakov
himself, always wary in these matters, was already in a pessimistic
mood when he wrote on 11 February to his friends the Popovs,
replying to their invitation to come and join them at Tolstoy's
estate, Yasnaya Polyana:

Of course, if it were possible to be transported without the slightest effort
to the snowdrifts of Yasnaya Polyana, then I would sit by the fire trying to
forget all about Molière, and Pushkin, and the comedy.

No, it's impossible. I envy you, and I hope you have a good rest, and I
thank you for the invitation . . .

Molière has had his première. The dress rehearsals were on the 5th and the 9th. People are talking of a success. At both of them I had to come out and bow, which I find a torment.

Today in *Sovetskoye iskusstvo* came the first arrow: Litovsky's review. He speaks disparagingly about the play, with great malice, even if relatively restrainedly; he writes inaccurately about the actors, with one exception.[24]

Later in her diary Yelena Sergeyevna described the gathering storm of criticism in the press, which did not correspond at all to the reception given to the play by the non-writing public. And then in an article in *Pravda* on 9 March 1936 entitled 'External Glitter and False Content', Bulgakov had much the same treatment meted out to him as Shostakovich had suffered:

The author has contrived to strip and denude this great theme of all that is serious and genuinely dramatic, of all great human feelings, and to substitute for them cheap effects and risqué situations in the spirit of the worst works by Dumas or plays by Scribe.

Bulgakov has taken as the basis for the story of Molière not the writer Molière, not the fighter and author of epoch-making works in the history of drama and the theatre, but Molière's entirely personal family life.[25]

MKhAT had in fact already pre-empted further criticism by removing the play from the repertoire even before the article was published. Yermolinsky describes Bulgakov's mood on the day of the publication:

The ninth of March was a day of mourning for him. He came to see me during the day. He was calm, and consulted me about financial matters. The banning of *Molière* complicated life even as far as simple everyday responsibilities were concerned. There were debts, and he had been counting on *Molière*.[26]

The banning of the play marked the end of Bulgakov's phase of work on Molière, with all the four works he had written since 1929 rejected and unpublished. He was never to see *The Cabal of Hypocrites* (*Molière*) performed again in his lifetime; this only became possible many years later, after the play's publication in 1962. Bulgakov's relations with MKhAT, which had hitherto always just survived the various crises to which they had been subjected, now finally gave way under the strain. Bulgakov had already been betrayed by Stanislavsky; and now the theatre took the play off with a haste which he found impossible to forgive.[27] He and his wife spent much of the spring and the summer after the ban

away from Moscow; and when they happened to spend some
time together with Gorchakov in the south, his condescending
manner towards them proved to be the last straw. When Bulgakov returned to Moscow in September, he handed in his resignation to MKhAT and broke off all his contracts with them.[28] He
soon found alternative employment as a librettist with the
Bol'shoy theatre;[29] but there is a sense in which the banning of
the Molière play constituted a defeat which finally broke Bulgakov's spirit.

   The Cabal of Hypocrites – to use its original, more pungent title –
does not pretend to be an historically accurate presentation of
Molière's life; it is a personal view of the playwright which uses
authentic materials, but rearranges them in order to concentrate all
the most significant factors which shaped his destiny into a compact
psychological study. One of the ways Bulgakov principally achieves
this effect is through his reorganization of the sequence of historical
events. The most important example of this is the way in which he
entirely reverses the chronology of the scandal over Molière's
Tartuffe, which allows him to introduce the theme of Molière's fall
from favour at court – an episode for which there is no historical
justification. In reality, the dispute and protests about the play took
place in 1664, and led to the play being banned before it had even
been completed; it was only in 1669 that permission to perform it
was granted, after which there was no further intervention from
Louis XIV. In Bulgakov's version, Molière is initially shown favour
by the King, and the play is allowed; some time later, however, it is
banned. The historical Molière, so far as we know, did not perceive
the 1664 banning of *Tartuffe* as a particularly devastating blow.
Indeed, the only evidence whatsoever that we have for any cooling
of relations between Louis XIV and Molière dates from much later,
in 1672, when the King awarded to the composer Lully the
copyright for 30 years of all the plays for which he had written
music, which included a number of Molière's.[30] This testifies,
however, more to the goodwill of the King towards Lully than to
any malevolence on his part towards Molière. Interestingly, the
stenographic record of the rehearsal held at Stanislavsky's home on
5 March 1935 suggests that the whole idea of having the King turn
away from Molière may not have formed part of Bulgakov's
original conception, and was a suggestion of Stanislavsky's which
Bulgakov for once welcomed:

Stanislavsky: By unmasking everybody, the charlatan doctors as well as the bourgeois, he set everybody against him. His only means of holding on was the patronage of the King, and when the King turned away from him, that really was a tragedy for him.

Bulgakov: It's a good idea – to put in a few phrases about the King withdrawing his favour from Molière.[31]

Bulgakov further distorts the facts in having Louis XIV take action against Molière because of a denunciation charging him with incest: the denunciation not only suggests that Molière's wife Armande Béjart was the daughter, rather than the sister, of Molière's former mistress, Madeleine, but also that Molière himself may have been Armande's father. The true story of the denunciation and its effects was quite the opposite. In 1663 Molière wrote *L'Impromptu de Versailles*, in which he made an insulting reference to a rival actor at the Hôtel de Bourgogne by the name of Montfleury. The latter's son took vengeance on his father's behalf not only by writing a riposte called *L'Impromptu de L'Hôtel de Condé*, in which Molière in turn was insulted, but also by writing to the King in December 1663 accusing Molière of having married his own daughter. It is not known what evidence Molière produced in his defence, but the fact that the King stood godfather to Molière's first child, born in January 1664, demonstrates that he dismissed the accusations. The issue was never raised again. So on two different occasions Bulgakov offers versions of historical events which seem to underline the King's role in Molière's downfall even though, as we shall see, the King is not ultimately accused in the play of full responsibility for his ruin. Bulgakov makes bold and free use of his materials, without actually inventing situations, distorting such forces as slanderous rumour only to present them in a more dramatic form; but he makes no attempt to portray these forces in strict proportion or chronological sequence, as a historian might seek to do. He gave a good account of this approach in the MKhAT newspaper *Gor'kovets* shortly before the play's 1936 première:

I wrote a romantic drama and not a historical chronicle. In a romantic drama complete biographical exactness is not possible or necessary. I put in a whole series of changes which serve to strengthen the play dramatically and embellish it artistically.[32]

Bulgakov adopts the same method with regard to the smaller details of the plot. Chambers states that the action of the play begins on 17 February 1662, and mentions two examples of anachronism in the first act.[33] But the events depicted in Act 1, which purport to take place in the course of a single evening, are in fact drawn from a great many different episodes in Molière's life, spanning eleven years in all. The troupe's first performance before the King was given on 28 October 1658, in the Guard Room of the Louvre; their first performance at the Palais Royal was on 20 January 1662; Armande and Molière were married on 20 February 1662, but she did not become pregnant until over a year later, in 1663; the whole episode of the boy hidden in the harpsichord dated from the time when Baron, the historical prototype for Moirron, was a very small child, and when Molière was still unaware of his existence; Baron only joined Molière's troupe in 1666, at the age of 13; and, finally, Madeleine Béjart did not leave the stage until after November 1669 – her last role was in *Monsieur de Pourceaugnac*, which received its première that month.[34]

Bulgakov resolves the problems which might be created by such a dense plot and complex time-scale through the invention of two characters who carry the structure of the play on their shoulders: Lagrange and Moirron. Little is known about Lagrange, an actor in Molière's troupe who kept a Register for the company in which were recorded all its performances and takings, and any events of outstanding importance. Through Lagrange Bulgakov establishes a narrative viewpoint which makes the play more coherent, singling him out as a character who will have some special function to perform:

Lagrange, who is not taking part in the performance, sits in the dressing-room plunged in thought. He is wearing a dark cloak. He is young, handsome, and dignified. The lamp casts a mysterious light on his face.

(219)

Our sense that Lagrange is rather an observer than a participant in the action is confirmed by a further stage direction in the first act, which invites us to look to him for a true interpretation of the comic dispute between Molière and Bouton:

Lagrange puts his head in his hands and weeps quietly.   (223)

Lagrange's entries in his *Registre* concerning Molière's marriage and his death mark the outer limits of the action of the play, which is lent a formal neatness through the repetition of the date, 17

February.[35] We are allowed to share the viewpoint of Lagrange, a sober and compassionate witness privy to all the most intimate aspects of Molière's life and endowed with a wisdom which enables him to appreciate the essential significance of events in the play. This permits Bulgakov simultaneously to suggest historical authenticity while stressing that he is presenting events through an individual, possibly subjective perspective.

While the figure of Lagrange provides the work's narrative clarity, the character of Moirron is vital to the compression and economy of the plot. One of Bulgakov's main sources for the play was Grimarest, whose 1705 biography of Molière will be discussed at greater length below; it is notable for the fact that one of Molière's actors, Baron, was Grimarest's main informant. Baron (1653–1729) had been employed as a very young boy by a M. Raisin, whom he assisted in the trick with the harpsichord. He later worked as an actor for M. Raisin's widow, and was spotted by Molière, whom he joined in December 1666. Armande, jealous of the attention Molière was showing Baron, made a scene and slapped him. Baron immediately walked out, and did not rejoin the troupe until 1670. In January 1671 a performance of *Psyché* gave rise to rumours that Baron and Armande were lovers. However, there is no evidence of any rift developing between Molière and Baron, and Grimarest goes on to give a touching account of the attentions shown by Baron to Molière at his death.

Bulgakov takes inspiration from this particular bias in Grimarest for one of the most successful inventions in his plot, the character of Moirron, whom he uses as the pivot for his anachronistic presentation of events. By compressing the events of Baron's life, he makes Moirron the instrument of Molière's downfall: the story of the harpsichord is carried forward and elaborated so that Moirron comes to overhear the secret of Armande's parentage. Moirron then acquires a motive for his denunciation through his affair with Armande and subsequent quarrel with Molière. This is made to coincide chronologically with the scandal over *Tartuffe*, so that the Cabal is able to make maximum use of the domestic storm. Moirron, a 'Judas' in Lagrange's view (270), is by no means the sole perpetrator of Molière's ruin, as the latter recognizes in his wry forgiveness of him in the last act; but he serves as the personification of fate's apparent ill-will towards Molière.

The symmetrical framework provided by Lagrange's entries is

reinforced by the fact that both the first and the last scenes of the play take place in Molière's theatre. Bulgakov, while principally interested in Molière's personality, was by no means as heedless of Molière's stature as a great dramatist as Stanislavsky supposed. These two scenes provide the audience with the necessary sense of Molière's passionate involvement with the theatre. The fact that, to all intents and purposes, he dies on stage, creates a convenient metaphor to express the paradox of his mortality as a man and his immortality as a writer. The body of the play is made up of some forty separate episodes, which combine to give a complex and comprehensive view of Molière's world and of the forces with which he has to contend; an approach later repeated by Bulgakov in *Posledniye dni* (*The Last Days*). The point is precisely that the writer–hero does not need to be at the centre of the stage for us to appreciate what factors determine his life; his fate depends not so much on his own actions as on those of the people around him. The succession of opening scenes combines to assure us of the uncertainties with which Molière is already beset, and makes explicit the tragedy of his life and vocation even before the Cabal sets about achieving his ruin. Molière is by no means just the victim of political intrigue; it is his destiny as a great artist to suffer.

Molière's transitory victory over Charron in the second act is succeeded by the revelation of a conspiracy against him, and by his discovery of Armande's infidelity. This confirms the pessimistic message of the first act, that hopes and aspirations are soon undermined by human fallibility. Molière's vulnerability has been exposed, and the rest of the play traces the disintegration of his personality under the pressures of betrayal, denunciation and rejection. By the fourth act only flashes of greatness remain, as in his wise handling of the melodramatically repentant Moirron. The tragedy already inherent in the play is now brought to a head, and the closing scenes describe a pathetic decline into insanity.

The tragic note is reinforced by Bulgakov's use at this stage of a sinister version of *Le Malade imaginaire*. This is historically accurate, since Molière did indeed collapse during the fourth performance of the play on 17 February 1673, although he actually died a few hours later at home. It is Grimarest who tells us that the collapse occurred as Argan the hypochondriac is being ceremonially initiated as a doctor, although this account continues by asserting that Molière pulled himself together and carried on with the performance.[36] Bulgakov, however, lends the scene a nightmarish quality which is entirely absent from the original. In Molière's version the scene takes place at the end of the play; Argan is to be mocked for his excessive faith in charlatan doctors by being invited to become one himself. Argan will of course believe every word of the comic mumbo-jumbo devised by some comedians, while his long-suffering family has a good laugh at his expense. In Bulgakov the episode assumes a completely different emotional character: a terrified Molière (Bulgakov deliberately uses the names of the characters in his own play rather than those of Molière's) is in bed, and is assailed by a series of apparitions which fill him with dread. He is caught up in a wild chant as he finds himself bewilderedly participating in an incomprehensible ceremony. The whirling exchanges are reaching a crescendo when Molière collapses, calling out for his old friend Madeleine, who has been dead for a year. Bulgakov here captures the delirium which preceded Molière's death, both as we know it from Grimarest's account, and as an appropriate rendering of the death as it relates to the tensions and events of the rest of the play. His last words are purposely stripped of dramatic significance:

Molière (suddenly falling in a comic way): Call Madeleine to me! I want her advice ... Help me! ...
        In the theatre: Ha-ha-ha-ha!
Don't laugh there in the stalls, wait, wait ...   (Falls quiet)   (282)

Bulgakov reminds us in Molière's remarks only of his common humanity.

The problem of determining where responsibility for Molière's ruin should lie is a complex one. While the two obvious candidates for blame are Louis XIV and the Cabal, Bulgakov sheds doubt on the possibility that either may be held fully responsible. The play does not simply argue that monarchy is evil, despite Molière's tirade against the King in Act 4:

The tyrant! ... He is a golden idol, and his eyes, would you believe, are emerald green ... All my life I've licked the spurs on his boots, and my only thought has been – don't crush me. And now he's crushed me just the same. The tyrant! ... I detest the tyranny of the King!   (273)

This outburst is vehement, certainly, but it is scarcely Molière at his most considered. In his state of extreme anxiety, Louis XIV becomes the scapegoat for evil which has largely been brought about by Charron. Bulgakov emphasizes that the speech is not to be taken strictly at face value by the way Bouton undermines the force of his words as he desperately attempts to suggest to imagined eavesdroppers that Molière is actually praising the King. On the one hand, the fact that he resorts to such a trick is an indication of the very real fear that he has of the repressive authorities; on the other, the fact that it is playacting – and poor playacting at that – stresses the pathetic absurdity of the scene.

The figure of Louis XIV is intriguing, designed to suggest the dual attitudes of hatred and fascination he evokes in Molière. Bulgakov is himself fascinated by the contrast between the monarch's absolute power and the helplessness of the writer. An interesting insight into the way Bulgakov wanted Louis XIV to come across on stage is afforded us by a selection of materials he provided for the actors during the course of work on the production, to assist them in building up their interpretations. This is just a selection of salient points from what is by far the longest and most detailed of the characterizations:

He raised the doctrine of divine right to a semi-religious dogma, expressed in the characteristic dictum ascribed, if not wholly reliably, to him: 'L'Etat, c'est moi!' (*Entsiklopedichesky slovar' Brokgauz–Efron* (*Brockhaus–Efron Encyclopaedic Dictionary*)).

He fascinated everyone. And the exterior did not prove deceptive, for Louis was a true King and did not shirk serious work (Prof. O. Iyeger, *Vseobshchaya istoriya* (*Universal History*)).

The King was uncommonly industrious, and was endowed with a regal exterior, a tactful manner, majesty, reserve, and the ability to dress even a refusal in a pleasant form ... There exist less favourable opinions. Saint-Simon insists that Louis was a narrow, cold person (Professor Savin, *Vek Lyudovika XIV* (*The Age of Louis XIV*)).[37]

These provide the basis for the portrayal of Louis as a man of undoubted power and self-assurance, but one who could combine genuine charm with his ruthlessness.

Louis stands in contrast to every other character in the play in the dignity of his behaviour. In the scene with De Lessac, he reveals himself a skilled and subtle handler of men; he deals with the cheat with elegant humour, as well as justice. This is further highlighted in the scene with Père Bartholomé.[38] On this occasion the clergy misjudge their enterprise and fail in their purpose of damaging

Molière's standing at court. But at the same time Louis displays a weakness which the Cabal will exploit – his pride. Charron tries to smooth the whole incident over:

He is up there, and you are on earth, and there is no-one else . . . Sire, there are no limits to your might, and never will be for as long as the light of religion shines over your State.   (240)

This formula, which Louis accepts as a reaffirmation of the divine right of kings, is in reality an expression of the Church's hold over him, for it is the Church which guarantees his position. For as long as Molière merely attacks the Church, as he had in *Tartuffe*, Louis will not disown his comedian; indeed, in the very earliest notes for the play Bulgakov apparently planned the scene between the King and the author of *Tartuffe* almost as a conversation between equals, with Louis deferentially discussing Molière's projected works.[39] The later version already portrays him as a much more patronizing figure; and as soon as the Church threatens the King's own dignity by implicating him in Molière's disgrace, Louis takes action against him. So it is only the initiative of the Cabal, using the executive power embodied in the King for its own ends, which brings about Molière's downfall. Louis himself, engaged in a higher game of statecraft, is callous about Molière's fate, though his fastidiousness is offended by the methods used to bring it about. Moirron becomes the butt of his scorn, a scapegoat for his distaste over the whole business. Louis leaves Charron and Odnoglazy to squabble over their clumsy attempt to engineer Molière's murder; and his exit, which closes Act 3, is a succinct expression of his superiority, and of his ultimately aesthetic concern for his own nimbus. Unhistorical though it is to suppose that an absolute monarch would stoop to closing doors himself, his final gesture is a symbolic washing of the hands.

Molière is fully aware of the identity of his real enemy, and when he attacks Charron there is a sincerity and a venom in his words which is missing in his later, more rhetorical denunciation of the King:

Ah, holy father! Are you satisfied? Is this for *Tartuffe*? I can understand why you have leapt so vigorously to the defence of religion. You are shrewd, my venerable sir. That's beyond dispute. My friends once said to me: 'You ought to write about one of those stinking monks.' And so I described you. Because where could you find more of a stinking monk than you?   (265)

Bulgakov stresses the personal aspects of the conflict between Molière and the leader of the Cabal, a silent and faceless body of conspirators.[40] The sinister men who wield real power are terrifying in the very elusiveness of their identity, and in the ruthlessness with which they work to prevent the artist revealing the extent of their hypocrisy and corruption. Any parallel which the reader might seek to draw with Bulgakov's own world reveals that he was treading treacherous ground indeed. For if we are to find a correlation between the figure of Louis XIV and that of Stalin, a corresponding one should be noted between the Cabal as the wielder of ideological power and the Communist Party; and it is they who are identified as the real source of harm in the play, while the character who appears to be the repository of absolute power remains in fact a figurehead.

What we know of the evolution of the text of *The Cabal of Hypocrites* suggests that it would be difficult to establish a putative master-text. As we have seen, the play was first reworked between 1929 and 1931, when Bulgakov removed from the text a number of details which provided a mysterious, demonic backdrop to the action. Once the play had been accepted for production at MKhAT, the text was again altered during the years of rehearsals as Stanislavsky sought to highlight the social and political aspects of the text. It is not yet possible to compare all the various drafts of the text or ascertain exactly which alterations Bulgakov agreed to or rejected between 1932 and 1936; but we can state with confidence that neither the text published in 1962, nor indeed the 1965 version which apparently restores virtually all the mystical elements removed in 1931, in fact corresponds to the text which seems to have been performed with Bulgakov's approval in 1936. In other words, the text appears to have undergone further editorial changes for the 1962 and 1965 editions; and until we have access to all the relevant archival materials we shall not be able to evaluate the grounds for these editorial decisions.

The basis used for the comparison of the 1936 text with the published versions is a draft of the play of which four almost identical copies have been preserved in the MKhAT Museum, one of them bearing a certificate that it was checked through on 18 December 1935. This date is so close to that of the première on 15 February 1936 that it is reasonable to assume that this text was more or less final.[41]

Certain features which were removed from the text before its publication in 1962 represent a regrettable loss in that they contributed to the vigour of the play's language. Such, for example, is a lively song written by Bulgakov for the musketeers, a drinking song about the Black Cat Inn, of no great significance for the plot but of interest as one of Bulgakov's rare excursions into verse form.[42] A further example of such emasculation comes in Act 2, Scene 1, when the cobbler is instructed by the King to insult the cardsharp. In the printed text this comes across as a facile joke, which turns on the complete inadequacy of his cursing. In the 1936 production the cobbler improvised a whole rhyming tirade against the cheat, threatening him with all sorts of dire punishments:

Ну держись! Чтоб ты себе на новом мосту, в великом посту ноги переломал и головой в лужу попал. Чтоб тебе жирная шлюха, поперёк твоего тощего брюха, помоями из окна вылила и нос твой крючком завила. Чтоб под святую пасху морду твою стёрли в краску и нож тебе в горло вогнали, чтоб ты мог понимать, как с королём в карты играть. Хорошо я его отделал, государь?

(Hold on, now! May you break your legs on the Pont Neuf during Lent and trip head first into a puddle! May some greasy slag pour dirty slops out of her window right down your skinny belly, and may she tweak your nose for you! May they rub your ugly mug in paint on the eve of Holy Easter, and drive a knife into your throat, so that you should learn how to play cards with the King!
Have I done him over like you wanted, Sire?)[43]

While this cursing is of no great literary merit, it does at least add colour – and point – to the scene.

One episode where there appears to have been a certain amount of hesitation is the moment in the Cabal scene when Moirron is being interrogated and two torturers are summoned and asked to bring a Spanish boot with them. In the published text, Moirron immediately assures them that this will not be necessary and begins to talk (252). This is the only point on which the various MKhAT texts diverge. In No. 327 a command is simply given that the boot should be placed on his foot, whereupon Moirron abandons his resistance. No. 322, the second prompter's copy, contains two alternative versions typed on separate pieces of paper. The first of these is extremely violent, with Moirron gasping out his confession as the torturers are urged to tighten the boot still more. The second has Moirron being persuaded to repeat what he had told Charron

earlier by the suggestion that a secretary was hidden in Charron's
room and has his confession already written down anyway. No. 82,
the assistant director's text, has a handwritten copy of the scene
where Moirron is actually tortured; and it is also included in
No. 44, the prompter's copy which was checked through in
December 1935. It seems probable, therefore, that it was the most
violent version which was actually performed. The removal of this
episode diminishes the character of Moirron, who acquires some
restored credit as a friend of Molière's through his initial valiant
resistance.[44]

Another small discrepancy between the 1936 version and the
published text comes in the Cabal scene again, where an exchange
between Charron and Brat Vernost' makes more explicit the extent
to which the news of Molière's incest delights them precisely
because it will embarrass the King, who is godfather to Molière's
child. Glad as they are to have vengeance on the author of *Tartuffe*,
the Cabal appreciates the usefulness of the incest scandal for their
higher ambitions.

A different kind of discrepancy suggests that some attempts were
made by the 1962 editors to restore, rather than to mask, Bulgakov's original intentions. This is the case where interpolations in
the 1936 versions we can only attribute to Stanislavsky are concerned. The principal example of this comes in the much-disputed
love-scene between Armande and Moirron. The 1962 and 1965
publications contain some exchanges only purporting to come from
Molière's comedy–ballet *Psyché* (246), for Bulgakov was absolutely adamant that he would not include any extracts from
Molière's actual writings in his play. This is why he went to the
lengths of composing some pseudo-Molière both for this scene and
for the closing scene, when Molière collapses. Stanislavsky, on the
other hand, was equally determined that the play would be much
improved by the inclusion of extracts from the originals, and it
would seem that, for the purpose of the 1936 production at least,
Bulgakov was overruled. In the MKhAT text Armande speaks a
line which virtually paraphrases a speech from *Psyché* (Act 4, Scene
4), and Moirron actually launches into a speech from *Dom Juan*
(Act 1, Scene 2).[45] None of this was retained in the 1962 and 1965
editions.

The 1936 and 1962 versions are also importantly at variance
concerning the vexed question of Armande's parentage; this is a

controversy of such importance to Bulgakov's prose biography of Molière that discussion of it will be deferred until the two works can be considered together. Yet it must be recognized that, for all these alternative readings, the text of *The Cabal of Hypocrites* which has survived is by no means a travesty of the author's intentions, perhaps because it was published under the supervision of Bulgakov's widow Yelena Sergeyevna. The more contentious elements have been smoothed down rather than eliminated; and the principal feature of Bulgakov's portrayal of Molière, the paradox of his literary greatness and his human fallibility, emerges despite everything from the text.

In the end, Molière figures almost as an unimportant victim of the struggle between the two powers of the King and the Cabal. In this work, as in *The Master and Margarita*, the writer is in a sense irrelevant to the affairs of the world; his significance is restricted to his ability to expose evil, and his artistic insights do not have to be measured in terms of the effectiveness of their attack on social issues. This is how we should interpret the remark omitted between 1931 and 1965 from the end of the play, about the cause of Molière's defeat: 'The cause of all this was fate.'[46] It is the writer's destiny to be defeated, and even if art is inherently subversive, still the artist has no alternative except to make some compromises with the State if his work is to be published or performed. And for as long as he retains his integrity in the composition of his art, the writer is under no obligation to go out and translate his thought into action.

The play sets out not to glorify Molière, but to invite our sympathy towards a man who was much tormented. He suffered not only because as a writer he drew upon himself the hostility of those social forces whose power he threatened to undermine, but also because writing is a vocation to which, it seems, vulnerable men are attracted. Their sensitivity, however, is accompanied by a weakness which prevents the writer from becoming a hero or a martyr. Molière is a man of volatile temperament, who can be aggressive and seem cruel at times; and yet those who love him sincerely can see through all that and recognize the suffering underneath. This trait of vulnerability characterizes many of Bulgakov's heroes, from Aleksey Turbin, the 'chelovek-tryapka' ('limp rag') in *The White Guard*, to the writer–heroes of Bulgakov's works of the 1930s; they also share a typical response to persecution in their longing for peace.

From all this it follows that Stanislavsky's attempts to present
Molière as a great literary and political figure were completely
inimical to Bulgakov's conception. This can be seen as the attempt
to express through the figure of Molière his view of the essential
tragedy of the writer's position, his alienated and yet fatally
dependent relationship to society. For Bulgakov this is true of
writers in any age, but it is of particular relevance to his own
society, which seeks to involve the writer in social and political life
to a greater extent than any other has done. It is in the sense that
Bulgakov believes all writers to share a common destiny that the
figure of Molière is a generalized one and the play non-historical;
but the personal affection Bulgakov felt towards Molière's writing
and his genuine interest in Molière's biography ensure that the
work is also a serious endeavour to evoke and penetrate the
historical figure.

The Life of Monsieur de Molière (1932–3)

In July 1932, at a time when Bulgakov was still optimistic about the
staging of his Molière play, he signed a contract with the publishers
of the 'Zhizn' zamechatel'nykh lyudey' ('Lives of the Great') series
for a prose biography of Molière. This was to be completed by 1
February 1933.[47] He got straight down to work on it, and by early
August he was already deep into his reading of materials for the
book, as we can see from his letter to Popov of 4 August 1932:

My dear friend Pavel Sergeyevich,
As soon as Jean Baptiste Poquelin de Molière releases my mind a little and
I get a chance to collect my thoughts, I will start writing to you with
avidity.
    A biography – ten printer's sheets – and in the heat, too – and in
Moscow, what's more!
    Yet I would like to be writing to you about serious and important things,
which is unthinkable for as long as Grimarest, Despois and other foreign
tourists are still on my desk.[48]

He worked on it steadily, except for a break from early September
to early November for the writing of The Follies of Jourdain, and
continued through the winter. The manuscript was delivered to the
publishers just slightly late, on 5 March 1933. The series editor
A. N. Tikhonov was extremely critical, particularly of the figure of
the narrator,[49] and sent it to Gor'ky in Sorrento for his opinion,

together with a letter replying to Gor'ky's criticisms of the series and of the authors who wrote for it:

You will be able to judge the extent to which even the most talented of them are ignorant and nonchalant as regards socio-political problems by Bulgakov's manuscript on Molière, which I am sending you.[50]

Bulgakov wrote to Tikhonov on 12 April protesting at his request that he should alter the whole narrative approach,[51] and the next day described the whole fiasco at length in a letter to Popov:

Well, now my Molierian days have begun. They opened with T[ikhonov]'s review. Dear Patya, it contained a multitude of delights. My narrator, who is in charge of the biography, is described as a casual young man who believes in sorcery and demons; he possesses occult skills, has a fondness for salacious stories, makes use of dubious sources and, worst of all, is inclined to royalism.

But that's not all. In my work, according to T., 'there emerge fairly transparent allusions to our Soviet conditions'!

Ye[lena] S[ergeyevna] and K[olya], when they had acquainted them-selves with the editor's missive, fell into a rage, and Ye. S. was even ready to rush off and have things out with him. Restraining her by her skirt, I was scarcely able to dissuade her from such domestic deeds of valour. Then I composed a letter to the editor.

When I had thought the business over at length, I decided it would be as well not to join battle. I just snarled a bit about the form of the review, but didn't bite. And in essence what I did was this: T. wrote that, instead of my narrator, I ought to put in 'a serious Soviet historian'. I informed him that I was not a historian, and refused to redo the book.

T. writes in the same letter that he has sent the manuscript to Sorrento.

And so, it is my honour to bury Jean-Baptiste Molière. It will be quieter and better for everyone. I am utterly indifferent to the idea of adorning a shop-window with my book-jacket. In reality I am an actor, not a writer. And, quite apart from that, I am fond of peace and quiet.

So there's your report on the biography you were interested in.

Please give me a ring. We'll agree on an evening when we can get together and draw into our conversation at table the names of those glorious comedians, sieurs Lagrange, Brécourt, Du Croisy and the commander himself, Jean Molière.[52]

But Gor'ky, who had done so much at the end of 1931 to get *The Cabal of Hypocrites* accepted, took sides against Bulgakov this time and sent Tikhonov a letter concurring with his opinion:

I entirely agree with your perfectly well-founded evaluation of M. A. Bulgakov's work. Not only does it need to be filled out with historical material and given social relevance, but its 'playful' style will have to be changed. As it stands it is not a serious piece of work, and you rightly point out that it will be roundly condemned.[53]

Gor'ky's point about the work's playfulness is a question to some extent of taste; but in demanding more historical material and criticizing it for its lack of seriousness or social significance, he calls into question Bulgakov's whole conception of the biography.

In fact, there is some reason to suppose that Tikhonov and Gor'ky were at least as concerned about the possible political consequences of publishing the work as they were critical of it on aesthetic grounds. Bulgakov's second wife, Lyubov' Yevgen'yevna, who had parted from her husband not long before, was working in the same publishing house as Tikhonov, and her recollection is that Gor'ky's real opinion of the work was somewhat different. Tikhonov told her that Gor'ky had been much more frank in conversation:

What can one say; it's talented, of course. But if we start publishing books like that we'll very likely get into trouble.[54]

For whatever reason, however, the biography was rejected once Bulgakov had made it clear that he was not prepared to make any alterations to it, and the question of its publication was never raised again in his lifetime. The series published it in the end in 1962, and even then only with a somewhat patronizing introduction and commentaries by an editor, G. Boyadzhiyev.

The question of the historical accuracy of the work raises the issue of Bulgakov's attitude to his sources and to the art of biography. An examination of his sources goes a long way towards confounding the view that his work was either shoddy, or else a crudely disguised comment on the contemporary scene. It is Bulgakov's prose biography rather than his play which has particularly provoked such attacks, since the attempt to invest a traditionally historical genre with a fictional viewpoint is more likely to make the reader uneasy. And since Bulgakov provided no bibliography, information about the works he used has to be deduced from the versions of events presented in the text, or sought in various documents relating to this period in his archives.

This is not the place to go into exhaustive detail about the various editions of Molière's works in Russian and French which Bulgakov referred to; suffice it to say that he consulted notes and introductory articles by many of the leading Russian Molière experts such as Yu. A. Veselovsky, Ye. V. Anichkov, K. L. Fel'i and others during the writing of the biography. He also owned a number of background works, such as a Russian translation of Scarron's *Roman comique*, which gives a good idea of theatrical life in provincial France in Molière's day; an edition in French of Madame de Sévigné's *Lettres*; A. N. Savin's *Vek Lyudovika XIV (The Age of Louis XIV*, Moscow, 1913), a good description of life at court with particular emphasis on social and political issues; and a *Petit Larousse* dictionary (Paris, 1910) to supplement the other encyclopaedias which he regularly used. Whereas in the play *The Cabal of Hypocrites* the sources used are evident for the most part only in general questions of interpretation, the biography is made up of episodes taken directly from specific sources, sometimes even as quotations or very close paraphrases, although these are never acknowledged. Bulgakov's decision not even to append a bibliography to this work was a measure of the unconventionality of his method which did little to recommend itself to the publishers.[55] In some places Bulgakov's own contribution amounts to no more than the narrative introduction and presentation of material, although he of course retains overall control of the work through his selection of episodes.

One of the basic sources used by Bulgakov for the biography was a work by M. V. Barro, *Mol'yer – ego zhizn' i literaturnaya deyatel'nost' (Molière – His Life and Literary Work*, St Petersburg, 1891). This provided him with a number of factual details, such as the ill-starred motto over Fouquet's gate 'Quo non ascendam', and the information about Chapelle's letter which was to be shown only to Mlle Menou; it also afforded him some anecdotes of extremely doubtful authenticity, such as the tale of the barber's chair in Pézenas where Molière is supposed to have sat observing men and manners, and the details of Charles Coypeau d'Assoucy's association with the troupe. Barro himself found all these items in French sources; but similarities in the presentation and style of certain episodes make it certain that Bulgakov himself went no further than Barro for these materials.

Another biography used by Bulgakov in a similar way was *Mol'yer – teatry, publika, aktyory ego vremeni (Molière – the Theatres, Audiences and Actors of His Time*, Moscow, 1922), a translation from the French of a work by K. Mantsius. This was the

source for details about the actor Bellerose, and for some of the
information about the Béjart and Poquelin families, including the
assertion, which Bulgakov dismisses, that Molière's father could
have served as the prototype for Harpagon in *L'Avare*. For the
most part these two books, like E. Despois's *Le Théâtre français
sous Louis XIV*, provided Bulgakov with uncontroversial details
and anecdotal materials which he lifted directly from the texts; it is
clear that he made no effort to check the stories which appeared
here, and certainly did not trouble to consult original sources.

Grimarest's *Vie de Monsieur de Molière*, the extremely controversial first biography of Molière published originally in 1705, is
used by Bulgakov in a variety of ways. His copy of the 1930 reprint
is preserved in his archive, and is apparently heavily laden with
annotations, as well as being accompanied by a notebook where
many passages have been copied out and comments made on the
text.[56] We have seen how it inspired him to create the figure of
Moirron in *The Cabal of Hypocrites*, and it can indeed be described
as the single most powerful influence on his interpretation, not least
in suggesting the title for his biography. Grimarest explains that he
used the form 'Monsieur de Molière' as a demonstrative indication
of respect, for which he came under strong attack, since comedians
were not supposed to be dignified with the title 'Monsieur'.[57]
Bulgakov would similarly have enjoyed redressing a slight, and the
title also served nicely to intimate the relatively domestic nature of
his approach.

In some instances Bulgakov takes long quotations directly from
Grimarest, adapting them only to suit his own narrative perspec-
tive. Compare, for example, his account of a conversation between
Molière's father and grandfather:

'Why have you taken to going so often to the theatre with him?' asked
Poquelin. 'You're not thinking of turning him into a comedian, are you?'
    The grandfather put down his hat, stood his cane in the corner, paused,
and then said: 'Please God that he should turn out to be as great an actor as
Bellerose.'   (26)

with Grimarest's version:

Le père, qui appréhendait que ce plaisir ne dissipât son fils, et ne lui ôtât
toute l'attention qu'il devait à son métier, demanda un jour à ce bon
homme pourquoi il menait si souvent son petit-fils au spectacle? Avez-
vous, lui dit-il, avec un peu d'indignation, envie d'en faire un comédien?

Plût à Dieu, lui répondit le grand-père, qu'il fût aussi bon comédien que Bellerose.[58]

There are many other examples of direct borrowings of this sort. In some instances, Bulgakov is more accurate about details than Grimarest; he does not follow him, for example, in dating *Psyché* to 1672 rather than 1671, nor does he make Grimarest's mistake of saying that Louis XIV granted the troupe 7000 livres (the actual figure was 6000)[59] when he bestowed upon them his royal patronage.

The scenes which close the biography are almost entirely taken from Grimarest, particularly in the great emphasis which is placed on the role of Baron in the proceedings. According to Grimarest, both Baron and Armande were deeply moved by Molière's last speech to them as he stood on the stairs in his house:

'Tant que ma vie a été mêlée également de douleur et de plaisir, je me suis cru heureux; mais aujourd'hui que je suis accablé de peines sans pouvoir compter sur aucuns moments de satisfaction et de douceur, je vois bien qu'il me faut quitter la partie: je ne puis plus tenir contre les douleurs et les déplaisirs qui ne me donnent pas un instant de relâche. Mais, ajouta-t'il en réfléchissant, qu'un homme souffre avant de mourir. Cependant je sens bien que je finis.' La Molière et Baron furent vivement touchés du discours de M. de Molière, auquel ils ne s'attendaient pas, quelque incommodé qu'il ne fût. Ils le conjurèrent, les larmes aux yeux, de ne point jouer ce jour-là, et de prendre du repos pour se remettre. 'Comment voulez-vous que je fasse? leur dit-il; il y a cinquante pauvres ouvriers qui n'ont que leur journée pour vivre; que feront-ils, si l'on ne joue pas? Je me reprocherais d'avoir négligé de leur donner du pain un seul jour, le pouvant faire absolument.'[60]

Bulgakov quotes almost complete phrases from this speech (212–13), but he intersperses additions of his own which cast an entirely new light on the exchange. He introduces the scene with a mildly flirtatious conversation downstairs between Armande and Baron, and while it is clear that they are anxious to avoid scandal, it is also obvious that they go upstairs with the utmost reluctance. They evidently consider Molière a bad-tempered, suspicious and eccentric old man. In Bulgakov's hands Molière's comments about the time having come for him to pass on take on a different significance: they are addressed to Baron, and the implication is that Baron will take his place when he has gone, not only in the theatre, but also with regard to Armande. Grimarest's sentimental scene becomes for Bulgakov the means of revealing Molière's bitterness and the extent of his domestic unhappiness. Bulgakov's borrowings from Grimarest are by no means unthinking; but he finds Grimarest's anecdotes and manner congenial, and adapts his materials to express his own imaginative intuitions about his hero.

One other important source for Bulgakov was the Russian version of a book by Jules Patouillet, translated as *Mol'yer v Rossii* (*Molière in Russia*, Berlin, 1924). This is where he found a discussion of the early Russian translations of Molière, which he used in his Prologue, including the extraordinary version of *Les Précieuses ridicules* composed by a jester at the court of Peter I. The actual quotation from the jester's text is to be found in the notes to Patouillet's book, and it seems probable that it was while working on this quotation that Bulgakov's eye was caught by a footnote on the next page:

In the commentaries to his translation of Fontenelle's *Conversations on the Plurality of Worlds*, which was finished in 1730 and printed in 1740, Kantemir explains the proper names which are mentioned (Copernicus, Descartes, Molière: 'Molière was a renowned author of French comedies in the reign of Louis XIV').[61]

This is, then, where Bulgakov found his second epigraph for the biography, to accompany the remark from Horace on satire referred to in Chapter 1. The choice of such a quaint description by Kantemir introduces the important theme of the relative merits of Molière and the King's claims to immortality, and comments humorously on the way that perceptions of them have evolved over the centuries.

It is interesting to compare Bulgakov's work with a biography written in the same period in the West, particularly as this affords us the possibility of assessing his historical accuracy in the context of Molière studies at that time. John Palmer, writing in 1930, describes some of the limitations imposed on the biographer by the materials available:

The initial task of the biographer of Molière is to recover him from the mass of legend that has accumulated about his name for the last three hundred years. Every stage in his career is encumbered with anecdotes, conjectures, libels and constructions ... There can be no summing up of the life and work of Molière. We can but show him at work, place him within his period and environment, and leave men free to take for themselves such pieces of him as they may require.[62]

Bulgakov's approach to the biography incorporates an awareness of our ignorance of the true facts of Molière's life, and this certainly puts in a different light his at times apparently cavalier use of sources. It is clear from Palmer that Bulgakov was not always up to date with the latest discoveries in the field, and a very important shortcoming of the biography is Bulgakov's failure to take advantage of the research published in the 1920s by G. Michaut, which to this day offers the most detailed and reliable investigation of Molière's life up to 1666.[63] This omission leads him to take for granted, for instance, the story that Molière had studied under Gassendi, a claim which Palmer is able to refute on the basis of evidence provided by Michaut.[64]

Another way of assessing the historical accuracy of Bulgakov's work is to examine his treatment of a key issue in Molière's biography, the unresolved controversy over Armande's parentage; whether Armande Béjart was not really Madeleine's daughter rather than her sister, and whether there is therefore any possibility of Molière having been her father as well as her husband. In *The Cabal of Hypocrites*, Bulgakov was unequivocal in stating that Armande was the daughter of Madeleine, although it is only in the 1936 MKhAT version of the text that the charge of incest is made entirely explicit by Molière's enemies during the interrogation of Moirron, who is horrified at the conclusions they draw from his confession:

Brat Sila (*Brother Strength*): In other words, my dear friend, you mean that Molière married his own daughter.
Moirron: I'm not saying that, holy father.
Brat Sila: But I am saying it. After all, you know that Molière lived for twenty years with Madame Madeleine Béjart.[65]

This is reinforced later in the same version of the play by the addition of another phrase to Louis XIV's explanation of the reasons why he is withdrawing his protection from Molière:

Because you presumed to ask me to stand godfather to your child by your very own daughter.

Perhaps the editors of the 1962 published text felt that this detail was historically too controversial to remain in the play, or simply that it was too offensive an accusation to make against the great dramatist, even when the rest of the play does not endorse the charge. Bulgakov is a little more tentative in his conclusions in *The Life of Monsieur de Molière*:

> What can one say about this tangled business, which is full of unreliable documents, circumstantial evidence, suppositions and doubtful facts? . . . This is my conclusion. I am convinced that Armande was the daughter of Madeleine, and that she was born in secret, in an unknown location, and of an unknown father. There is no specific proof to show that the rumours of incest were correct, that is, that Molière married his own daughter. But there is no proof either which would absolutely refute this dreadful story.
>
> (138)

Bulgakov's sources differ quite considerably in their opinions of the truth: Barro presents the evidence for Madeleine having been Armande's mother without finally committing himself;[66] Mantsius dismisses the charges as vile slander;[67] Grimarest takes it for granted that Madeleine was her mother and refers throughout to Armande as 'sa fille', but names Madeleine's erstwhile lover, the Duc de Modène, as her father.[68] Bulgakov's contemporary John Palmer comments on the way in which generations of biographers have tried to prove that Armande was not Molière's daughter:

> The generous and unlearned were content to deny the imputation on the grounds of decency . . . We will merely observe that none of the friends of Molière, during his lifetime, is recorded as having said a single word to invalidate the general belief that Armande was the daughter of Madeleine.[69]

Bulgakov accepts the argument that there may have been a conspiracy to persuade the world that Armande was the daughter of Madeleine's mother, Marie-Hervé Béjart; but the evidence for this is shown by Palmer to be invalid. There was a notorious document which stated that Armande's mother was Marie-Hervé, and Bulgakov suggests that it must be fake because it describes as minors children who must long ago have attained majority (132–3). Palmer points out that since the age of legal majority at the time was 25, there are no grounds for discrediting the document; but at the same time Palmer still does not deny that Madeleine may have been Armande's mother.[70] Bulgakov's editor Boyadzhiyev, referring to the authority of Michaut and Eugène Rigal, reproaches him for having allowed himself to be persuaded by slander either about Armande's father or about her mother.[71] Yet other modern commentators seem on the whole to endorse Bulgakov's conclusions: Alfred Simon notes that Molière and Madeleine spent the summer of 1641 together (there is some confusion as to whether Armande was born in 1642 or 1643), but suggests that:

S'il semble à peu près sûr qu'Armande était la fille de Madeleine et non sa soeur, il n'en résulte pas qu'elle fût la fille de Molière.[72]

In fact, while Bulgakov's use of materials was idiosyncratic, his work displays sufficient scholarship to make it a serious contribution to the study of Molière. Historical authenticity was after all not his primary purpose. He did not seek out primary sources; Lagrange's *Registre* had been available in a facsimile edition since 1876, for instance, but we know that he did not consult it.[73] His use of sources was unconventional: he was more concerned to make a varied range of materials the basis for a personal interpretation of the subject than to fall in with the normative style adopted by the scholarly biographer. Bulgakov is not interested in mere historical fact, which he evidently considers lifeless. For him, the personality of Molière only comes to life when refracted through the eyes of another writer, and whereas references to biographers of Molière or historians of the period are wholly lacking from the text, references to other writers abound. Horace, Kantemir, Goldoni, Griboyedov, Pushkin, Gogol, George Sand, Zotov, Scarron, Gassendi, Alfred de Vigny, Loret, Voiture, Ménage, La Fontaine, Boileau and Corneille are some of the writers who appear in Bulgakov's work in order to state their opinions of Molière, create works inspired by his life, or acknowledge his influence on their writing. Bulgakov's aim in invoking this literary tradition is to convey something of his sense that the writer's world is a closed one, that it is a craft largely appreciated by the practitioners of it, while the rest of society remains indifferent or even hostile to it. He brings out the difference between the normal approach of the biographer, whose concern is the historical facts about the man of genius, and his own, which seeks to evoke the human qualities of that genius.

Bulgakov selects telling and vivid details from a range of respectable sources such as Mantsius, Barro, Savin, Despois, Patouillet and others; yet his main source is Grimarest, who would never be used by a conventional biographer without some explanation of his limitations and bias, and whose claims to veracity have been dismissed by virtually all Molière scholars. The reader will not appreciate the nuances of Bulgakov's interpretation, therefore, unless he already has a detailed knowledge of Molière's life; so that Tikhonov's reservations about the biography, like Stanislavsky's anxieties about *The Cabal of Hypocrites*, are to some extent understandable if we construe them as expressing a concern that these works would simply be above the heads of the audiences for whom they were intended. The aim of Bulgakov's art is always to stimulate, never just to educate, and it is in this sense that it can be seen as the art of an intellectual élite. The public's response to the works when they were published, however, suggests that Stanislavsky and Tikhonov may have underestimated their audiences.

The most striking feature of the work itself is the Prologue, where the narrative stance adopted by Bulgakov creates a certain intimacy and serves as a focussing point for the humour with which he treats the vagaries of Molière's behaviour and temperament. Apart from establishing the manner of what is to follow, Bulgakov states in this, the only major fictional passage in the work, his attitude towards Molière and towards his own creation too. He is, as it were, warning the reader not to approach the biography with too many preconceptions, and endeavouring to forestall criticism by asserting the unconventionality of his approach from the very beginning. We may regret that he did not carry this bold conception through to the rest of the work, which loses in interest what it gains in conventionality.

Even the opening paragraph sets out to undermine what might have been our expectations of the work: rather than naming the hero and invoking his greatness, Bulgakov stresses the ordinary humanity of the infant:

On 13 January 1622 a certain midwife who had studied her craft in the maternity home of Maison Dieu in Paris under the direction of the celebrated Louise Bourgeois, delivered sweet Madame Poquelin, née Cressé, of a first child, a premature infant of the male sex.   (9)

The only fame referred to here is that of the now long-forgotten – and, indeed, fictional – head of the school of midwifery, Louise Bourgeois. This is already a prelude to the theme of the uncertainty of greatness and immortality which is to flavour our appreciation of the course of the relationship between Louis XIV and Molière in the book. But Bulgakov will also emphatically assert his admiration for Molière, which should be borne in mind by the reader as we

follow Molière through the series of apparently trivial or unflatter-
ing incidents which are depicted in the body of the book. As the
narrator tells the midwife:

Madame Poquelin will not give birth to such a child again, nor will any
other matron have such a child for centuries to come.   (10)

He later develops the theme of the relative claims of political and
creative power to immortality in a comment on a line from
Campra's opera *Aréthuse*:

'The Gods rule heaven, and Louis the earth!'
   This man who ruled the earth never took his hat off to anyone, except to
ladies, and would not have come to visit Molière on his death-bed. And
indeed he did not come, nor did any prince. The man who ruled the earth
considered himself immortal, but in this, I imagine, he was mistaken. He
was mortal, like everyone else, and consequently blind. Had he not been
blind, perhaps he would have come to see the dying man, because he would
have seen interesting things in the future, and would possibly have wished
to have a part in true immortality.   (14)

The point is finally driven home in the conventional metaphor of
Molière as the 'king' of French drama, which carries ironic value in
the particular context of an absolute monarchy. Its relevance in the
context of Stalin's Russia needs scarcely to be indicated. Our
impression of Molière's greatness is, however, to be tempered with
compassion for him as a weak and suffering individual: the narrator
addresses him as 'you, my poor, bloodstained master!' (13), an
accolade which aligns him with Bulgakov's other tragic creators.
   The author makes it clear that his aim is not to add yet another
scholarly tome to the body of literature on the subject:

My concern is different: my hero's plays are going to be produced for three
centuries on all the stages of the world, and it's not clear when people will
stop putting them on. That's what I find interesting! That's the sort of man
who will develop out of this infant!   (13)

In order properly to penetrate this charismatic mentor of world
theatre, Bulgakov sets his first-person narrator in Molière's world
and transforms him into a writer as well:

And so: I am wearing a long coat with huge pockets, and in my hand I hold
not a steel pen, but a goose quill.
   Wax candles stand burning in front of me, and my mind is working
feverishly.   (10)

In an ingenious extension of the birth image which opens the work, Bulgakov ends the Prologue with a theatrical flourish: having digressed in his conversation with the midwife into a discussion of Molière's significance as a writer, the narrator turns back to the new-born baby:

Have you understood me? Then be careful, I beg you! Tell me, did he scream? He's breathing? – He lives!   (14)

This joyful exclamation proclaims that it is not only Mme Poquelin who has produced her child, but also Bulgakov who has produced and introduced his character.

After this the work returns to a more conventional narrative of Molière's life, following chronologically through his early disasters to his successful plays, the history of which is given in exhaustive detail. Bulgakov's main concern is with Molière as a professional: he is fascinated by his dedication as the leader of his troupe, and the way in which he sustains his efforts as an administrator while continuing to create new works. He describes Molière's career in terms of a consuming passion which allows him no peace; the theatre does not relinquish those whom it has bewitched:

Alas! The Hôtel de Bourgogne and the Marais were far from having exhausted all the possibilities for those who suffer from a wholly incurable passion for the theatre ... The reading of Corneille, which had inflamed my hero's imagination at night, the unforgettable impressions at street performances, the smell of that stifling mask which, once you have worn one, you will never take off, all finally corrupted the hapless lawyer ... This man could not exist outside the theatre for a second.   (22, 44, 57)

The biographical novel avoids showing us Molière at work; and it ornaments its narrative with only a few direct quotations from his plays. What Bulgakov evokes is the constant tension and urgency which accompanies the writing of new works, and he demonstrates how the stress of needing new and great successes wears Molière down. Although he often compromised in order to get plays put on and to retain the King's favour, Molière was also stubborn in his efforts to get his controversial plays performed. Bulgakov comments admiringly on his behaviour after the disastrous reception of the first three acts of *Tartuffe*:

And what did the author of this ill-starred play do? Burn it? Hide it away? No. When he had recovered from the upheavals at Versailles, the

unrepentant playwright sat down to write the fourth and fifth acts of
Tartuffe. (158)

He also relishes the way Molière followed *Tartuffe* not with a
conciliatory work, but with *Dom Juan*, which was certain to create
at least as much of a scandal. This proof of Molière's irrepressible
boldness belies a suggestion made by Bulgakov's posthumous
editor Boyadzhiyev that he is portrayed in the book as a meek and
compliant figure:

The playwright's personal attitude towards the King and the grandees, for
all its external respectfulness, was devoid of those traces of servility which
from time to time clearly emerge in Bulgakov's book. It would be possible
to demonstrate with facts that Molière wasn't that concerned with success
among the powerful of this world, since for the artist what was decisive was
success amongst the mass of the spectators, those who filled the expanses of
the parterre.[74]

The view that Molière's satire was above all written for the benefit
of the masses is patently naive.

Molière does not come through unmarked from this lifelong
struggle; it weakens and embitters him. When his old friend
Boileau urges him to abandon the stage and content himself with
his writing, Molière retorts:

Not once in my life have I succeeded in writing anything that has given me
even the slightest satisfaction. (204)

His art has proved a torment from which he has been unable to
escape, a vocation which isolates him from society and renders his
life a constant battle. Bulgakov traces the development of his personality from the idealism of Molière's youth, when his passion for
the theatre was as stimulating and liberating a force as it was to be for
Maksudov in *A Theatrical Novel*, to the misery of old age, when his
art has become a curse to him and the character of the man of genius
has been completely undermined by the rigours of his career.

But Bulgakov nevertheless retains his faith in the superiority of
the writer over the philistinism of the authorities, who can be relied
upon for stupidity as well as inconsistency. When Louis XIV
eventually decides to allow *Tartuffe* to be staged, the narrator poses
a sardonic question:

Who will throw light on the tortuous path of the life of a comedian? Who
will explain to me why a play which it was impossible to perform in 1664
and 1667 should be possible to perform in 1669? (185)

The argument that political expediency rather than moral and protective purposes governs the actions of the censorship derives of course from Bulgakov's own experience of its vagaries; his own *The Days of the Turbins*, banned in 1929, was unexpectedly permitted again in January 1932, the year in which he began work on this biography. Many of the passages which, through the narrator's voice, constitute a general statement on the plight of the writer, can be taken by analogy specifically to apply to the Soviet situation, and to reflect Bulgakov's views. At the same time, the immediate political overtones of the work remain subordinate, as in *The Cabal of Hypocrites*, to his concern with the historical figure.

Bulgakov's ironical narrative style has prompted Konstantin Rudnitsky to describe the work as a 'belletristic biography'.[75] The element of fiction not only allows Bulgakov to introduce ideas not strictly germane to his purpose, and a humorousness untraditional to the biographical genre; it also blatantly questions the possibility of a biography conveying something which we could with confidence define as 'the truth'. Bulgakov's biography offers a view of the writer in society, while at the same time it seeks to understand the reality behind one dramatist's greatness.

The Follies of Jourdain (1932) and *L'Avare* (1935–6)

On 16 July 1932 Bulgakov signed an agreement with Yury Zavadsky's Theatre Studio for a translation of *Le Bourgeois gentilhomme*. It was written very rapidly, during September, October and the first half of November 1932; and the gay tone of the whole work and the exuberance of the writing may reflect the happy mood Bulgakov was in at the time of his marriage to Yelena Sergeyevna, which brought to an end a protracted period of personal unhappiness.[76] The play was delivered to the theatre on 18 November 1932, was not accepted for production, and remained unpublished until 1965 when, according to Colin Wright, it was included in an edition of Bulgakov's plays as a last-minute substitute for *Zoyka's Apartment*, which was thought too controversial.[77]

Bulgakov may well have shared the view of *Le Bourgeois gentilhomme*, with its Turkish interlude, expressed by his narrator in the biography of Molière:

Molière's idea was significant and witty . . . On the whole, I must observe that the Turkish play doesn't give me personally any pleasure at all . . . In short, I would not have thanked either the Chevalier Laurent d'Arvieux for his words of advice, nor the court for its commission, nor the utterly exhausted and agitated Molière for the writing of an interlude which spoils a good play! . . . Alas! it must be admitted that those 'balaba' truly signify nothing at all, and there is nothing amusing about them.   (194–6)

Molière had himself been hampered in the composition of the play by the knowledge that he must at all costs include some Turks, who were to be mocked as a political gesture in retaliation for the arrogance shown by a Turkish embassy to the French court; and by the knowledge that, since the play was first to be performed at Chambord for the King, the dramatic element must necessarily be subordinated to the King's known taste for plays with plenty of music and ballets.[78] The work which resulted has always been a great success with European audiences, although it does present considerable difficulties to producers. Pierre Descaves, the general administrator of the Comédie Française who accompanied them on a tour of the Soviet Union in 1954, reports a pertinent comment made to him there by a Soviet writer:

On peut dire que Molière est l'un des dramaturges préférés du peuple soviétique et que la Comédie Française, pour sa première tournée officielle, a eu raison d'amener à Moscou ce *Tartuffe*, si représentatif et déjà familier au public russe, et *Le Bourgeois gentilhomme*, pièce moins connue à cause des difficultés de la mise en scène. Cependant le Théâtre Central pour Enfants à Moscou vient d'inscrire à son programme le *Bourgeois*, et les metteurs en scène s'inspireront évidemment de la présentation française de la comédie.[79]

It seems probable, therefore, that Bulgakov was not only following his personal inclination, but also recognizing the Theatre Studio's need for a simplified version of the work in the way he approached what was to be more an adaptation than a simple translation of the play. It has not yet been possible, however, to establish the exact nature of the theatre's commission, and it seems likely that they had been envisaging something that would keep closer to the original than the work Bulgakov offered them, and that this was the reason for the rejection. In fact, Rudnitsky reports that when the play finally received its première in a Krasnoyarsk theatre forty years later, it was a remarkable success.[80] It is indeed a subtle and interesting work, deserving of more attention from critics and theatres than it has hitherto received.[81]

In its plot and cast the play follows the original quite closely, although its scale and scope are far narrower. The story of Jourdain, his foolish pretensions to grandeur, and the devices used by those around him to abuse those pretensions and finally expose them are all to be found in the later piece. Much of the dialogue paraphrases Molière's text in content, without obeying the conventions of form typical of his style. Indeed, one of the fundamental differences is the way that the inherent seriousness and formality of French classical comedy are set aside in the modern rendering. Bulgakov wisely refrains from the attempt to reconstruct the style of the period, and opts instead to heighten the elements of farce which lie at the back of Molière's conception. Moments such as that when Mme Jourdain disrupts the love-scene between her husband and Dorimène by arriving on the dining-table are more redolent of twentieth-century surrealist humour than of the age of Molière.

The most striking divergence from the original lies in the framework in which Bulgakov sets Molière's plot. Bulgakov's cast-list is not of the characters of *Le Bourgeois gentilhomme*, but of the members of Molière's troupe who are to play the major roles. The list corresponds to the 1670 cast-list for the première of *Le Bourgeois gentilhomme*, but with some significant exceptions. The part of Cléonte's *servant* Covielle is to be played by an *actor* named Covielle; this may merely be a misprint. There are several other discrepancies among the minor roles. Molière's music master becomes the drama and music master, which will provide the justification for the insertion of an extract from *Dom Juan* into *The Follies of Jourdain*. Hence also the addition of the names of Dom Juan and the Statue of the Commander to the cast. Jourdain's philosophy tutor acquires the name Pancrace in Bulgakov's version; this is actually the name of another Molierian philosopher, the Aristotelian Pancrace from *Le Mariage forcé*. An examination of that play reveals that Bulgakov actually composed his character from a combination of Pancrace and of his fellow-philosopher, the Pyrrhonist Marphurius. Brindavoine, who in Bulgakov's play acts both as Molière's servant and as Jourdain's servant, has a name borrowed from one of Harpagon's lackeys in *L'Avare*. However, the major discrepancy between the 1670 cast-list and Bulgakov's lies in the attribution of the main role, Jourdain, not to Molière as in 1670, but to Madeleine Béjart's younger brother Louis, who had also been a member of the troupe since its very inception. In Bulgakov, the alteration is explained away as being due to Molière's illness; but an examination of the historical facts reveals that this must have been a deliberate distortion on Bulgakov's part. The première of the play took place in October 1670 in front of Louis XIV at Chambord. But an entry in Lagrange's *Registre* earlier that year, at the end of March, reads as follows:

Il y a eu du changement dans la Troupe. Le Sr. Bejard, par deliberation de toutte la Troupe a este mis a la pansion de 1000 livres, et est sorty de la Trouppe.[82]

Louis Béjart could not, therefore, ever have played the part of Jourdain, and we must seek a deeper significance in Bulgakov's exclusion of Molière from the cast. It should be added that the device of using the names of Molière's actors for the cast is itself Molierian; he used it in 1663 for his one-act comedy *L'Impromptu de Versailles*, where the roles are distributed to the underprepared actors in a manner which is echoed in the opening scene of *The Follies of Jourdain*.

The structure of a 'play within a play' is already present in *Le Bourgeois gentilhomme* in the form of the Turkish ballet. Bulgakov elaborates this form by adding both an outer framework and interpolations from other plays by Molière with the purpose of making the play's theatricality more conspicuous, and in order to make the audience more aware of the presence and nature of theatrical illusion.

The framework gives Bulgakov the opportunity to comment on the actor's lot; it is not, as we might expect from an author who had made such a close study of the troupe, a portrayal which particularly carries the flavour of the period. There are few realia to create any impression of historical authenticity, and the characterization is extremely economical. Louis Béjart, the central figure here, is someone about whom we in fact know very little; which is perhaps why he was chosen to replace Molière, to whom an audience would relate with its own preconceptions. Béjart takes a detached and melancholy view of his profession:

I don't feel the slightest desire to fall into the embraces of the muse just at the moment . . . O, dark maw which has swallowed me up every evening for the last twenty years, so I am not to escape you today either.   (291)

His ironic comment on the muse's embrace serves to bring theatrical art down to a mundane level, and this is reiterated at the end of the play when, his work over, he is finally free to wander off and join his friends at the inn. The contrast between this low-key final scene and the brilliance of the farce which has preceded it does not, however, function in such a way as to undermine our feelings about the magic of the theatre. The realities of the actor's life may be mundane, but the product of his art remains a cause for wonder.

Bulgakov effects the transition from the framework to the inner play in a complex and humorous fashion. Béjart grandly decrees that the theatre should be prepared for the performance:

Magically light up M. Jourdain's drawing-room for me!   (293)

The audience is amused when this does indeed 'magically' happen. Béjart begins to change his clothes for the role of Jourdain, pausing only to assume a narrative guise for the audience's benefit:

Ah, I'd forgotten that the audience was here. Let's go into my bedroom, Brindavoine. And as for you, ladies and gentlemen, this is what's happening ... It's morning. Monsieur Jourdain's day is beginning. The music master is peeping through a crack, watching Brindavoine dress Jourdain ... We've begun.   (293)

He retreats to the back of the stage in a gesture of modesty which in fact marks his transition into the fictional character, and the *audience*, which had been watching *Béjart* changing, finds its perspective blending into that of the *music master* watching *Jourdain* being dressed. By the time the audience has absorbed this parallel, the magic of the illusion is complete; a masterly exposition of theatrical sleight of hand on Bulgakov's part.

Once left behind, however, the framework does not entirely disappear. Bulgakov wishes us to be sufficiently aware of the illusion not to be totally caught up in it, so he slips in tiny details irrelevant to Molière's text, whose function is to remind us of the outer setting. Such, for instance, is Jourdain's remark about his lameness:

Jourdain: I'm rather embarrassed, you see, that I have a limp.
Dancing master: Who's got a limp? You? Where did you get that idea from, Monsieur Jourdain?
Jourdain: Do you mean to say it's not noticeable?
Dancing master: It's not noticeable at all.   (296–7)

This seemingly trivial exchange has no significance – and there is no justification for it in *Le Bourgeois gentilhomme* – until we recall

that in real life the actor Louis Béjart was lame. The character of
Jourdain momentarily slips away to reveal Béjart, and we are
reminded that we are watching a theatrical fiction – and then the
text reverts to the level of *Le Bourgeois gentilhomme* once more.
As so often in Bulgakov's works, it is the case that certain subtleties
of detail are left to be picked up only by someone who has a close
knowledge of the subject. A further confusion of the various levels
of the play, though in this case a rather simpler one, occurs when
the drama master produces an extract from Act 5, Scene 6 of *Dom
Juan* for Jourdain as an example of dramatic prose. Nothing more
alien to the mood of *Le Bourgeois gentilhomme* could be conceived. This incongruity should, we imagine, strike Mme Jourdain
as she comes bustling unexpectedly into the room; but here the
notion of theatrical illusion is mocked and exposed as she shoos the
astonished Statue of the Commander out of the house. She destroys
the illusion by her practicality, and transports herself almost out of
the level of *Le Bourgeois gentilhomme* to that of the audience of
The Follies of Jourdain by her lack of credulity.

The ending of the play appropriately offers a stripping away of
the same layers of illusion. Whereas in *Le Bourgeois gentilhomme*
the ending consists of a harmless charade, with Jourdain being
mocked for his pretensions all unawares, Bulgakov takes the plot a
stage further and shows Jourdain discovering the ways in which he
has been tricked. In an anguish and bewilderment which remind us
of the terrifying transformation Bulgakov wrought on *Le Malade
imaginaire* for the ending of *The Cabal of Hypocrites*, Jourdain
cries out:

What's going on here? I don't believe anything! I don't believe anyone!
(336)

First of all the supposed Turks remove their turbans to reveal their
true selves – that is, Cléonte and Covielle – thereby dismantling the
first level of the illusion. Jourdain is now distraught:

Everything is deception in this world! . . . I really am going mad, it seems!
Hold me!   (337)

During this outburst he turns on his wife and accuses her of not
being herself. The audience itself is taken by surprise as the false
woman is stripped of her costume to reveal the actor Hubert, who
had complained at the beginning of the play about always being

given women's parts.[83] After this change of direction Jourdain, still more or less playing his part, calls upon the philosopher Pancrace to console him in his confusion. However, the latter answers him not as Jourdain, but as Béjart, with the news that they have come to the end of the play. *Le Bourgeois gentilhomme* is instantly left behind, and we return to the outer setting. Béjart issues instructions for the shutting-up of the theatre, which reminds the audience of *The Follies of Jourdain* that the performance they are watching must also soon come to an end; and Béjart strolls off for his drink, leaving us to sort out all the mystification.

Critical writing on this play has, for the most part, viewed it as an unoriginal work. Lyubimov, writing in 1966, suggests that *The Follies of Jourdain* simply represents an exercise in imitation:

> Just as the important artists of a new age used sometimes to copy the canvasses of the great masters of the past, in order to penetrate the most inaccessible secrets of their art, so Bulgakov composed his play on motifs from Molière.[84]

Four years later Konstantin Rudnitsky echoed this opinion, extending it to embrace Bulgakov's 1935–6 translation of *L'Avare*:

> It was a witty and original attempt to resurrect and collect together in one work the most durable, perhaps eternal comic devices which the genius Molière had deployed, and at the same time to bring to life the atmosphere of a theatrical performance in Molière's time ... the translation of *L'Avare* and the comedy about Jourdain were significant for Bulgakov only inasmuch as they brought him closer to Molière and helped him to get inside Molière's plays, to understand their mechanics.[85]

Wright also pursues this line of argument, and relegates *The Follies of Jourdain* to the status of a second-ranking work in the Bulgakov canon:

> *Half-Witted Jourdain* is a successful imitation – rather than adaptation – of Molière's play, the atmosphere of which Bulgakov had captured very well. Indeed, one has the impression of reading a Molière text ... It bears witness to his skill as a playwright, but it remains a dramatic exercise, a curiosity, which can hardly be compared with his original works.[86]

This roll-call of disparagement is completed by Ellendea Proffer's view that 'there is something rather mechanical about this pastiche'.[87]

Bulgakov's purpose is clearly more sophisticated than has been assumed hitherto, and it is doubtful even whether the play can truly

be seen as a straightforward redeployment of Molierian techniques. Where they are present, they may be being used in a
manner more parodistic than respectful. Like other seventeenth-
century dramatists, for instance, Molière characteristically constructed his plays from a multitude of brief scenes, which followed
swiftly upon one another with little regard for the plausibility of the
timely appearance of each character on stage. In *The Follies of
Jourdain* this device is used to exaggerated effect in the transitions
between acts: Nicole exclaims with considerable naiveté when
Cléonte turns up at the start of Act 2 'Oh, you've arrived at exactly
the right moment, Monsieur Cléonte! And we were just wanting to
send someone for you!' (28). The technique contributes here to
Bulgakov's larger purpose of drawing the audience's attention to
the artificiality of the theatrical process. A more direct reflection of
Molière's style is to be found in some of the dialogues, where an
attempt is made to convey not just the sense, but also the rhythms
of the original. This is only really true, however, of the great set
pieces, such as the dispute between the teachers, or the quartet of
Lucile, Cléonte, Nicole and Covielle, all taking exaggerated
offence at imagined slights before making up again.

But Bulgakov looks directly to Molière for favourite themes or
character-types much more than he does for stylistic features. One
favourite target of Molière's satire, most notably in *Les Précieuses
ridicules*, were the 'marquis'. So Bulgakov takes the figure of
Dorante, the disreputable marquis in *Le Bourgeois gentilhomme*,
and goes to great lengths to blacken his character, in order to stress
this typically Molierian concern. In *Le Bourgeois gentilhomme*
Dorante behaves badly towards Jourdain because he wants to
secure Dorimène, whom he loves; but in Bulgakov's version even
the sincerity of his love is called into question:

My affairs are in a poor way, gentlemen. And the worst of it all is that he's
in love with Dorimène, not knowing that I've proposed to her. But at the
same time I can't not marry Dorimène. Unless I get my hands on her
fortune I'll fall into the clutches of my creditors. True, my role is not
particularly attractive, but what can you do?   (307)

Later, he stoops to blackmailing the servant Covielle, making him
understand that he will only keep quiet about the deception to be
practised on Jourdain if he is bribed to do so.

The features described above scarcely warrant our considering
the play *The Follies of Jourdain* a serious study of Molierian

techniques. One might argue that a comparable number of Molierian characteristics are to be found in Bulgakov's earlier *The Cabal
of Hypocrites*, which rather goes to refute the suggestion that *The
Follies of Jourdain* represents a new departure for Bulgakov in that
narrow respect. *The Cabal of Hypocrites* certainly includes its own
share of typically Molierian characters: Bouton, for example, is an
archetypal Molierian servant in his combination of buffoonery and
wisdom, and his absolute devotion to his master. Even the Archbishop Charron acquires the additional title of 'marquis' in the
cast-list, which is obviously quite unjustifiable in historical terms,
while it enhances our sense of him as a wicked character.

It is equally difficult to accept that Bulgakov's translation of
L'Avare represents a considered exercise on his part in the study
of Molière's style; written, as Yelena Sergeyevna points out in a
letter of 4 January 1936, in great haste, it is an undistinguished
rendering of the original into a fluent Russian which precisely
makes no attempt to capture the style of the play.[88] Wright has
stated that the work was first published in 1939, and then reprinted
in 1952; but a close examination of the two editions reveals that
the later one has been substantially rewritten – and improved –
although no explanation of the alterations is provided.[89] In both
cases the editor was S. Mokul'sky, and it seems probable that he
chose to 'reuse' Bulgakov's translation rather than the hundreds of
others available to him as a personal favour to Bulgakov's widow
Yelena Sergeyevna. He may have been responsible for the
improvements himself, or he may have asked Yelena Sergeyevna
to work on the text; she, after all, like Lyubov' Yevgen'yevna
before her, was much more fluent in French than her husband, and
she had translated Maurois's biography of George Sand since
Bulgakov's death.[90] We may indeed speculate on the extent of her
collaboration with Bulgakov on the original translation of
L'Avare.

Conclusions

Why did Bulgakov have such an intense, heartfelt relationship to
Molière? Because the greatest writer of comedies in the world, whose
plays would have audiences rocking with laughter for three centuries, led
a dreadful, tragic life; and Bulgakov could not help but look into the

chasm of this contradiction. In exploring Molière for himself, he was discovering himself at the same time.[91]

Kaverin's sensitive analysis of the significance of Molière for Bulgakov is confirmed in another account given by a friend of Bulgakov's from MKhAT, Pavel Markov:

In his own words, Bulgakov had always 'been attracted by the personality of the mentor of many generations of dramatists, a comedian on stage, an unlucky man, a melancholy and tragic figure in his personal life'.[92]

In uncovering those aspects of Molière's life and personality to which he himself could most closely relate, Bulgakov also opened his study out to a consideration of the writer's vocation in general. In his play *The Cabal of Hypocrites* and in his prose biography, Bulgakov combined a historical approach with the expression of his affinity with Molière as an individual and as a writer; he also paid tribute to the central position occupied by Molière in the European dramatic tradition. A close reading of Molière provided the initial impetus for *The Follies of Jourdain*, although the work later developed into a light-hearted but subtle exploration of the nature of theatrical illusion. His sense of personal empathy with Molière is evoked in an anecdote reported by Ellendea Proffer, to the effect that in the next world Bulgakov declared that the first person he would call on would be Molière.[93] After the defeat of all his Molière projects, Bulgakov was to write to Popov and refer to his eponymous hero as though Molière had been a dear and intimate friend:

After the death of *Molière* we feel quiet, sad and despairing.[94]

3

Pushkin and Gogol – Bulgakov's Russian masters?

During the period from 1929 to 1936 when Bulgakov was working on Molière, two other writers also came particularly to occupy his attention. His 1930 stage adaptation of Gogol's *Myortvye dushi* (*Dead Souls*) was followed in 1934 by a film scenario of the same novel, as well as a second film scenario, this time of *Revizor* (*The Government Inspector*). And in 1934–5 he wrote his biographical play about Pushkin, *Posledniye dni* (*The Last Days*). But where Bulgakov's response to Molière had engendered a compact and coherent series of works, the return to the nineteenth century and to Russian subjects produced a rather more fragmented response. Pushkin is absent from the play which treats of his biography; and Bulgakov shied away from writing any works about Gogol, preferring instead to evoke his presence through lyrical narrative devices. The question naturally arises as to whether this is due to any particular feelings on Bulgakov's part about his Russian forebears, as opposed to the European tradition; whether he felt that in the Molière works he had expressed his views on the writer in such a comprehensive manner that there was now room to embrace new concerns as well as consolidating his earlier themes; or, indeed, whether the painful lessons he had learned from the hostile reception of his Molière works had not simply made him wary of treating too explicitly in print of his favourite theme of the writer. This chapter will endeavour to throw some light on these questions, as well as considering the issues raised by the works themselves.

Since, as a biographical play, *The Last Days* offers an obvious parallel with *The Cabal of Hypocrites*, the subject of Bulgakov's relationship with Pushkin will be considered first, especially in the light of statements made by him in his fiction and in his correspondence throughout his career. However, before looking at *The Last Days* itself, we will examine the correspondence between Bulgakov and his co-author, Vikenty Veresayev, which provides unusually rich material for an analysis of Bulgakov's working methods and of his approach to Pushkin. The problem of Bulgakov's view of Gogol will come later, concluding with a brief consideration of Bulgakov's stage adaptation of *Dead Souls*, and an examination of the textological problems appertaining to his two other adaptations of Gogol.

Bulgakov and Pushkin

And my God, how it has all come to pass! What poet from the past or the present has *not* been a negro, and what poet have they not killed?[1]

Marina Tsvetayeva

Bulgakov's relative indifference towards poetry has already been mentioned; and although on one occasion at least he made an explicit exception of Pushkin, there is nevertheless no reason to suppose that if Pushkin occupied a special place in Bulgakov's pantheon, it was particularly in his capacity as a master of poetic form. As with Molière, Bulgakov's interest is focussed specifically on the writer's biography, and on the way in which society and posterity have responded to his achievements; this is the theme of *The Last Days*. At the same time, Bulgakov naturally comes to that work with a close knowledge of Pushkin's works, and they provide a significant proportion of the literary references in Bulgakov's writing from the beginning to the end of his career. Scattered references from Pushkin provide both incidental matter and important thematic material, with certain of Pushkin's works proving especially rich sources. In *The Days of the Turbins*, for example, the junkers sing the refrain from Pushkin's poem *Zimny vecher* (*Winter Evening*), which also figures in *The Master and Margarita*; the poem provides the epigraph for the story *V'yuga* (*The Snowstorm*) as well, before going on to be used most extensively as the leitmotif for *The Last Days* itself.[2]

Pushkin's *Yevgeny Onegin* (*Eugene Onegin*) plays a striking role in Bulgakov's writing. When the name appears in his works, it is almost always on occasions when sinister forces are – or are thought by the protagonists to be – at work. In the 1924 story *Khansky ogon'* (*The Fire of the Khans*), the philistine visiting the estate of Arkhangel'skoye refers sneeringly to the parasitical aristocracy who once owned it as 'Onegins'.[3] In *The Fateful Eggs*, which also dates from 1924, the unfortunate Aleksandr Semyonovich attempts to charm the monster by playing it the waltz from Tchaikovsky's opera *Eugene Onegin* on his flute, but without success:

The eyes in the undergrowth instantly lit up with an implacable hatred of that opera.[4]

In *The White Guard* (1925), the villain Shpolyansky – whose prototype was apparently Viktor Shklovsky[5] – is repeatedly identified by his supposed physical resemblance to Onegin:

Mikhail Semyonovich was black-haired and cleanshaven, with velvety sidewhiskers, and he bore an extraordinary resemblance to Yevgeny Onegin ... You are so good-looking that you can even be forgiven your appalling resemblance to Onegin! Listen, Shpolyansky ... It's indecent to look like Onegin. Somehow you're excessively healthy ... Mikhail Semyonovich really did look like Onegin in the snow ... The black Onegin sidewhiskers disappeared. (125–7, 234)

In the same novel, the hero Aleksey recalls as one of the less pleasant features of his schooldays the complicated discussions they had in class about the contrast between Lensky and Onegin. As with *Faust*, and indeed with *Pikovaya dama* (*The Queen of Spades*), Bulgakov's perception of the literary text is very often mediated through its musical setting. In its guise as an opera, *Eugene Onegin* reappears in *The Master and Margarita* as a feature of Ivan's nightmare pursuit of Woland through Moscow:

In each of these windows burned a light under an orange lampshade, and from all the windows, all the doors, from under all the gates, from roofs and attics, from basements and courtyards there burst forth the hoarse roar of the polonaise from the opera *Eugene Onegin*.

And all along his difficult way he was for some reason inexpressibly tormented by the omnipresent orchestra, to the accompaniment of which a ponderous bass sang of his love for Tat'yana. (470)

While it is difficult to construct a coherent justification out of these examples for viewing Bulgakov's unusual response to *Eugene Onegin* as a significant theme in his writing, there is nevertheless an interesting paradox in his interpretation of Onegin as a diabolical figure, particularly in the light of his less-than-satanic Mephistophelean characters.

This extensive use of literary reference indicates the extent to which an awareness of Pushkin's texts accompanied Bulgakov throughout his career. Beyond this, however, Pushkin acquired a much more explicit importance for Bulgakov as the symbol of a culture which was under threat even in its own time, and which appeared to be being ignored, forgotten and rejected in the modern world. This symbolic evaluation of Pushkin may date from an experience which Bulgakov describes in his obviously auto-biographical *Cuffnotes*. The occasion was a talk given in Vladikav-kaz by Bulgakov on 26 October 1920, in his capacity as a member of the local department of culture. He had decided to defend Pushkin in response to an earlier lecture by some iconoclast who had mounted an attack on Pushkin as a bourgeois decadent:

He referred to Pushkin unfavourably, but in passing. And promised a separate lecture on him. On a night in June he did a glorious job on Pushkin. For his white trousers, for his 'I look ahead without appre-hension', for his general 'Gentleman-of-the-Bedchamberism and spon-taneous servility', his 'pseudo-revolutionary spirit and hypocrisy', for his bawdy verses and his attentions to women.

Pouring sweat in the stifling heat, I sat in the front row and listened to the lecturer ripping Pushkin's white trousers to pieces. When at last, refreshing his dry throat with a glass of water, he proposed in conclusion that Pushkin should be tossed into the stove, I smiled.[6]

Bulgakov decided to take up the challenge, and composed a vindication of Pushkin full of quotations from his verse; according to the fictionalized account in *Cuffnotes*, these included *Stansy* (*Stanzas*), *Vakkhicheskaya pesnya* (*Bacchic Song*), *Exegi monu-mentum* and *Zhil na svete rytsar' bedny* (*Once There Lived a Poor Knight*). But his eloquence was to no avail, the audience remained indifferent, and he himself was subsequently pilloried in the press as a bourgeois reactionary. Reverberations of this experience are to be found in a number of his later works.

A first example of this reaction is to be found in *The Fateful Eggs* (1924), where Bulgakov reiterates his distaste for Meyerkhol'd's theatre, which he had already attacked in his 1923 *Stolitsa v bloknote* ('Biomekhanicheskaya glava') (*The Capital City from my Notebook* ('Biomechanical Chapter')).[7] Now he speaks with some glee of:

The theatre of the late Vsevolod Meyerkhol'd, who perished, as we know, in 1927, during a production of Pushkin's *Boris Godunov*, when the trapezes with the naked boyars collapsed. (79)

Evidently the most suitable revenge that Bulgakov can dream up for someone who, in his opinion, is guilty of travestying the classics,

is to prophesy that he will succumb during one of his own productions. Later in the same story, the opera *The Queen of Spades*
features in an entirely different way from the role played by the
music from *Eugene Onegin*; here it is a genuine part of an ironically
presented idyll, as Rokk plays his flute on a quiet evening:

Fragile Liza from *The Queen of Spades* blended her voice in a duet with the
voice of passionate Polina, and was borne off into the moonlit skies, like a
vision of an old and nevertheless infinitely precious régime, enchanting to
the point of tears.   (96)

A year later, this notion of Pushkin as a central element in 'an old
and infinitely precious régime' is brought out by Bulgakov in his
novel *The White Guard*. Not only is the epigraph to this lament for
an age of heroism and gallantry a passage from *Kapitanskaya
dochka* (*The Captain's Daughter*) evoking the coming of the storm,
but the association is made quite explicit in the opening description
of the Turbin household: various images are used to indicate the
comfort and security of the home they cherish – the tiled stove, the
carpets, the portrait of Aleksey Mikhaylovich with a hawk perched
on his wrist, and also –

the bronze lamp under its shade, the best bookcases in the world, with their
books giving off an odour of mysterious, old-fashioned chocolate, with
Natasha Rostova and the Captain's Daughter.   (15)

The year, however, is 1918, and the storm of revolution in the
Ukraine is imminent:

It had already long ago begun to sweep down from the north, and it was
bearing down and bearing down without stopping, and the further it came
the worse it got. The elder Turbin had returned to his native city after the
first blow had fallen, shaking the hills above the Dnepr. Well, people
thought, it will soon stop now, and the life which they write about in the
chocolate books will begin, but not only did it not begin, all around things
were getting more and more dreadful ... The walls will collapse, the
startled hawk will fly up from the white gauntlet, the light in the bronze
lamp will go out, and the Captain's Daughter will be burnt in the stove.
                                                                       (15)

Here there are no consoling words to suggest that 'manuscripts
don't burn'.

Pushkin is also represented in Bulgakov's stories by the statue
erected in his memory on Tverskoy Boulevard in Moscow. In the
1922 stories *Moskva krasnokamennaya* (*Redstone Moscow*) and

Chasha zhizni (*The Cup of Life*) he is pictured gazing down with ironic detachment at Moscow under NEP; by 1925, in *Pokhozhdeniya Chichikova* (*The Adventures of Chichikov*), he is being exploited by the rascally Chichikov as a NEP enterprise, functioning spuriously under the name Pampush (short for 'pamyatnik Pushkina' – 'Pushkin monument').[8] Mentioned (literally in passing) in the story *Ploshchad' na kolyosakh* (*Accommodation on Wheels*, 1926),[9] the image receives its final elaboration in *The Master and Margarita*. The poet Ryukhin, discomfited by Ivan's attacks on the hack work he produces for the May Day celebrations, is returning to Moscow in a truck from Stravinsky's asylum when they pass by Pushkin's statue:

'Now there's an example of real good luck . . .' At this point Ryukhin stood up to his full height in the back of the lorry and raised his fist, for some reason attacking the iron figure, who hadn't laid a finger on anyone. 'At every step in his life, whatever happened to him, it all turned out to his advantage, it all furthered his glory! But what did he do? I can't understand it . . . Is there something special about those words: "The storm with darkness . . ."? I don't understand . . . He was just lucky, he was lucky!' Ryukhin suddenly concluded with venom, as he felt the lorry moving off under him, 'and that White Guard officer fired at him, fired at him and shattered his thigh, and guaranteed him immortality . . .'   (489)

This is of course not just envy, but an indication both of Ryukhin's philistinism and of the pangs of an uncomfortable conscience; hence the scorn with which he describes D'Anthès as a 'White Guard officer', not implying thereby that Pushkin can be compared to a heroic Red martyr, but that he is an equally suspect reactionary. This modern hostility to Pushkin is further illustrated in Nikanor Ivanovich's dream later in the novel, where he sees a performance of *Skupoy rytsar'* (*The Miserly Knight*):

Before his dream Nikanor Ivanovich had absolutely no knowledge of the works of the poet Pushkin, although he knew him as a person very well, and several times a day would utter such phrases as: 'And I suppose Pushkin's going to pay for the flat?', or 'And so you mean Pushkin unscrewed the lightbulb on the landing?', 'And so it's Pushkin who's going to pay for the heating oil, is it?'   (583)

This episode not only indicates that magic forces are at work – how could Nikanor Ivanovich dream a play he's never read? – but also, since he then fails to appreciate the play and is delivered to the asylum cursing Pushkin for all he is worth, demonstrates the

philistinism of the new age. Pushkin's works may have been saved
from the flames which threatened to engulf them in *The White
Guard*, but they have survived only to be spurned alike by the
uneducated Nikanor Ivanovich, and by Ryukhin, the representative of the new cultural élite.

The writing of his play about Pushkin, *The Last Days*, occupied
Bulgakov during 1934 and 1935. His decision in the autumn of 1934
to devote his whole attention to Pushkin may have been stimulated
by his friendship with several Pushkinists, who would be able to
feed his interest with new materials and advise him about sources.
One of these was his close friend Pavel Popov, who had written to
him in October 1931 of the excitement he felt at the prospect of
handling some of Pushkin's manuscripts:

> Starting from yesterday, I have moved on to Pushkin. In the former
> Pushkinsky Dom there are 22 of Pushkin's notebooks which have never
> been published. True, they are all preparatory notes and materials for the
> history of Peter the Great, which never got written, but you feel a certain
> frisson when you embark on the editing of such a text. The last excerpt in
> these books was copied out by Pushkin on the morning of the duel.[10]

Over the next year, he continued to work on Pushkin, and to write
to Bulgakov about it:

> I don't only love Pushkin, I love you as well . . . I've worked on nothing but
> Pushkin recently, it's time I moved on to Bulgakov.[11]

Between 1934 and 1936, that is to say throughout the period when
Bulgakov was working on Pushkin, Popov's research bore fruit in
the shape of a number of articles.[12] And in December 1939 he
wrote to Bulgakov, who by then was desperately ill, to tell him that
his edition of an archive containing information about Pushkin's
financial and domestic affairs towards the end of his life was shortly
to be published. He apologized for having allowed a passage in his
introduction to be excised; it referred to the work of Soviet writers
preparing to celebrate Pushkin's jubilee, and since, as he
announced to Bulgakov in the same letter, the Pushkin play had at
last been accepted for the MKhAT repertoire, the exclusion of his
remark was particularly irksome:

> It's turned out stupidly: after all, if anyone's going to be interested in the
> book, then it will be the producers of your play, and it would have been
> good if this had been anticipated in the foreword.[13]

A point mentioned in this letter from Popov was obviously another factor in Bulgakov's decision to write the play, namely the forthcoming hundredth anniversary of Pushkin's death. This was an occasion for genuine celebration of the poet's achievement, as well as for a demonstration of national fervour; and it was therefore an opportunity for writers like Bulgakov, who continued to attract suspicion, to display his dedication in a patriotic cause.

There had been numerous works on Pushkin and plays about him written in the 1920s and 1930s; but the anniversary itself inspired a wide range of artists, from Tsvetayeva, who in the summer of 1936 translated eighteen of Pushkin's poems into French, to Shostakovich in the same year composing his first settings of Pushkin for voice and piano (op. 46); there has even been an unsubstantiated suggestion that he may have considered writing an opera on the basis of Bulgakov's play.[14]

For Bulgakov, the event drew together a number of different concerns: it was an opportunity to investigate more closely the biography of a writer who had been of considerable importance to him for many years; it was an occasion to try his hand again at writing a biographical play; and it was a chance to restate in a less problematic form several of the issues raised in The Cabal of Hypocrites, which was still bogged down in rehearsal at MKhAT. Perhaps he believed that a study of persecution under the Tsarist régime would be less open to charges of subversive allegorical intent than a work set in seventeenth-century France. The nature of the anniversary had naturally provoked a particular interest in the circumstances surrounding Pushkin's death. This suggested to Bulgakov the idea of focussing much more narrowly than he had done with Molière in order to explore the very last days of Pushkin's life; thus suggesting a title to the committee at MKhAT in 1939, who felt the original title – Pushkin – to be inappropriate for a play in which the poet did not actually appear.[15]

Work on the play began in October 1934, and on this occasion Bulgakov decided to invite a collaborator to join him. He appears not to have asked Popov, but turned instead to the Pushkin scholar Veresayev (real name Smidovich), who was an old and trusted friend some twenty-four years Bulgakov's senior. Veresayev had originally been a member of the 'Sreda' group with Gor'ky, Serafimovich, Bunin and Kuprin, where he was known for the inflexibility of his opinions; this earned him the nickname

'Kamenny most' ('Stone Bridge').[16] Bulgakov had first become aware of him as the author of *Zapiski vracha* (*Notes of a Doctor*), which provided a model for his own *Zapiski yunogo vracha* (*Notes of a Young Doctor*); and in the fragments of a diary which have survived, he speaks of attending a lecture where Veresayev spoke about his book on 14 February 1922. Bulgakov was impressed by his intelligence and readiness to confront difficult questions.[17] Bulgakov then called on Veresayev, and their friendship became established during 1923.[18] Subsequently Veresayev, who reviewed possible publications for 'Nedra', was asked to look at *The White Guard*, which he thought very good, if unsuitable for that particular publishing-house. He insisted, however, that *The Fateful Eggs* should be published immediately.[19] It was he who drew Gor'ky's attention to Bulgakov's work in 1925, and thereafter he took an active interest in the progress of Bulgakov's career. In May 1926 he presented him with an inscribed copy of his recently published translations of Homer,[20] and in August of the same year he was writing to Bulgakov as 'mily' ('dear') Mikhail Afanas'yevich and telling him how he had been pulling strings to help him get better housing.[21] At some stage Veresayev lent him 5000 roubles, which prompted him to write a friendly letter to Bulgakov in July 1931:

I don't know why we see one another so rarely; whether it's because you're very busy, or whether you find that you have little in common with me – in that case I won't protest. But if the reason is that you're embarrassed about the thing which I beg you not to be embarrassed about, and of which, when I see you, I *absolutely and truly* never think, then that is very sad for me. I'm always very delighted and happy to see you.[22]

This letter evidently reached Bulgakov at a moment of crisis, for he replied with a dramatic appeal for advice, in turn provoking a concerned response from Veresayev:

I've received your letter; and not from your words, but from the letter itself I sensed how gravely unwell you are and how your mind is troubled. Advice? I don't understand what you want advice about. But I continue to think that your hope of a trip abroad is completely insane . . . It is difficult to give advice to someone in your situation, but all the same I am determined to say one thing. Suppose a man was told: 'You can't have children.' At that point he would say to himself: 'Then what's the point of having sexual relations? I'm finished.' And a monstrous thing happens: his health goes to pieces, he is consumed inside by exasperating dissatisfaction, he sees naked girls in his dreams and can't stop thinking about anything else. Are the creative needs of a writer any less than his sexual needs? And is it possible, without destroying his entire being, for him to say to himself: 'They won't print me; so I'll abandon writing.' It's a fundamental mistake.[23]

Two years later, in 1933, Bulgakov was still in Veresayev's debt and wrote to him of a recent trip to Leningrad, where he had made futile attempts to make the theatres there pay him the money he was owed:

Yelena Sergeyevna sends telegrams via the Vseroskomdram organization and wheedles small advances out of them, and I just dream of the day when she will get her way, and I will return my remaining debt to you and be able to say once more what you have done for me, dear Vikenty Vikent'yevich! Oh, I'll always remember the years from 1929 to 1931![24]

During 1934, he continued to correspond with Veresayev about all sorts of matters: his move to a new flat in Nashchokinsky Pereulok, the question of finding a summer dacha, and the right tactics for applying for a two-month trip abroad from September; whether to mention illness or not, and the problem that he does not feel strong enough to travel without Yelena Sergeyevna.[25] This last is again a long and intimate letter, a token of their closeness; when Bulgakov's plans for travel abroad, not unexpectedly, fell through again, Veresayev was swift to express his sympathy:

I feel so grieved for you! What an incessant nervous strain! And how much strength is needlessly wasted on it, strength which would be so useful for literature! Dear, oh dear! ... I hug you warmly and wish you spiritual strength. And what is Italy to you? As though it were not possible for you to find rest and peace here at home.[26]

In asking Veresayev to work with him in October 1934, therefore, Bulgakov was seeking the assistance not only of an expert, but of a friend of long standing. The initial agreement was that Veresayev would take responsibility for the collecting of materials, while Bulgakov would do the actual writing. Yelena Sergeyevna was rather puzzled by the decision to share the work out, and asked her husband for an explanation:

'I must,' replied Bulgakov firmly. 'After all, he helped us at the most difficult time.'[27]

This cryptic remark, together with the fact that the play appears to have been more or less completely planned before Bulgakov approached Veresayev, suggests that in some senses Veresayev's collaboration was superfluous; and this was indeed the first objection which Veresayev himself raised to the project. As far as Bulgakov was concerned, however, Veresayev's name would presumably lend academic respectability to the enterprise and improve the work's chances of being performed, and there may also have been some sense in which the invitation was a way of repaying Veresayev for all his past kindness. It is certainly true that, after all their disagreements finally resulted in Veresayev withdrawing his name from the work, Bulgakov was insistent that he should still receive his half-share of the royalties. Yelena Sergeyevna herself does not discuss Bulgakov's motives for the invitation in the introduction to her selection of the correspondence between the two men; she merely gives the following account, based on diary notes made at the time:

Mikhail Afanas'yevich proposed to Veresayev that they should write the play together. Vikenty Vikent'yevich, when we went to see him on 18 October, was extremely touched and agreed to the proposal. He got quite carried away and began to talk about Pushkin, about the tragic nature of his destiny, and about the fact that Natal'ya Nikolayevna was by no means a shallow person, but an unhappy woman. At first Vikenty Vikent'yevich was perplexed by the fact that the play was to be without Pushkin, but having thought about it, he agreed.

They decided that Bulgakov would do the writing part, and Vikenty Vikent'yevich would take charge of the selection of materials.[28]

The survival of the correspondence exchanged between Veresayev and Bulgakov during the summer of 1935 is a happy circumstance which allows us to chart the course of their disagreements, and to assess Bulgakov's intentions with regard to the text. The letters, most of which have been published, reveal that their disagreements were to some extent a matter of personality and temperament, and that Veresayev's irascible disposition in particular made it difficult to reach compromises once disputes had arisen. The correspondence also reveals, however, that certain of their disagreements derived from fundamental differences in their ideological and aesthetic conceptions of the work. Yelena Sergeyevna identifies the main area of conflict in a commentary which also sets out the essential features of Bulgakov's approach to his major theme, the theme of the artist's destiny:

Veresayev aspired towards a profoundly historical play, and was insistent that all the dates, facts and events should be precisely observed. Bulgakov was, of course, in agreement with this. But in his opinion it wasn't enough. An artist's fantasy and his personal understanding of these historical facts were also necessary. When he had the idea for the play, Bulgakov saw the opportunity to speak out on his cherished theme of the right of the writer to his own, unique view of art and of life. In his historical plays – *Molière*, *Pushkin*, and *Don Kikhot* (*Don Quixote*) – he made use of the past in order to express his own attitude to the modern world, which preoccupied him just as it preoccupied us and continues to preoccupy us to the present day ... This is the correspondence of two honourable, principled men of literature. After all the torments to which they subjected one another in those summer months of 1935, their relations remained friendly as before, and their mutual love and respect did not suffer in the least.[29]

The incompatibility of Veresayev's desire to create a strictly historical drama and Bulgakov's desire to colour such a drama with themes of more universal significance was not immediately apparent, however, and when the exchange of letters began in May 1935, Veresayev's queries and complaints were for the most part focussed on points of detail. Judging by the tone of Veresayev's first letter, relations between the two men had already become strained; the immediate reason for the letter was that Bulgakov had agreed to read the play to the troupe at the Vakhtangov theatre when Veresayev considered that it was still far from ready. He also complained that none of the details about which he had expressed reservations – Saltykov's phrase about his 'incognito', Dubel't's quotations from the Gospels, and D'Anthès's shot at the picture – had been altered. He then went on to claim for himself a rather larger role in the writing of the play than had been originally envisaged:

This by no means signifies that I am prepared to content myself with the role of a humble purveyor of material, not daring to pass judgement about the merits of the way the material is used ... I find the image of D'Anthès fundamentally incorrect, and I cannot as a Pushkinist take responsibility for it. That sturdy, exuberant, conceited, insolent fellow, who feels marvellously at ease in St Petersburg, in your version snivels and suffers from attacks of spleen.[30]

In fact Veresayev was already by this stage submitting to Bulgakov his own versions of certain scenes and exchanges, which Bulgakov repeatedly dismissed for their lack of stage sense or their crude overstatement of the characters' positions with regard to the tragedy. On this occasion he pointed out how often he *had* altered the text in order to accommodate Veresayev's criticisms, and adduced documentary evidence to justify the three details on which Veresayev had cast doubt. The major issue for the moment, however, remained the figure of D'Anthès. Bulgakov dismissed Veresayev's alternative version out of hand:

Let me reply to you: I in my turn consider your image of D'Anthès impossible in stage terms. He is so thin, trivial and emasculated that he could not possibly be put into a serious play. One cannot present a little officer straight out of a ball or an operetta in the capacity of the murderer of Pushkin, who perished so tragically ... It's a question of Pushkin's life in this play. If you give him unserious partners, Pushkin will be diminished ... The real trouble is that Pushkinists (and I will undertake to prove this) *have no image of D'Anthès at their disposal and know nothing about him.* No-one has any facts about him. You have to think D'Anthès up for yourself.[31]

The proof which he here promised to collect took the form of a large number of excerpts concerning D'Anthès – some sixty in all – from a wide range of sources, which indeed effectively demonstrate the difficulty of establishing a definitive and coherent portrait of the man. This was despatched to Veresayev with a rueful comment:

The real problem is that the study of Pushkin, as I am now bitterly convinced, is not a precise science.[32]

Bulgakov was not only determined to adapt the material provided by Veresayev to suit his overall conception, but he was also clearly sensitive to the limitations of that material in purely historical terms.

For the moment, Veresayev was won over, although the appeasing letter he sent Bulgakov on 6 June 1935 was rather confused, and really opened up a much more serious area of disagreement:

In your heart you are thinking: 'It would be best of all if Veresayev stopped interfering in this business and allowed me complete freedom henceforth; let him try to "socialize" the play, just so long as I am free autocratically to reject his attempts, without wasting time on long altercations.' ... There can only be one boss, and in our case only you can be that boss ... All this doesn't mean that I am refusing to give you what help I can in the future, inasmuch as you will accept it as simple advice that doesn't bind you to anything.[33]

Bulgakov's refusal to switch the emphasis from the personal tragedy to a more politicized interpretation was at the root of many of their differences over points of detail. Veresayev continually sought to bring out the political positions of all the characters: it was he who insisted that Nicholas I should make disparaging remarks about Pushkin's 'Decembrist' poems and his history of Pugachov, which in the latter case was quite in contradiction of the historical evidence;[34] that scornful remarks should be made about liberalism and Carbonarism in the scene between Stroganov, D'Anthès and Heeckeren; and that Pyotr Dolgorukov should make explicit his pretensions to the Russian throne, a suggestion that Bulgakov rejected on the grounds of sheer implausibility, commenting that the next scene would have to depict Petya's departure for Siberia.[35]

Since peaceful relations appeared to have been restored, it was with genuine astonishment that Bulgakov received Veresayev's missive of 1 August. Veresayev announced that all his friends had criticized the later part of the play, finding the duel and death scenes dull and lifeless; and he claimed that they considered the figure of d'Anthès to have been rendered in a romantic hue derived from Leonid Grossman's colourful and unreliable account in his *Zapiski D'Arshiaka* (*Notes of d'Arshiak*).[36] The upshot was that Veresayev had embarked on the composition of a completely independent play, and was proposing that his version should be offered to theatres as an alternative to Bulgakov's. Bulgakov immediately replied with a reminder to Veresayev of his undertaking in June to keep to their original division of responsibilities; and he reaffirmed his belief that the play was now virtually ready, barring a few details which Veresayev had promised to provide.[37] He followed this up on 16 August with a systematic attack on the drafts which Veresayev had sent him, criticizing them for the woodenness and heavy-handedness of the characterizations. In particular, he categorically rejected all those passages where characters were made to recount rather than act out significant events, stressing that the whole dramatic illusion was destroyed once characters were allowed to express an awareness of their own significance:

You have gone over the knots of the play that I had tied with such trouble, over precisely those places where I had avoided head-on attacks, and with enormous precision you have undone all those knots, after which the costumes simply dropped off the protagonists, and wherever the play had been made most subtle, you have put great fat dots on my i's.[38]

He argued that Veresayev's determination to include a reference to Heeckeren's known involvement in speculation, like his desire to have Dolgorukov actually enunciate his Imperial aspirations, was absolutely unacceptable:

All this bears no relation either to the tragic death of the poet, or to D'Anthès, or to Natal'ya, and altogether has no right to existence in this play.[39]

Bulgakov had constructed the play in such a way that it radiated out from the central figure of the poet, and nothing irrelevant to the poet's destiny, whether it fell into the category of local colour as in the examples above, or whether it involved a politicized interpretation of events, was going to be included in the play if he could help it. Bulgakov now insisted that Veresayev should decide whether he was prepared to put his signature to the play as it stood. Veresayev's answer made it clear that there was no more room for negotiation:

I didn't expect any other reply from you. The basic source of our disagreements is clear to me: it is your organic blindness to the social aspects of Pushkin's tragedy. This blindness was notable in you before, but now, flushed with the praise of your supporters, it is even more difficult for you to feel the defects of your play in this respect ... Do what you like with the play, deliver it to the theatre in whatever form you feel appropriate. I for my part will retain the right, inasmuch as it will prove possible for me, to campaign for the excision from your beautiful play of the often astonishingly unnecessary violations of historical truth, and for the strengthening of its social background.[40]

Discussion of the play as such came to an end with this letter, and their correspondence thereafter dealt with their formal rights to the work, the question of drawing up a contract, and the issue of who had the right to read the play to theatres and other official bodies – a right which Bulgakov considered exclusively his own, since he had at the very beginning taken responsibility for all negotiations with theatres. In fact, he was very anxious that Veresayev should neither read the play to too many people, nor broadcast their disagreements too widely; he foresaw serious problems for the work if Veresayev should attack it on ideological grounds and attempt to disrupt the production – a threat which, fortunately, Veresayev did not actually put into effect. The coolness in their relations culminated in Veresayev's formal declaration of 19 December 1935 that he was withdrawing his name from the work, although in an informal note accompanying the letter he at least offered his services if he could be of any use during the production.[41]

Subsequent events bear out Yelena Sergeyevna's claim that Bulgakov's friendship with Veresayev survived the hostility stirred up by the two of them in the summer of 1935. When *The Cabal of Hypocrites* was banned in March 1936, Veresayev wrote in very sympathetic terms to commiserate, and not just because the ban ruined their hopes now of getting the Pushkin play staged at the Vakhtangov theatre:

I am deeply shocked by the taking off of your play. Your creative journey is unavoidably hard. I wish you spiritual strength to bear this new blow. I embrace you warmly.[42]

Four days later an article in *Sovetskoye iskusstvo* criticized the as yet unperformed and unpublished Pushkin play in terms which confirmed that it could not be saved:

Pushkin himself is not brought into the play. The authors give no explanation at all of this fact. But maybe Pushkin is spoken about so much and so well in the play that his presence on stage would be superfluous? Alas, this cannot be said. All that is shown in the text is that Pushkin is the author of 'The storm with darkness veils the sky . . .'. And that's it. The authors don't even hint at the existence of other works by Pushkin. We need scarcely ask about the image of the poet, the social roots of his tragedy, or any reflection of the era in the story of his life and death.[43]

The title of the article, 'An Attempt on Pushkin', indicated that the play was being viewed as a defiance of the Establishment view of the poet as it was to be enshrined in the adulatory pieces written for the jubilee. In May the Vakhtangov theatre tried to persuade Bulgakov to make alterations to the work so that it would be more acceptable, but he refused; and by the autumn of 1936 it was clear that the enterprise was doomed. Bulgakov, by now weary after a whole series of setbacks, wrote gloomily to Veresayev:

May Pushkin rest in peace, and may we do the same![44]

The depression caused by the failure of yet another of his works lasted well into the following year, as we can see from a letter to Popov in March 1937:

Many people told me that 1936 was, as they said, a bad year for me because it was a leap year; there is such a superstition. I can assure you that it is a false superstition. I can now see that, as far as I'm concerned, 1937 is at least as bad as its predecessor.

Amongst other things, I'm going to court on 2 April; those sharks from the theatre in Khar'kov are making an attempt to extract money from me, playing on the misfortune with *Pushkin*. At the moment I can't hear the word 'Pushkin' without shuddering and I curse myself hourly for having had the ill-fated idea of writing a play about him.

Certain of my well-wishers have chosen a rather strange method of consoling me. More than once I've heard suspiciously unctuous voices: 'Never mind, after your death it will all be printed!' I'm very grateful to them, of course.[45]

Bulgakov evidently did not hold Veresayev at all responsible for the disaster with the play, and their correspondence continued intermittently, if a shade less warmly, right up until Bulgakov's death. Their letters were mostly brief notes, including reports from Bulgakov about the progress and eventual success in the spring of 1937 of their legal battle with the Khar'kov theatre, which was claiming compensation now that the play had been officially banned.[46] It is interesting that when the reasons for the ban were reported in *Sovetskoye iskusstvo* in February 1937, no account was taken of Veresayev's disclaimer of responsibility for the play:

A number of plays distorting historical truth were taken out of the repertoire by the All-Union Committee (*Molière*, *The Bogatyrs*). Bulgakov and Veresayev's play about Pushkin was not licensed for production: it showed Pushkin not as a poet of genius, but as the hero of a domestic drama.[47]

And indeed a letter from Veresayev to Bulgakov in the autumn of 1937 revealed that he too had fallen into disfavour with the authorities:

About eighteen months ago you borrowed a thousand roubles from me, expecting to be able to return it in the autumn of the same year. This you were unable to do because the Shakespeare business went wrong.

My circumstances have now taken a sharp turn for the worse. My biography of Pushkin has been banned, they don't want to reprint my old things, and I'm not writing any fiction. I've undertaken a translation of *The Iliad* and *The Odyssey*. This is work that will take me six or seven years, and until it is completed it won't keep me fed.

If it is at all possible, I would be very grateful if you would return the money you owe me.[48]

The loan dating from the spring of 1936 relates presumably to the time when Bulgakov's hopes of solving his perennial financial problems had been dashed by the banning of *The Cabal of Hypocrites*; it therefore provides further evidence that the bitterness between the two men lasted little beyond 1935. Veresayev remained in contact, and in December 1939 Popov wrote to Bulgakov of Veresayev's friendly concern about his illness:

Today I called on Vikenty Vikent'yevich and learned some interesting news concerning you that I hadn't known before: namely, about your Pushkin, and about the fact that it's been included in the 1940 plan . . . V. V. was very, very kind, and spoke about you very sympathetically and touchingly.[49]

Only with the last letter in their correspondence does a sour note again enter the history of their friendship: it dates from late January 1940, when Bulgakov was already in the terminal stages of his illness. Because of this, it is addressed to Yelena Sergeyevna, who with her power of attorney had just signed what Veresayev considered to be an extremely unprofitable contract with MKhAT for *The Last Days*; the play was at last going to be staged, presumably as part of MKhAT's contribution to pre-war patriotic fervour. It is an ill-tempered and insensitive letter, full of reproaches which indicate Veresayev's genuine anxiety about his financial predicament, but this does not necessarily indicate any continuing resentment on his part against Bulgakov.[50]

Defining the purpose of the collaboration between the playwright and the scholar remains a difficult task. Views on the major issues and on details were exchanged, and in certain instances Veresayev was able to persuade Bulgakov to alter emphases and to introduce references of political significance. Certainly a good deal of animosity was generated in the course of their debates, as one would expect from any collaboration between such forceful and individualistic writers. But the hypothesis that Veresayev's contribution was ultimately not necessary to the writing of the play still cannot be dismissed. For while Veresayev was undoubtedly a Pushkinist of high repute, with access to an extremely wide range of materials, it is also true to say that a series of important publications during the 1920s would have enabled Bulgakov to assemble much of the material himself, especially with the guidance of both Veresayev and Popov. Bulgakov's use of sources therefore emerges as an important issue, since it should enable us to determine Veresayev's exact contribution. An examination of the sources will also show where Bulgakov departed from conventional

or received interpretations in order to create his personal image of
Pushkin.

Although access to the notebooks Bulgakov used when working
on sources remains restricted, it is nevertheless possible to establish
a more or less comprehensive account of them through other
means.[51] Evidence is to be found in the play itself, in the correspondence between Bulgakov and Veresayev, and in the two publications of extracts from the notebooks which have so far been
placed at our disposal; additional information has been supplied by
Chudakova in a range of publications.[52] Since this evidence satis-
factorily accounts for virtually all the material Bulgakov appears to
have used, we cannot expect any significant additions to emerge
when the notebooks are finally made available.

The most striking conclusion to emerge from an examination of
these materials, especially in view of all Veresayev's criticisms, is
the extent to which it was *his* works above all which supplied
Bulgakov with his interpretations. Foremost among these was his
two-volume *Pushkin v zhizni* (*Pushkin in his Lifetime*), a comprehensive anthology of contemporary evidence and comments
classified in such a way as to build up a chronological picture of
Pushkin's life. It is obvious, therefore, that Bulgakov used the
latter part of the second volume most intensively, although since
there is some blending into the play of episodes from earlier
moments in Pushkin's life, the whole of the second volume has to
be taken into consideration. Veresayev's other major anthological
work, his *Sputniki Pushkina* (*Pushkin's Companions*, 1934), was
also used; this is a series of brief portraits of all the people who
were closest to Pushkin, his fellow-poets, his family, his friends
and the authorities. Bulgakov may also have consulted some of
Veresayev's shorter monographs, such as his *Duel' i smert' Pushkina* (*Pushkin's Duel and Death*, 1927), or his *Zhena Pushkina*
(*Pushkin's Wife*, 1935). An example of Bulgakov's reliance on
Veresayev is provided in the letter he wrote him in May 1935
where he produced a list of quotations to prove his point about
D'Anthès; as it turns out, the sixty references could have been
culled almost without exception from Veresayev's *Pushkin in his
Lifetime*.[53] He shows that Veresayev, who had been so eclectic in
his collecting of materials for his own anthology, is now evincing
historical partiality in insisting on one particular interpretation of
D'Anthès; at least Bulgakov, when he chooses to portray

D'Anthès in a certain light, is prepared to admit that he has invented him.

The Pushkin scholar P. Shchogolev has commented on the inadequacy of the materials relating to the end of Pushkin's life:

> It seems that there is no period of the poet's life about which there is such a plethora of anecdotes, contemporary memoirs, and correspondence, and yet there are extremely few materials of a documentary nature amidst this abundance, and critical investigations of what materials there are simply do not exist in the literature of Pushkiniana.[54]

This criticism to some extent applies to Veresayev's own work, where the materials are presented with only occasional indications as to their reliability; so that, for example, discredited or disputed statements by Natal'ya Nikolayevna's daughter A. P. Arapova stand side by side with incontrovertible accounts of the same incident by more impartial observers. This is not to suggest, of course, that Veresayev was not himself aware of the relative merits of the testimonies. What makes his book so fascinating is that it provides an accurate picture of the way Pushkin's society looked at him or chose to write about him, rather than trying to offer a supposedly impartial and objective portrayal of the poet. This approach afforded Bulgakov an ideal assortment of materials, since his concern was always more with perceptions of the writer than it was with strict historical authenticity. As with Molière, when it came to portraying Pushkin Bulgakov was happy to trust to his own blend of reliable and discredited sources, with a generous admixture of personal intuition.

A detailed reading of *Pushkin in his Lifetime* reveals how exhaustively it was used for minute realia, which are scrupulously included in the text. Bulgakov turned to this work for the exact details of Pushkin's dealings with the money-lender Shishkin, such as the figure for Pushkin's total debt of 12,500 roubles, and the fact that Aleksandra Nikolayevna's silver eventually had to be handed over in order to stave off the sale of items previously pawned. The suggestion that Benkendorf may have arranged for the police not to go to the scene of the duel, which they might otherwise have prevented, also comes from the collection. Nicholas I's remark that he often passes in front of Natal'ya Nikolayevna's windows, but that the blinds are always drawn, is taken from the memoirs of Nashchokin, which Veresayev quotes; and the details concerning Stroganov's presence and advice at the moment when the challenge

is received by Heeckeren are also all to be found in his book. Even
the closing scene, which one critic has described as 'clearly invented', is based on Veresayev's selections from the memoirs of A. I.
Turgenev, who accompanied the body on its undignified last
journey.[55]

Veresayev's *Pushkin's Companions* was similarly used by Bulgakov for details about a number of characters, particularly Pushkin's
manservant, Nikita Kozlov; Chudakova has suggested that the
work may even have drawn Bulgakov's attention to this figure's
dramatic potential with its comment that:

The old fellow Nikita Kozlov passes before us at the very back of the stage
in Pushkin's life, as a dim, lifeless shadow.[56]

The work was also the prime source of information about Kuko-
l'nik; in particular, it was the source for the story of the ring which
Nicholas bestowed on Kukol'nik as a reward for the patriotic play
he had written, and which then became the subject of disrespectful
sneering by Saltykov.[57]

Bulgakov draws on Veresayev's materials for details of the
language and behaviour of most of the characters of the play; but
there are some exceptions, notably in the case of the Goncharova
sisters. Veresayev's monograph *Pushkin's Wife* was published in
1935, at the time of the writing of the play, so we may safely assume
that Bulgakov was acquainted with the work even if he did not
possess a printed copy. Here he would have found the following
conclusion about Natal'ya Nikolayevna, Pushkin's wife, whose
involvement with D'Anthès precipitated the tragedy:

Natal'ya Nikolayevna alone failed to notice anything, and was utterly
unaware of the approaching storm. She may well have been indifferent to
Pushkin, she may well not have loved him, she may have got carried away
by D'Anthès to the point of entirely forgetting herself, but she might have
noticed what was happening to Pushkin![58]

Bulgakov's view of Natal'ya is independent of Veresayev's impa-
tience here. Some commentators have suggested that his portrayal
of her is a particularly sympathetic one; Chudakova, for example,
argues that in his final judgement of her as blind rather than guilty,
Bulgakov was drawing a conclusion surprisingly – and unwittingly –
close to that given by Marina Tsvetayeva in her 1929 *Natal'ya
Goncharova*:

Guilt is removed from Natal'ya Goncharova from the very start . . . There is nothing bad or depraved in Natal'ya Goncharova, nothing that you wouldn't find in thousands like her . . . She is innocent because she's a doll, she is innocent because it was fate, she is innocent because she didn't love Pushkin.[59]

The particular moment which has given rise to the view that Bulgakov's is a sympathetic interpretation is the touching moment in the third act when Natal'ya complains to her sister Aleksandra that the lot of a great poet's wife is not easy:

Why has no-one ever asked me whether I am happy? People only know how to demand things of me. But has anyone ever pitied me? What else is wanted of me? I've borne him children, and all my life I hear poetry, nothing but poetry . . . So recite poetry, all of you! Zhukovsky's happy, and Nikita's happy, and you're happy . . . and leave me alone.[60]

Elsewhere, however, Bulgakov portrays her in such a way as to reverse this impression, and indeed invents material which is not to be found either in Veresayev or in his other sources in order to achieve this effect. Thus Natal'ya is credited with having arranged a second rendezvous with D'Anthès, to which he fails to come because he is at that very moment engaged in his duel with Pushkin (63). In fact, A. I. Turgenev's memoirs, cited in *Pushkin in his Lifetime*, record that Natal'ya went out only to collect her children on the afternoon of the duel, and there is no evidence elsewhere to suggest that she sought any further meetings with D'Anthès after the single rendezvous with him at the flat of Idaliya Poletika.[61] The portrayal of Natal'ya at the time of Pushkin's death is also somewhat slanted; while there is plenty of evidence for her hysteria and for her refusal to believe that Pushkin was really going to die, Bulgakov omits any references to Pushkin's deep concern for her and his requests that she should attend him and feed him, as was attested by several accounts in Veresayev's work.[62] Bulgakov's version suggests that she had no part to play in Pushkin's final moments, and excludes any hint of the affection towards her of which many of those who attended him spoke. Overall, then, Bulgakov's view of Natal'ya deviates from his sources in a negative, not a positive direction.

By contrast, Bulgakov presents Aleksandra Nikolayevna, Natal'ya's unmarried elder sister, as Pushkin's good angel; she and Zhukovsky, whose role is also particularly emphasized in Bulgakov's interpretation, are shown as the poet's only true friends (apart from the minor figure of Nikita) in a hostile society. Several observers cited in Veresayev suggested that Aleksandra was in fact Pushkin's mistress, as well as being the sincere devotee of Pushkin's poetry which Natal'ya signally failed to be.[63] Bulgakov leaves the issue ambiguous, but certainly hints at the possibility of Aleksandra being in love with Pushkin in the conversation between the two sisters which is interrupted by Danzas with the news of the duel (63). His glowing portrayal of Aleksandra certainly brings out more clearly his negative presentation of Natal'ya.

The third Goncharova sister, Yekaterina, does not appear in the play, although she is referred to in her capacity as D'Anthès's new wife, whom he is intending to betray by running off with her sister Natal'ya Nikolayevna. The brief mention of her is nevertheless interesting inasmuch as it provides a different angle on the dispute between Veresayev and Bulgakov about the latter's use of Grossman's *Notes of d'Arshiak* in his portrayal of D'Anthès. It turns out that Veresayev had himself decided to include a highly questionable statement by Grossman in his *Pushkin in his Lifetime*; it is one of only a very few modern sources quoted in the work.[64] Grossman claimed that the first child of D'Anthès and Yekaterina was conceived out of wedlock and was born in April 1837, only three months after the wedding, which took place just before the duel in January 1837. In his 1935 study *Pushkin's Wife*, Veresayev even uses this information as though it were undisputed fact; W. N. Vickery has since pointed out, however, that the information is highly suspect, and that Grossman himself in the 1936 *Vremennik Pushkinskoy kommissii* (*Annals of the Pushkin Commission*) changed his mind and gave the date of the child's birth as 19 October 1837.[65] But Veresayev evidently raised no objections when Bulgakov used the information from Grossman he had found in *Pushkin in his Lifetime* for the scene where Heeckeren complains to D'Anthès (within just one month of the wedding!) about the effects of Yekaterina's pregnancy on his peaceful household (51). So Veresayev's reproaches to Bulgakov about using Grossman come to seem a little sanctimonious, given Veresayev's own acceptance of his embroidered anecdotes.

Bulgakov's direct use of Grossman's book was in fact fairly modest; he drew on it principally for details of the Heeckeren household, such as the decoration of D'Anthès's room with carpets and a collection of weapons, and the fact that Heeckeren was a collector – in reality a smuggler – of exotic knick-knacks.[66] The book also provided the basis for the incident which Veresayev criticized as implausible, when D'Anthès fires a shot at the wall:

Near the mirror hung a painted caricature from a humorous Parisian broadsheet, depicting the sharply-pointed head of Louis-Philippe as a huge, smiling pear.

'It's my favourite target,' declared Georges gaily.

And, taking a special type of pistol from the wall, he let off several shots at the Charivari picture, unfailingly hitting the same spot with one bullet after another.[67]

Veresayev's complaint that the blind Stroganov would suffer a heart attack at this point is perhaps a legitimate one, but Bulgakov insisted on retaining the scene, explaining that he wished it to serve as a reminiscence of Silvio's shot in Pushkin's story *Vystrel (The Shot)*.[68]

Apart from his extensive use of Veresayev and this limited use of Grossman, it is remarkable how few other works Bulgakov chose to consult. One important study he would have known was P. Shchogolev's *Duel' i smert' Pushkina (The Duel and Death of Pushkin)*, probably in the third edition of 1928. Ellendea Proffer mistakenly suggests that Bulgakov displayed great percipience in identifying Dolgorukov as the author of the offensive anonymous letters sent to Pushkin and his friends, a fact which she says was confirmed only in the fourth edition of 1936.[69] In fact, Shchogolev's well-known investigation using the services of a handwriting expert was first published in the 1928 edition, so that Bulgakov could easily have benefited from his discoveries in this respect.

Another work used by Bulgakov was an article by Lents entitled 'Priklyucheniya liflyandtsa v Peterburge' ('Adventures of a Livonian in Petersburg'), extracts from which he could have found in *Pushkin in his Lifetime* before he consulted it in the original. This was the main source for the character of the eccentric Saltykov, and an example will demonstrate how faithfully Bulgakov followed the original on this occasion:

With the utmost seriousness he used to tell stories which he didn't believe himself, and invented for his own use a history of Russia; he would refer to it in discussing historical facts in such a way that the listener was at a loss to decide whether he really was in a distinguished household conversing with an intelligent man, or with a madman . . . At precisely six o'clock he would return home on foot, trot with small, ringing steps through the first room, where the table was already laid, and come with his hat still on his head into the drawing-room next to the library ... His wife, daughters, sons and guests used to spend the time before the meal in this second room ... Near the first window in the drawing-room stood a little table just for him, with microscopic sandwiches and a whole battery of vodkas on a heavy silver tray. He would down one small glass of vodka, place a minuscule piece of bread in his mouth and, still wearing his hat, without exchanging greetings with anyone, as though he were absolutely on his own in the room, he would proceed, tapping loudly with his Spanish cane, through the library into his study. He used to call this his 'incognito'. He would emerge from his study an entirely different person; he would greet all the assembled circle, extending a finger to one guest and making a dry bow to more distinguished visitors, and then he would say; 'Let's go through to the table.'[70]

In this passage we find the answer to Veresayev's point that Saltykov's talk of an 'incognito' had no historical justification, as well as a refutation of Wright's claim that this scene, like those at the office of the Third Department and at the post-station, was simply invented by Bulgakov.[71]

Of the remaining identifiable sources, none seem to have contributed significantly to Bulgakov's presentation of characters or events in the play. Extracts from Pushkin's correspondence are to be found in Bulgakov's notebooks, suggesting that he read the letters in order to immerse himself in the atmosphere of the period as well as, more specifically, to gain a sense of Pushkin's state of mind at the end of his life.[72] Bulgakov also read Pushkin's *Dnevnik* (*Diary*), which he used for the episode when Pushkin infuriates the Tsar by wearing a frock-coat to a ball rather than the uniform of a gentleman of the bedchamber, as was required of him by his rather undignified position at court.[73] Chudakova cites a number of other less significant sources: an edition by Shaposhnikov of Yazykova's letters about Pushkin, a gift to Bulgakov from the editor which adds little to the play; Grech's *Zapiski o moyey zhizni* (*Notes on my Life*), which provided a prototype for the figure of Bogomazov in the shape of V. F. Bogolyubov; Shil'der's *Iz pisem Nikolaya k brat'yam i drugim* (*From Nikolay's Correspondence with his Brothers and Others*), which suggested certain details in the portrayal of Nicholas I; and Chulkov's *Imperatory* (*Emperors*), from which extracts were copied into Bulgakov's notebooks.[74] The only other identifiable source is mentioned in Bulgakov's letter to

Veresayev in May 1935; this was Kostomarov's *Avtobiografiya* (*Autobiography*), which he found in Lemke's *Nikolayevskiye zhandarmy i literatura 1826–1855 gg.* (*Literature and the Gendarmes under Nikolay, 1826–55*), and which he cited to justify Dubel't's frequent quoting from the Bible.[75]

Two conclusions may be drawn about Bulgakov's use of sources for this play. The first is that although a great majority of the materials were provided by Veresayev, it seems that Bulgakov could have found virtually all of them in Veresayev's published works if he had so wished; a handsome dedication might therefore have done just as well as an invitation to co-authorship, and we must seek in Bulgakov's debts of gratitude to Veresayev the real reason for the invitation. Once their collaboration had been officially established, Bulgakov was able to call on Veresayev for additional materials when necessary; but he ultimately allowed Veresayev little scope to influence the content of the play, and the concessions to the need to sketch in the political background to Pushkin's death if the play were to be licensed for performance remained fairly minor. The second conclusion is that, as with the Molière play, Bulgakov selected materials more with an eye to their vividness than to their authenticity. He then created a play which, for all the boldness of his decision to exclude the poet himself from the action, would evoke his history more faithfully and uncontroversially than the Molière play had done.

Pushkin's absence from the play caused some consternation among theatre producers and audiences at the time of its first production, which eventually reached the stage in 1943, and has continued to do so ever since. Yelena Sergeyevna later explained Bulgakov's decision to exclude the poet from the stage primarily as a question of taste:

It seemed unacceptable to him that even the most talented actor should come out onto the stage in a curly wig, with sidewhiskers, and laugh Pushkin's laugh, and then start to talk in ordinary, everyday language.[76]

This view was seconded by Paustovsky:

This showed Bulgakov's reverence for Pushkin (what actor would be capable of playing Pushkin in a way that would not diminish his image in our eyes?), his artistic tact, the severity and daring of a master.[77]

Certainly these considerations would have been uppermost in Bulgakov's mind, since he abhorred vulgarization. Writing a play

about a poet without actually putting him on stage is also consistent
with his deeply-held conviction that the writer is a being isolated
from the society which determines his mortal fate. In opting, after
the problems he had encountered with *The Cabal of Hypocrites*, to
sidestep controversy and leave Pushkin out, he was not essentially
altering his approach to the problem of portraying a creative genius
in the theatre. Whereas the Molière works had concentrated on the
man himself, Bulgakov broadened his perspective here to examine
the daily life of the central figure through a portrayal of the people
around him, who represent the social, economic, political and
domestic pressures which interfere with the task of creating art.

In order that the play should succeed in these aims, it was vital
that the absence of Pushkin should be compensated for in a
rigorous organization of plot and theme, to exclude any material
irrelevant to the main subject. The events of the play unfold with
growing intensity, the settings shifting from Pushkin's tense household to an evening of malicious gossip at Saltykov's literary soirée,
then on to the society ball, which Pushkin attends although
repeatedly singled out as an outsider; from there the scene switches
to the offices of the secret police, working through the night to
protect the Tsar from the poet's writings, before moving on to
Heeckeren's house and the receipt of the challenge – a challenge to
the authors of Pushkin's domestic humiliation, certainly, but also
perhaps to all the enemies we have seen on the stage beforehand.
After the duel, we return to the domestic scene to see its relative
peace and security shattered by Danzas's news of Pushkin's wound;
and after the death of the poet, the remainder of the play is devoted
to showing how the episode is dealt with in such a way as to ensure
that no serious disturbances should ensue. Pushkin is the main
subject of conversation in all these scenes, and the other *dramatis
personae*, all of roughly equivalent significance and none of them
characterized in any great depth, figure in the play only inasmuch as
their actions relate to the poet's fate. In paring away all that is
irrelevant to Pushkin, Bulgakov heightens the tension in order to
communicate the unremitting persecution suffered by the poet and
the inescapability of his fate. Even after his death, society continues
impersonally to 'deal' with him as it did during his lifetime.

In other words, Bulgakov leaves the audience to create their own
picture of Pushkin. In doing so, he was indubitably relying on the
audience's prior knowledge of Pushkin's history, as well as on its

presumed sympathy for the poet. Otherwise, the picture is built up indirectly through the various characters' feelings about him: loyal Aleksandra hopelessly and uselessly loving the man and his art; Natal'ya Nikolayevna unloving, unsympathetic to his art, and visibly more interested by other men; Zhukovsky in awe of his talent, protective, but despairing over his reckless behaviour at court; the Saltykov salon eager to slander him and belittle his achievements; Nicholas I playing cat and mouse with him, threatening and patronizing him while flirting with his wife; D'Anthès and Heeckeren arrogant and contemptuous of the cheated husband and scribbler. Even those most sympathetic towards him wish him at least in part to be other than his true self.

But the essential way in which Pushkin's presence is conveyed on stage is through his poetry, which is used sparingly but to strong effect. Readers of the play are offered an epigraph from *Eugene Onegin*:

И сохранённая судьбой,
Быть может в Лете не потонет
Строфа, слагаемая мной.

(And perhaps the stanza I've composed, preserved by destiny, will not sink into Lethe's waters.)[78]

The suggestion that the poet's work can take on its true significance after the death of the man himself was a cherished belief of Bulgakov's which was to inform the whole of *The Master and Margarita*; and Rudnitsky points out that it was a concept which bound *The Cabal of Hypocrites* and *The Last Days* together:

The two plays agree on one thing; a confident prophecy of the inevitable – albeit even posthumous – triumph of the truth torn by the artist from a life that is transient and mutable, and rendered back to life for eternity.[79]

The poems serve to provide a commentary on the major themes of the play, but also help to identify the predicament of the characters with whom they are associated. *Eugene Onegin* reappears in the play on the day of the duel, when Aleksandra and Zhukovsky tell their fortunes from the work; they turn up only verses of bitterness and regret:

Познал я глас иных желаний,
Познал я новую печаль;
Для первых нет мне упований,
А старой мне печали жаль ...

Приятно дерзкой эпиграммой
Взбесить оплошного врага . . .
Ещё приятнее в молчанье
Ему готовить честный гроб.   (60–1)

(I have come to know the voice of other desires, I have come to know new sorrow; of the first I can have no hope, and my former sorrow I regret . . . It is agreeable with an impertinent epigram to enrage a blundering enemy . . . It is even more agreeable to prepare him an honest grave in silence.)[80]

These lines capture Pushkin's despair and foreshadow the tragedy which his friends are no longer capable of preventing. Pushkin's *Pora, moy drug, pora* (*It's time, my friend, it's time*, 1834) reinforces the mood of resignation in its longing for peace and renunciation of worldly concerns. The poem is read by Nikita Kozlov, who puzzles over the text copied out in an exercise book, recognizing the authenticity of its sentiments but unable to work out the significance of the 'pobeg' ('flight') which appears to be the solution offered by the poet (56–7). He is no more able to help Pushkin than Aleksandra and Zhukovsky.

Another work used by Bulgakov in the play is Pushkin's 1836 poem *Mirskaya vlast'* (*Worldly Power*); this mockingly describes the way guards have been posted to protect Bryullov's painting of the Crucifixion, and asks:

К чему, скажите мне, хранительная стража?
Или распятие – казённая поклажа,
И вы боитесь воров или мышей? . . .
Иль опасаетесь, чтоб чернь не оскорбила
Того, чья казнь весь род адамов искупила,
И, чтоб не потеснить гуляющих господ,
Пускать не велено сюда простой народ?   (46)

(To what purpose, tell me, this protective guard? Or is the Crucifixion state property, and do you fear thieves or mice? . . . Or are you afraid lest the mob insult Him, whose execution redeemed the whole race of Adam; and, in order not to crowd the strolling gentlefolk, have orders been issued not to admit the common people?)

Pushkin's comment on the way the State takes over both religion and art and establishes authority over them is of no little relevance to Bulgakov's message to a modern audience.

But the play is dominated by the refrain of Pushkin's 1825 poem *Zimny vecher* (*Winter Evening*), with its imagery of storm and darkness juxtaposed against the light–dark imagery of the rest of the play, dramatizing the turmoil in Pushkin's mind. *Winter Evening* is sung by Aleksandra as the opening of the play, thus providing the spoken text with its epigraph. Subsequently the poem becomes associated with Bitkov, the 'Judas' who follows Pushkin and spies on him, and whose unconscious sympathy for the poet increases as he is caught up in the beauty of his verse. Bitkov's new sensitivity to poetry marks a stage in his moral development, since the end of the play sees him coming to an awareness, if not of his guilt, then at least of the disreputableness of his actions. Both he and the policeman Dubel't (who retains the lines of Pushkin's poem after hearing Bitkov recite them just once) are indicators of the power that poetry might have to penetrate even to those who are working to stamp it out. It would nevertheless be wrong to read any optimism into the play on this account. In the closing scene of the play, Bitkov's recollection of lines from *Winter Evening* is blended into the real snowstorm raging outside over the poet's corpse:

Yes, he wrote poetry ... And there was no peace for anyone with those poems ... not for him, not for the authorities, nor for me, God's servant, Stepan Il'yich ... Goodness, what a storm ... The very best lines he wrote: 'The storm with darkness veils the sky, whirling round the blizzards. Now like a beast it starts to howl, now like a child to sob ...' Do you hear, that's right, just like a child. (77–9)

It is astonishing that when the play was finally performed in 1943 this last scene was considered to be problematic by the Repertory Committee, who were most concerned that the police spy should not be seen to repent of his actions. Nemirovich-Danchenko, who was supervising the production in its final stages, was prepared to concede that a full-scale repentance would not be necessary so long as it was made clear that Bitkov was at least beginning to come to an awareness of the harm he had been involved in.[81] But the Committee was not satisfied at the idea that the audience should even catch a glimpse of the stirrings of Bitkov's conscience, and eventually insisted on more drastic alterations to the ending of the play. These were made, and one of the Committee members, A. V. Solodovnikov, voiced their approval of the change:

You have done well to transfer Pushkin's verses to Turgenev, rather than leaving them for Bitkov to speak. It's a step in the right direction.

Pushkin's heritage is not transmitted to Bitkov, it is of no importance to us what effect it has on him; Pushkin's heritage is transmitted to the people, to the progressive forces.[82]

This destroyed one of the most original characterizations – and Bulgakov's only significant invention – in the play. The ideological implications of such a change are puzzling: Bitkov, the common man, is shown to be incapable of shrugging off his despicable role or appreciating the national poet's verse, while the officer Turgenev, who has consented to take part in the discreet removal of the body from St Petersburg, is granted the honour of speaking the verse instead.

At the same meeting, Solodovnikov went on to recommend that more of Pushkin's verse should be included in the play, in order that it should end on an optimistic note; he wanted the audience to be left not with an impression of the swirling storm, but rather with the promise of a new dawn. This suggestion was gracefully dismissed by Nemirovich-Danchenko, who pointed out that it would contradict the essential message of the play. Solodovnikov was no doubt motivated in his suggestion by the fact that the production was taking place in war-time, so that the Committee was presumably seeking for ways of instilling vigorous optimism in the audience. In actual fact, the MKhAT production already contained more direct quotation of and references to Pushkin's verse than had been originally envisaged by Bulgakov; these had been added by Yelena Sergeyevna at the theatre's request in 1942.[83] In the most substantial of Yelena Sergeyevna's alterations, the scene between Zhukovsky and Nicholas I where the latter expresses his mistrust of Pushkin's flattering poems is expanded to include references to his *Druz'yam* (*To My Friends*, 1828) and to *The Captain's Daughter*; but her alterations do not materially affect the sense of the play as Solodovnikov's would have done.

Bulgakov further enriches the texture of his play with references to poetry other than Pushkin's. The inflammatory power of poetry is most strongly evoked in his use of Lermontov's *Smert' poeta* (*Death of a Poet*), which is recited by a student outside Pushkin's house on the night of his death (72–3). Lermontov's poem was in fact one of the original sources for the Russian and later Soviet interpretation of Pushkin's death as murder, or at least as being part of some sort of conspiracy. But whilst scholars have continued to document the extreme hostility of court circles towards Pushkin, and their evident delight at the news of his killing, it remains true that in objective terms Pushkin's death was the result of a duel which he himself had initiated, and which he had a fair chance of surviving, especially since he was a practised and redoubted marksman. Bulgakov certainly chose to use the suggestion which he had found in *Pushkin in his Lifetime* to the effect that Nicholas I (or, strictly speaking, Benkendorf) chose not to prevent the duel; but at the same time he does not suggest that Nicholas I is therefore to be held solely and directly responsible for the poet's death.[84] Instead, he adduces a number of different factors contributing to the misery of his last days. Ellendea Proffer has argued that the play really seeks justly to apportion the blame for Pushkin's death, thereby becoming something of a detective story.[85] But I would argue that the play, on the contrary, avoids putting the blame on any particular factors, and rather seeks to demonstrate the wide range of circumstances which conspired to render Pushkin's *life*, rather than his death, tragic. By going beyond the basic issue of how to apportion the blame for Pushkin's death to a broader consideration of the poet's plight during his lifetime, Bulgakov enables *The Last Days* to bear a more universal message. Yelena Sergeyevna recalled that he thought of Stroganov's blindness in the play as a symbol of the blind fate which in the end was responsible for destroying Pushkin.[86] Through this evocation of the ultimate power shaping the writer's destiny, Bulgakov reiterates the message contained in the censored last line of *The Cabal of Hypocrites*: 'The cause of all this was fate.'[87]

Apart from Lermontov's poem, with its provocative questions about the poet's death, Bulgakov also makes use in the play of Zhukovsky's *A. S. Pushkin* (1837); we see this in the actual process of composition, as Zhukovsky attempts to come to terms with his friend's death. The poem, of which Bulgakov cites only snatches, dwells on the new, serene and strangely fulfilled expression on Pushkin's face after death, and explores the notion that the poet accedes to a higher vision beyond death:

Было лицо его мне так знакомо, и было заметно,
Что выражалось на нём – в жизни такого
Мы не видали на этом лице. Не горел вдохновенья
Пламень на нём; не сиял острый ум,
Нет! Но какою-то мыслью, глубокой, высокою мыслью
Было объято оно: мнилося мне, что ему

В этот миг предстояло как будто какое виденье,
Что-то сбывалось над ним, и спросить мне хотелось: что видишь?

(His face was so familiar to me, and I was struck by what was expressed on it; we had not seen the like on this face during his lifetime. It was not the flame of inspiration which burned on it; nor was it sharp wit gleaming, no! But it was suffused with some thought, a profound, noble thought; and it seemed to me that at that instant some vision had appeared before him, that something was taking shape above him, and I felt like asking: what do you see?)

This is again a familiar Bulgakovian theme. Both Lermontov's and Zhukovsky's poems are examples of, as it were, poetry in action: Lermontov's carrying a powerful call to freedom, and Zhukovsky's, spontaneous and prosaic, an unaffected evocation of the visionary. These are contrasted in the play with the limp erotic verse of Benediktov who, significantly, cannot even remember it well enough to recite it off by heart (24–5). He belongs to a literary world whose works we do not hear, because their principal occupation is not in the end the creation of great literature, but the destruction of great poets. Bulgakov seems here to have been recalling Sologub's memoirs of Pushkin:

He had many literary enemies, who gave him no peace and wounded his irritable pride by proclaiming, with the self-assurance characteristic of those gentlemen, that Pushkin had grown weaker and had written himself out, which was an utter lie, but all the same a hurtful lie.[88]

The distance from Saltykov's salon to Griboyedov House, both equally fired by envy and philistinism, is not so very great.

To sum up; Pushkin, though absent (except in current Soviet productions) from the stage, remains the pivot of the play. Nothing in the play happens which is not related to his fate, and characters are measured by the degree of their understanding of him. Pushkin's poetry provides the fabric of the play; sometimes the influence of his language can be detected on the overall tone of the work, and sometimes it seems to be parodied, as in Nicholas I's sentimental speech to Natal'ya at the ball, or in D'Anthès's spleen. Pushkin's absence is by no means a non-presence; when he flits across the back of the stage as a shadow, it is first as a man weary and ill, then at the ball angry and alien, his humiliation indirectly echoed in the figure of the negro servant, and finally as a mortally wounded body. There is no need for him to speak, for his very silhouette serves to express to the audience the consequences for Pushkin of what is being enacted at the front of the stage. Pavel Markov suggests that there may be a sense in which, in purely dramatic terms, the play suffers from his absence:

But the theme of the artist, the theme of the ruler of men's thoughts, the theme of poetry undoubtedly benefited from it. Bulgakov was afraid of violating our notion of Pushkin through the gross corporeality of a stage incarnation. What was more important for him was the way in which society lived off Pushkin's creations, responding to him either with indignation or with enthusiasm.[89]

But if a production succeeds in incorporating all the elements whereby Bulgakov compensates for the lack of his hero, the audience finds itself presented with a very tautly structured piece. Pushkin is excluded from the action because he is persecuted, because society does not allow the poet the right, the freedom, the responsibility or the peace to carry out his work. To describe the play as a play without Pushkin is therefore to miss the whole point of Bulgakov's approach.

This attitude may be compared with that of Tsvetayeva, who in a 1931 poem, the first in her collection *Stikhi k Pushkinu* (*Poems to Pushkin*), describes her distaste for the way in which artists are taken over by the state and deified:

Бич жандармов, бог студентов,
Желчь мужей, услада жён,
Пушкин – в роли монумента? . . .

К Пушкинскому юбилею
Тоже речь произнесём:
Всех румяней и смуглее
До сих пор на свете всём,

Всех живучей и живее!
Пушкин – в роли мавзолея?

(The scourge of gendarmes, the god of students, the gall of husbands, the delight of wives, Pushkin – in the role of a monument? . . . We will also pronounce a speech for the Pushkin jubilee: more ruddy and swarthy than ever anyone in the world, more tenacious and livelier! Pushkin – in the role of a mausoleum?)[90]

She would surely have welcomed Bulgakov's discreet presentation of Pushkin in the play, and his avoidance of the necessity for 'the genius' to be portrayed by an actor. Another comment of hers on

Pushkin's approach to historiography illuminates Bulgakov's own approach to the writing of a play about a historical figure:

Pushkin's Pugachov is a riposte by the poet to the historical Pugachov, the riposte of a lyric poet to the archive: Yes, I know, I know it all as it was, and how it all was, I know that Pugachov was base and pusillanimous, I know it all, but I don't want to know that knowledge of mine, I counter that not-mine, alien knowledge with my own knowledge. I know better.[91]

In the same way, for all his study of archival materials, Bulgakov's Pushkin is not the archivist's or the historian's Pushkin; for Bulgakov too knows better, and reserves for himself the right always to interpret history according to his own lights. Bulgakov's purpose here is not to pass final judgement on the guilty, nor to establish some sort of absolute historical truth; he asserts the primacy of the artist's perception of history, as he ultimately asserts the power of literature – and here, despite his personal reservations about the genre, of poetry – over the philistines. The play succeeds in evoking Pushkin's plight in a manner that is all the more engaging for being individualistic, while at the same time exploring the perennial Bulgakovian theme of the conflict between society and the artist.

Bulgakov and Gogol

'And so, dead souls ... And here I am, at the end of my career as a writer, obliged to compose adaptations. What a brilliant finale, don't you think?[92]

Between 1929, when Bulgakov first embarked on his study of Molière, and the mid-1930s, which saw the writing of the play about Pushkin, he also produced a series of works based on those of Gogol. In 1930–2 he created a stage version of *Myortvye dushi* (*Dead Souls*) for MKhAT, and this was followed in 1934 by two film scenarios, one of *Dead Souls* and one of *Revizor* (*The Government Inspector*).[93] Whilst the film scenarios never reached the screen, the adaptation of *Dead Souls* for MKhAT was accepted after considerable rewriting, and proved an extremely successful production: by the 1970s it was the fourth most frequently performed production for MKhAT in the Soviet period, surpassed only by *The Days of the Turbins*, *An Ideal Husband* and *Anna Karenina*.[94] As adaptations, these works afford interesting material about the ways in which Bulgakov responded to his literary heritage, even if they are inferior in quality to Bulgakov's major works on Molière or *The*

Last Days. The question these adaptations prompt, given his affectionate and knowledgeable familiarity with Gogol, is whether any special significance can be attributed to the fact that Bulgakov chose *not* to write about him as he had written about Molière and Pushkin. For while Gogol did not inspire Bulgakov to the kind of biographical writing which grew out of his interest in Molière and Pushkin, the influence of his writings and of his personal history on Bulgakov's literary development is of considerable importance, and his identification with his predecessor's fortunes is particularly strong. Popov records Bulgakov's high esteem for Gogol in his memoirs:

He continually set Gogol up as a model for himself, and loved him, along with Saltykov-Shchedrin, better than any other classic writer in Russian literature.[95]

This is confirmed in a letter Bulgakov sent Popov in 1926, which was evidently an answer to some sort of questionnaire:

Among writers, I prefer Gogol. In my view, no-one can compare with him. I read *Dead Souls* at the age of nine. I regarded it as an adventure story. In my opinion, there came a second period in Gogol's creative life when he wrote himself out ... In his *Correspondence* he revealed his soul.[96]

Bulgakov's personal identification with Gogol is also attested to by Valentin Katayev in his book *Almazny moy venets* (*My Crown of Diamonds*), where Bulgakov figures in the guise of 'sineglazy' ('blue-eyes'):

Although blue-eyes was a doctor by training, he once confessed to me that he had always thought of himself as a writer like Gogol.[97]

Katayev reveals that although the two of them never really got on (Bulgakov disapproved of Katayev's amorous interest in his sister), they found common ground in their love of Gogol. They even considered publishing a magazine together, which was to satirize the absurdities of NEP; Bulgakov had got as far as choosing the name for the publication – 'Revizor' ('The Government Inspector'), but they were not in the end given permission to publish it.[98]

In Bulgakov's stories of the early 1920s, Gogol fulfils a role similar to the one we have identified in his interpretation of Pushkin: a great writer of the past who symbolizes all that is under threat in the new culture. The point is made in light-hearted fashion in the stories *Lestnitsa v ray* (*A Staircase to Heaven*, 1923) and

Biblifetchik (*The Libriwaiter*, 1924), where the workers' earnest
endeavours to acquire some sort of culture are in both cases
expressed in terms of their wanting to read the works of Gogol
together with Bukharin's *Azbuk kommunizma* (*ABC of Commu-
nism*).[99] The ironic incongruity of this juxtaposition mocks the
indiscriminate tastes of the new readers. The theme is developed in
Cuffnotes, where Gogol figures alongside Pushkin and
Dostoyevsky as one of the classic authors whose works are dismissed out of hand during the lecture by the radical speaker, who
calls instead for the creation of an entirely new culture.[100] The final
outrage which causes the narrator of this story to flee the city of
philistines (based on Vladikavkaz) and try to make a living for
himself in Moscow, comes when the local Literature Department
acquires a new head:

My cup is overflowing. At twelve the 'new direction' arrived.
  He came out and announced:
  'We'll persue a diff'rent polisy. We don't need any more of this
pawnography, *Woe from Wit*, *Government Inspectors* . . . Gogols . . .
Magols . . . We'll rite our own plays.'
  Then he got into his automobile and drove off.[101]

For Bulgakov such cultural illiteracy represents a desecration of his
most cherished values.
  In 1930–4 Bulgakov's knowledge of Gogol was extended and
deepened in the course of his reading of primary and secondary
sources for his work on the various adaptations, and a new
immediacy comes to characterize Bulgakov's sense of kinship with
him. It is typical, for instance, that at this time he should turn to
Gogol's fantastical descriptions in order to describe some aspect of
his own experiences. In January 1932 Bulgakov's fortunes suddenly
improved after the difficult period since 1929 with the news of the
revival of *The Days of the Turbins* at MKhAT. He was shrewd
enough to realize, however, that his future was still by no means
assured, and he complained in a weary letter to Popov of the
swarms of people who besieged him with questions, determined to
know what it all meant. On seeing that he was unwilling or unable
to provide them with a satisfactory explanation, they had begun to
devise their own:

And they gave such wonderful explanations, Pavel Sergeyevich, that
everything went dark before my eyes. It all ended with a very familiar

figure with a sharp nose and the crazed eyes of a sick man running in to see me one night. 'What does it mean?' he exclaimed.

'What it means', I replied, 'is that these citizens, and above all these literary men, are acting out the 9th chapter of your novel, which I, great teacher, adapted in your honour. You yourself said: "... in their heads there was commotion, hubbub and contradiction, there was disorder in their thoughts ... they revealed their mistrustful and lazy natures, full of unceasing doubt and eternal fearfulness".

Cover me up with your cast-iron greatcoat!'

And he covered me up, and now I could hear the theatrical rain coming down more distantly; and my name thundered out, and the Turbins', and 'Shalyapin is coming and Kachalov has had his leg amputated'!! (Kachalov is indeed unwell, but all the same you can't just go around slicing the legs off People's Artistes! And Shalyapin, it seems, is not coming, so they were wasting their time disconnecting the telephone at the Bol'shoy!) They ought to have their tongues torn out![102]

Here Bulgakov appeals to Gogol for protection, like Pushkin, through the image of his statue in Moscow; he envisages him as some kind of benign spirit who will defend him from the gossips who remind him of the inhabitants of the town of N. in *Dead Souls*. Where he had earlier referred to Molière as his master and Pushkin as his commander, he now addresses Gogol in turn as his 'great teacher'.

Among the things that Bulgakov learned from Gogol were certain tricks of style; Kaverin has asserted that:

Reading Bulgakov, you can't help beginning to feel that to Dostoyevsky's well-known aphorism 'We have all emerged from under Gogol's greatcoat' one ought to add 'and from Gogol's *Nose*'.[103]

This extension of Dostoyevsky's famous (but probably apocryphal) comment to Bulgakov's prose results in the imputation to it of a mucous quality which the critic presumably did not intend; nevertheless the influence of Gogol's style is discernible in Bulgakov's prose, especially in his early stories. The short sentences, laconic manner, frequent exclamations, and apparently detached observation of a distorted reality which we associate with *Nos* (*The Nose*) and with *Zapiski sumasshedshego* (*Notes of a Madman*) find reflection particularly in his feuilletons and in the *Diaboliad* collection. Bulgakov did not adopt the most typical Gogolian characteristic, his use of absurd hyperbole, nor does he indulge in alogism to a comparable extent. In his mature work he tends to seek the grotesque and the ridiculous directly within situations, rather than undermining situations in the Gogolian manner through a blatantly surreal use of language. One characteristic which he borrows is Gogol's habit of giving his heroes eccentric names; Paustovsky, recalling Bulgakov's skill at devising nicknames for the staff at school, mentions that two at least were never able to shrug off their Gogolian names of Masloboy and Shpon'ka again.[104] Bulgakov then went on to invent equally comic names for the characters of his stories; Archibal'd Archibal'dovich, Buton-Netselovanny, Aristarkh Platonovich, Baklazhanov and so on. He even draws on a glossary of Ukrainian words provided by Gogol at the beginning of Part 2 of *Vechera na khutore bliz Dikan'ki* (*Evenings on a Farmstead near Dikan'ka*) for the name of one of the characters in *The Master and Margarita*, Varenukha.[105]

Chudakova, who has taken a particular interest in the stylistic and thematic kinship between the two writers' works, has identified specific links between *Notes of a Madman* and *Cuffnotes*.[106] In both stories the narrator finds reality bewildering because of his illness, while at the same time exposing the essentially absurd nature of that reality. Chudakova argues that, through its use of direct quotation, Bulgakov's work explicitly invites a parallel with *The Nose* as well;[107] and she pinpoints in both works a breakdown of language as being symptomatic of a complete alienation from the world. She also identifies in the story *Diaboliad* an echo of typical Gogolian themes, such as the hopeless quest which forms the basis for the plot of Gogol's 'Petersburg' stories, and a sinister elusiveness of identity which drives the narrator to the point of insanity. Chudakova concludes that the main difference between the two writers' approaches is that Bulgakov ultimately has more faith in the capacity of the hero, however downtrodden, to survive against the oppression of 'byt' ('mundane reality').

There is undoubtedly a common interest between the two writers in the absurd, and in comic situations which slip over into the terrifying. But as far as the stylistic echoes are concerned, it is important to distinguish between Gogol's dislocation of language in *Notes of a Madman*, a measure of Poprishchin's alienation from reality which only reflects upon that reality by association, and Bulgakov's, where the broken language is realistic, accurately and directly portraying the *actual* absurdity of the language of the new

culture. This is particularly exemplified in the acronyms which the
narrator has to struggle to understand:

I'm the director. Dir. Lito. I'm getting the hang of it.
Dirsubart. Poped. Litcollegium . . .
'Litodir?'
'Dir. Dir.' . . .
. . . A grey fence. A poster on the fence. Huge bright letters. A word. Oh
my fathers! What sort of a word is that? Vlamatwan. What on earth does it
mean? What can it mean?
Vladimir Mayakovsky's twelfth anniversary.[108]

The adaptation of Gogolian material or devices not only marks
Bulgakov's real stylistic and thematic indebtedness to his master,
but in this instance serves a sharp satirical purpose which belies
Chudakova's view of Bulgakov's relative optimism about mankind.
   In a different article, Chudakova endeavours to extend her
theory to *A Theatrical Novel*, where she argues that the narrative
style adopted by the text's supposed author, Maksudov, is
consciously modelled on Gogolian devices and techniques.[109] But
apart from a rather unconvincing account of the similarities
between Chichikov's negotiations with Sobakevich and Maksudov's haggling with the theatre over payment for his play, she is
unable to produce much textual evidence to support her view. This
is hardly sufficient to justify the elaborate explanation she then
gives of the possible function of this imitation:

By assimilating this 'alien world' through Gogolian speech, Maksudov
discovers in himself powers to resist it.
   Even in Bulgakov's early prose Russian literature figures as inward
support for the hero in his resistance to the alogism of 'byt'. It functions as a
measure of a norm, helping him to recognize violations of that norm, to
become aware of them and to counter them with definite values; and this
function of Russian literature also becomes apparent in *A Theatrical
Novel*.
   The free reworking of Gogolian speech in the novel combines in a
complex manner the self-affirmation of the author–narrator with the
assertion by him of the unbroken traditions of Russian literature. 'Classic'
Gogolian devices which have become the heritage of the modern world are
put forward polemically; as not having been rendered obsolete, nor having
been surpassed by the contemporary prose which Maksudov reads when he
is thinking about his second novel . . . *By the very manner of the narration*
Bulgakov demonstrates who it is that became, not only for his hero, but
also for himself, a living point of orientation during his work on *The Master*

and Margarita, the novel which he began four years after completing his first novel, and which he finished only just before he died.[110]

While Chudakova's specific argument in relation to *A Theatrical Novel* remains tenuous, her comments assume a much greater interest when applied to Bulgakov himself, for she touches upon the key issue of the way Bulgakov relates to the literature of the past, using it as a standard against which to measure an abhorrent modern culture. Just as the influence of Tolstoy can be most clearly traced in Bulgakov's first novel, so the explicit stylistic influence of Gogol diminishes as Bulgakov establishes an independent style after the mid-1920s. But Gogol can be said to have continued to inspire the lyrical and satirical themes of Bulgakov's mature work even as Bulgakov grew away from his diction.

One early example of Bulgakov's direct responses to Gogol is not strictly an adaptation so much as a reworking of a Gogolian creation into a new genre; this was his 1922 *Pokhozhdeniya Chichikova (The Adventures of Chichikov)*, subsequently published in the 1925 *Diaboliad* collection. Bulgakov conceived this work independently, rather than having it thrust upon him, as was the case with his adaptations of the 1930s. Within the framework of a dream, Bulgakov takes the characters from *Dead Souls*, adds a few from *The Government Inspector*, and lets them loose on Moscow under NEP. Chichikov discovers that the city is entirely given over to speculation and corruption, and that there is plenty of scope for his criminal imagination. Soon he is the most successful speculator in the city, and the narrator is called in by the bemused authorities in a last, desperate attempt to restore order. His mission accomplished, the narrator is offered whatever reward he chooses:

'Thank you. Ask for whatever you would like.'
So there I was, hopping by the telephone. And I almost poured into the receiver all the budget proposals which had been torturing me for so long: 'Trousers ... a pound of sugar ... a 25 candle-power lightbulb ...'
But suddenly I remembered that a self-respecting man of literature ought to be disinterested, so I wilted, and muttered into the telephone: 'Nothing, except the bound works of Gogol that I recently sold in the flea-market.'
And ... bang! There on my table was an edition of Gogol trimmed in gold!
I was so delighted to see Nikolay Vasil'yevich, who had more than once consoled me during gloomy, sleepless nights, that I bellowed:
'Hurrah!'

And . . .
Epilogue
. . . of course, woke up. And there was nothing: no Chichikov, no
Nozdryov, and, chiefly, no Gogol . . .
'Ho-hum . . .' I thought to myself, and began to dress, and once again life
went strutting ahead of me in its humdrum way.[111]

This satire on life under NEP has at its basis a concept which was
to be elaborated in a much more sophisticated manner in *The
Master and Margarita*, for the characters arrive in Moscow having
been released from the realm of shadows by a joker–demon so that
they should wreak havoc on Soviet Russia, much as Woland's suite
invades Moscow in the 1930s. The ending of the story is a comic
comment on the dire economic situation and the chronic shortage
of basic goods, let alone books; it also suggests more subversively
that the State cares so little for culture, as symbolized by the works
of Gogol, or is so worried by the parallels that might be drawn
between the world of *Dead Souls* and the present day, that the only
hope for someone who wanted to get hold of Gogol's works would
be for a dream to come miraculously true. If this seems an
exaggerated interpretation, it should be noted that Bulgakov's
story was never published as a separate book, even though archival
sources show that the original publishers, 'Nedra', gave permission
for this in April 1926, and that a contract was drawn up with the
'Zemlya i Fabrika' publishing-house in May of the same year.[112]
Boris Thomson has pointed out that 'dozens of variations on
Gogol's Chichikov and Khlestakov began to appear in books and
plays from 1924 onwards', and that this became a recognized way of
satirizing the Soviet Establishment under the guise of a critique of
Tsarism.[113] Bulgakov's 1922 work appears to have been an early
example of this particular genre, and the interest of the work
certainly relates to its force as a satire, rather than to its ingenuity as
an adaptation of Gogol. It draws on Gogol for its essential material,
but the plot, theme and style all belong to Bulgakov.

It is paradoxical that, as Gogol's significance for Bulgakov as a
mentor diminished, he found himself increasingly involved in
commissions to make adaptations of his works. When Bulgakov
joined the production staff of MKhAT in 1930, he was almost
immediately appointed to assist with a new production of *Dead
Souls*. He was by no means enthusiastic about the task of writing a
new adaptation of the novel to begin with, and by May 1932 he was

entirely disillusioned by the theatre's whittling-down of his creation to a safe and respectful illustration of Gogol's masterpiece. He reflected on the history of the production in a letter to Popov shortly before the première:

I gaze at my shelves and shudder with horror: who's next, who will I have to adapt tomorrow? Turgenev, Leskov, Brokgauz–Efron? Ostrovsky? But the latter, fortunately, adapted himself for the stage, evidently foreseeing what would happen to me in 1929–31. Briefly . . .
(1) You *cannot* adapt *Dead Souls* for the stage. Take that as an axiom from a man who knows the work well. I have been informed that there exist 160 adaptations of it. Maybe even that's not quite accurate, but in any case *Dead Souls* cannot be staged.
(2) And how then did I come to undertake the task?
  I didn't undertake it, Pavel Sergeyevich. It's a long time since I have undertaken anything, since I do not control a single one of my steps, but Fate seizes me by the throat. As soon as I was appointed to MKhAT I was brought in as an assistant producer on *Dead Souls* (Sakhnovsky is the senior producer, then there's Teleshova and me). One glance at the notebook with the adaptation written by an invited scenarist was enough for everything to go green before my eyes. I understood that on the very threshold of the theatre I had met with a calamity: I had been appointed to a non-existent play. Not a bad début, eh? Its not a long story. After protracted torture what had long been known to me but which many people, unfortunately, didn't know, became clear: in order to stage something, you have to have written it yourself. And, to cut a long story short, I was the one who had to write it.
  My first plan: that the action should take place in Rome (don't stare at me!). Since he sees Russia from 'a beautiful distance', we'll see it that way too!
  My Rome was destroyed as soon as I reported on my outline. And I terribly regret my Rome.
(3) No Rome, so no Rome. Precisely, Pavel Sergeyevich, I carved it up! Just carved it up. And I dismantled the play, down to each separate stone. Literally into shreds . . .
  What happened to Nemirovich when he read it! As you see, it's not the 161st adaptation, nor even an adaptation at all, but something altogether different . . . (All over the place the text is given to other characters, not at all the same ones as in the *poema*, and so forth.)
  Vladimir Ivanovich was in a state of horror and fury. There was a great battle, but the play nevertheless went forward in that form. And work on it has been going on for about two years! . . .
  When will *Dead Souls* be premièred? In my opinion, never. If it's premièred as it is now it will be a terrible failure on the Main Stage.
  What's the problem? The problem is that in order to put on Gogol's

enchanting phantasmagoria, you have to have producers of talent in the
Theatre.
So there you are, Pavel Sergeyevich!
And anyway, I don't care. I don't care. And I don't care![114]

Bulgakov had wanted to avoid a simplistic rendering of the original,
a faithful but lifeless illustration of the text. As described in this
letter, he dismantled the dialogue of the novel with the help of the
producer, Sakhnovsky – to whom Bulgakov eventually conceded
one sixth of the royalties in recognition of his contribution – and
fitted it back together with additional materials from other works
by Gogol, transposing dialogue from one character to another,
and sometimes disrupting the original chronology.[115] The most
important instance of this chronological transformation is the
compression of all the events of Part 2 of *Dead Souls* into two final
scenes on stage: Chichikov is arrested even before leaving the town
of N., and is then released from prison to escape in his 'ptitsa-
troyka' ('winged troyka') after paying the authorities an enormous
bribe. Other inventions of Bulgakov include the elaboration into a
whole scene of the episode in which Chichikov first gets the idea of
buying the dead souls; and a fantastical extension of the story of
Captain Kopeykin, culminating with the arrival of Captain Kopeykin in the flesh, as a courier sent on to announce the arrival of a new
Governor-General, rather as in *The Government Inspector*.[116]

As Bulgakov explains in the letter, his boldest ambition had been
the attempt to frame the work in the broader perspective of Gogol
sitting in Rome, contemplating his beloved Rus' from afar, torn
between his admiration for the beauties of Italy and his guilty
nostalgia for the homeland he cannot bear to live in. Bulgakov was
anxious to preserve the tension in *Dead Souls* between the comic
and the lyrical; and he hoped to achieve this by the introduction
into the work of a narrator, the 'chtets' ('reader'), who would bring
the narrative viewpoint of the novel to life and also invoke the spirit
of Gogol himself. This involved a complex characterization, which
will be discussed at further length below.

The theatre, however, rejected most of the important innova-
tions proposed by Bulgakov and Sakhnovsky, and embarked on
rehearsals in 1930. Towards the end of 1931, Stanislavsky intervened and insisted that the original grotesque and hyperbolic sets
designed by Meyerkhol'd's erstwhile pupil, Bulgakov's friend
V. V. Dmitriyev, should be abandoned; they were replaced by sets

which above all strove for historical authenticity.[117] When the
production was finally premièred at the end of 1932, it inevitably
attracted unfavourable comparison with Meyerkhol'd's sensational
1926 production of *The Government Inspector*, and it was criticized
as being typical of MKhAT's cautious and academic approach.[118]
As Milne points out, however, Bulgakov's original scheme for the
work would have pre-empted such attacks through his ingenious
approach, and it was really Stanislavsky's determination to draw
the audience's attention away from the text back to the actors
which made the MKhAT production seem such a conservative
response to Meyerkhol'd's challenge. Interestingly, Bulgakov, who
had hated Meyerkhol'd's *The Government Inspector*, seems to
some extent to have wanted to follow his example in highlighting
the grotesque potential of Gogol's text.[119] But the essential point
made in Bulgakov's May 1932 letter to Popov was that what he had
written was 'not an adaptation at all, but something completely
different'; it would be more appropriate to consider his version of
the novel, at least in intention, as an independent work, concerned
not just with the plot of *Dead Souls*, but, much more importantly,
with the artist behind the work, with the theme of 'Gogol and his
novel *Dead Souls*'.

In March 1934 Bulgakov signed a contract with Soyuzfil'm for a
film scenario of *Dead Souls*.[120] In essence he approached the
cinema version in the same way as his stage adaptation, although
once again most of his inventions were ultimately rejected in favour
of a more pedestrian interpretation of Gogol's text. The scenario
was written at some speed during the busy summer of 1934 and was
completed in a first draft by July. The Bulgakovs went to Leningrad
to take electric-shock treatment for their health; and they were
visited there by the Assistant Director of the First Cinema Factory,
Vaysfel'd, together with Ivan Pyr'yev, the producer of the film, in
order to discuss the draft. On 10 July 1934 Bulgakov sent a letter to
Popov in Moscow:

The thing is that I've searched the whole hotel room and the second copy
isn't here. Which means they took both away instead of one.
   And I'm now sitting and having to think how to redo it.
   Lyusya maintains that the scenario turned out extremely well. I showed
it to them in a rough draft, and was quite right not to have wasted time
correcting it. Everything that I liked best about it, that is to say the scene of
Suvorov's soldiers in the middle of the Nozdryov scene, the separate,

lengthy ballad of Captain Kopeykin, the funeral service on Sobakevich's estate, and above all, Rome, with the silhouette on the balcony; all of that was utterly annihilated. The only thing I'll be able to save is Kopeykin, and even then only by cutting him. But oh, God, how I regret Rome!

I listened to everything that Vaysfel'd and his producer had to say, and immediately said that I would redo it; they were even rather astonished.[121]

So once again Bulgakov had endeavoured to introduce a narrative perspective to the work, involving the figure of Gogol writing *Dead Souls* in Rome, silhouetted against the background of the city as he stood on his balcony. He had also hoped to exploit the visual possibilities of cinema to bring some of Gogol's vivid similes and digressions to life; an example here is the reference to Suvorov's soldiers, who in Gogol's text appear when Nozdryov advances on Chichikov with the excessive zeal of a lieutenant who imagines he is taking part in one of Suvorov's battles.[122] Bulgakov had wanted to give physical reality to the narrator's elaborate image, once again bringing the narrator into the focus of the audience's attention so that they should be aware of his voice as well as of the mere events of the plot.

It might be asked why Bulgakov on this occasion put up so little resistance to the rejection of his ideas; the answer is to be found in the final section of his letter to Popov, where he reports on the fate of his play *Blazhenstvo (Bliss)*, which he was hoping to get accepted for production in Leningrad:

An incident took place here relating to *Bliss* which goes beyond the bounds of plausibility.

A room in the Astoria Hotel. I read the play. The director of the theatre, who is also a producer, listens, expresses complete and apparently genuine enthusiasm, plans to put it on, promises me money, and tells me that he will be back in forty minutes to have supper with me. Forty minutes later he returns, eats, says not a word about the play, and then disappears into the ground and is no more to be seen!

Some people have suggested that he vanished into the fourth dimension. Such are the wonders that occur in this world![123]

The message of this episode was clearly that some sort of pressure had been applied on the producer to abandon the project, so it may be that Bulgakov simply decided at this point to play safe with *Dead Souls* rather than expose himself to further difficulties which, quite apart from any other considerations, would entail significant financial loss.

But Bulgakov's problems with the film scenario were by no means over. During the rest of 1934 and the spring of 1935 the studio kept insisting on alterations to highlight the social themes in the work and play down Bulgakov's individual interpretation. Although Bulgakov did provide them with alterations as required, these often proved unacceptable to the studio.[124] Another problem was that the producer, Pyr'yev, had begun to make his own alterations to the text and consequently to put forward claims to a share in the rights over it; however, the publication of most of the correspondence relevant to the issue by G. Fayman proves conclusively that Bulgakov at least never accepted Pyr'yev's claims to co-authorship.[125] This raises important questions about the authenticity of the text of the scenario published in *Moskva* in 1978 under both their names, especially since the editor himself points out that the reasons given by Pyr'yev for the eventual abandoning of the project are as implausible as they are discreditable. Pyr'yev claimed to have turned against the film after reading the attack on Shostakovich in *Pravda* in January 1936, which had filled him with a sudden zeal to find a way of confronting contemporary issues in film, rather than looking back in reactionary fashion to the nineteenth century.[126] But since the project had in fact been discarded long before the *Pravda* article appeared, the real motives for the abandoning of the film remain obscure.

The editor of the text in *Moskva* goes on to explain that the scenario had been altered by Pyr'yev in 1965 even before it was edited again for the 1978 publication; and it becomes difficult to believe that the text corresponds at all closely to Bulgakov's original intentions, or even to the text as it stood when it last left his hands. Indeed, one has only to read the opening lines of the *Moskva* text, which place the author's voice against the background of St Petersburg on a dark, misty evening, to be struck by the distance between this setting and Bulgakov's repeatedly expressed desire to place the work and its narrator against the backdrop of the warmth and sunlight of Rome.[127] In both versions of *Dead Souls*, then, Bulgakov was largely thwarted in his endeavours to pay tribute to Gogol as the author of his masterpiece; and the published versions of the scenarios are less rewarding to the student of Bulgakov than the drafts and plans expressive of the author's original intentions.

Bulgakov's final adaptation of Gogol was *The Government*

Inspector, also written in 1934, and published by Wright in 1977 on the basis of a very limited edition of 1935.[128] Here the textual problems are reversed. Bulgakov signed a contract for the work with Ukrainfil'm in mid-August 1934, and a first draft of it was ready by the middle of October.[129] In late November he reported that he had had fruitful discussions with M. S. Korostin, whom he would be happy to have as the producer of the film.[130] He was extremely busy over the following few weeks, and Yelena Sergeyevna noted in her diary that he was less than enthusiastic about the work on *The Government Inspector*:

I can feel how much the work on *The Government Inspector* is beyond Misha's strength, how much he is agonizing over it. Working on other people's ideas for money.[131]

The second draft of the work was sent to the studio on 9 January 1935, and a third draft on 28 February (Yegorov's reading of this date as 8 February is an error).[132] During this period, however, it became clear that Korostin was taking upon himself a considerable share of the work, and this was formally recognized by Bulgakov in a letter to the studio of 5 March 1935, where he asked that payment for the work should be equally divided between them, dating back to 1 February 1935.[133] Bulgakov then took less and less interest in the adaptation, and an agreement of 26 September 1935 readjusted the proportions so that Bulgakov should receive only 25% of the money.[134]

The text that we have, therefore, is ultimately mostly the work of M. S. Korostin. Indeed, he assured a recent interviewer that he had a version already prepared when he first came to work on the project with Bulgakov, which would also explain Yelena Sergeyevna's remark about 'other people's ideas'.[135] While we can detect certain features in the text reminiscent of Bulgakov's humour, the fact of his renouncing his rights over the work at a time when he was in financial difficulties must argue for the work being accorded only a very tentative place in the Bulgakov canon.

In the 1930s Bulgakov's conscious relationship to Gogol was through the direct medium of his works, which he adapted with some reluctance. The important feature of the adaptations of *Dead Souls*, however, was the endeavour to introduce a narrator to the productions, and it is in this device that we can recognize Bulgakov's characteristic fascination with the figure of the creator standing behind the work and guiding it with his voice. In July 1930 Bulgakov and Sakhnovsky summed up their view of the function the 'chtets' ('reader') should fulfil in the production in a plan they submitted to MKhAT for consideration:

As for the 'chtets' or 'authorial character', it should be said that he is not a figure who simply delivers the lyrical digressions to the audience and supervises the action in the performance, but a character who has to convey and bring out for the audience the tragic divide between the Gogol who is seeking a positive hero, and the Gogol who belongs to the reality which he felt obliged to mock and display in such destructive satirical colours.[136]

Bulgakov then elaborated his view of the role of the 'chtets' in a letter to Nemirovich-Danchenko in November 1930:

These are my thoughts regarding the role of the 'chtets' (the presenter of the performance) in my adaptation of *Dead Souls*.

A repeated analysis of the text of my adaptation, and in particular of the Plyushkin scene, has shown that it would be possible to try to extend the role of the presenter of the performance with the aim of weaving the role organically into all the scenes of the play, so as to make the presenter in the full sense of the word the conductor of the play.

To achieve this it will be necessary to undertake an extremely careful and sensitive study not just of the text of the 'poema' *Dead Souls* but also of other background materials, such as Gogol's letters and the works of certain of Gogol's contemporaries ...

It should be added that the play will naturally become more weighty with the introduction of the role of the 'chtets' or presenter, but strictly on condition that the 'chtets', having opened the play, should then guide it in direct and lively motion together with the rest of the characters, that is, that he should take part not only in the 'reading', but also in the action.[137]

Some years after the production, Sakhnovsky, who always regretted that their original plans had come to nothing, described the sources they turned to in order to achieve the desired effect of authorial presence in their character of the 'chtets':

We were considerably assisted in our quest by the correspondence to and from Gogol, stories and remarks about Gogol by S. Aksakov, Annenkov and Smirnova, individual sections in *Vybrannye mesta iz perepiski s druz'yami* (*Selected Passages from Correspondence with Friends*), and articles and letters written by Belinsky, Herzen, Chernyshevsky and Zhukovsky ... But the most important thing for us was Gogol's text. In front of us lay the tenth edition edited by Tikhonravov, and a Brokgauz edition edited by Kallash.[138]

The emphasis here on biographical material indicates the extent to which Bulgakov wanted the character of the 'chtets' to arise out of authentic contemporary perceptions of the writer's personality, while the identity of the 'chtets' as narrator is of course largely established in the manuscript through material selected from the narration of *Dead Souls* itself.[139] The digressions which Bulgakov chose to put in the mouth of the 'chtets' in addition to his basic narrative function most typically bring out the note of personal melancholy and anguish which colours the satirical comedy of the original, and which Stanislavsky hoped to eliminate in order to stress the text's denunciatory force. Bulgakov's version ended with the 'chtets' describing Chichikov's departure and concluding with a moving address to the open road and a wry comment on the poet's lot:

Ah, the road, the open road! How often, like a dying, drowning man, have I seized upon you, and you have magnanimously carried me away and saved me. Oh, without you, how difficult it would have been to struggle with the paltry burden of trivial passions, to walk hand in hand with my worthless heroes! So often I would have liked to strike elevated chords and fetter my admirers to my triumphant chariot! But no! Your path has been determined, poet! They call you base and worthless, and you will not gain the sympathy of your contemporaries. They will take your soul and heart away from you. They will attribute all the qualities of your heroes to you, and your very laughter will crash back down upon you. O, dear friend! What subjects there are! Have pity on me. Perhaps my descendants will pronounce reconciliation over my shade.
(*A lamp is lit*)
... and I looked around me and, as before, saw Rome at the hour of sunset.[140]

Bulgakov here combines phrases from Gogol's correspondence and variants to the novel to create a speech which is still in keeping with the narrator of *Dead Souls*.[141] At the same time, the passage embraces the perspective of Gogol writing the words in Rome and perceiving Russia as if in a vision. This opens up a path from Gogol's narrator to Gogol himself; and since the famous passage about the artist's characters from Chapter 7 of *Dead Souls* is here self-assertively reshaped by Bulgakov, the sentiments expressed are brought to encompass the figure of Bulgakov as well. Gogol's views on the fundamentally tragic and misunderstood nature of the writer's destiny, the problems of writing about fallible heroes, and the risks of satirical art all touch very acutely upon the concerns closest to Bulgakov's heart.

Bulgakov's affinity with Gogol also finds expression in a specific way through the theme of the city, which is a recurring and unifying feature of Bulgakov's writing. Their shared Ukrainian background may have been an additional factor in establishing Bulgakov's initial enthusiasm for Gogol; and he evokes Gogol's affection for Kiev in his own 1923 story *Kiev-gorod* (*The City of Kiev*), expressing his fervent hope that the city will recover from all the upheavals it has suffered during the Revolutionary period:

I hear the quiver of new life. It will be rebuilt, its streets will begin to hum again, and the regal city will stand again above the river that Gogol loved.[142]

Gogol is associated for Bulgakov, however, not only with Kiev, which without being named is lovingly evoked in *The White Guard* as 'the City'; but also, as we have seen, with Rome. This association may have been fostered in Bulgakov's mind even in his schooldays by a teacher of Russian literature whom Paustovsky here recalls:

During lessons on Gogol Selikhanovich brought to life before us the Rome of Gogol's day; its layout, its hills and ruins, its artists, carnivals, the very air of the Roman Campagna and the blueness of the Roman sky. Strings of distinguished people connected with Rome processed before us, summoned to life by a magical power.[143]

This memory assumes a special interest in the light of the significance which the image of Gogol writing and living in Rome was to have for Bulgakov's adaptations many years later.

One consequence of this fascination with Gogol and Rome was that when Bulgakov thought, as he so often did, of travelling abroad, his ambitions extended beyond Paris, where his two younger brothers now lived, and which he longed to visit as the city of Molière, to a hope that he might one day visit Italy.[144] In a letter which Bulgakov addressed to Stalin in May 1931 appealing for permission to travel during the summer, he even appeared to identify his desire to see the world with Gogol's almost pathological inability to stay put in Russia for any length of time:

Highly respected Iosif Vissarionovich!
    The more I think about it, the greater grows in me the desire to be a modern writer. But at the same time I have seen that, in depicting the modern world, it is impossible to remain in that highly attuned and calm state which is necessary in order to carry out a great and harmonious piece of work.

The present is too animated, too mercurial, it irritates the senses; *and the writer's pen shifts imperceptibly into satire* ... It has always seemed to me that in my life some great self-sacrifice awaits me, and that precisely in order to serve my native country *I shall be obliged to go and develop somewhere far away from it* ... 'I knew only that I was going away not at all in order to delight in foreign lands, but rather in order to endure, just as though I had had a presentiment that I would recognize the worth of Russia only outside Russia, and that I would attain love for her far away from her.'

N. Gogol

I fervently request you to intercede on my behalf with the Government of the USSR that I might be sent on leave abroad from 1 July to 1 October 1931.[145]

In this extraordinary missive the first two paragraphs consist of quotations from Gogol's *Avtorskaya ispoved'* (*An Author's Confession*), one of his most reactionary pieces of writing, where he sought to defend his *Selected Passages from Correspondence with Friends*.[146] The sentiments which he expresses are unambiguous in their painful consciousness that conditions in Russia do not lend themselves to the writing of anything but unacceptable satire, and in the event Bulgakov may have been fortunate that his request for support was merely ignored.

Chudakova has argued convincingly that Bulgakov's fascination with Gogol's Rome had a further consequence for the text of *The Master and Margarita*.[147] She has shown that Bulgakov used Gogol's own descriptions of the city, his story *Rim* (*Rome*), and accounts given by friends of Gogol, such as Annenkov, as an inspiration for his descriptions of both Moscow and Yershalaim in the novel. The textual references adduced by Chudakova demonstrate the ways in which the language, rhythms, mood and authorial perspective of the later work echo Gogol's, although she quite rightly does not attempt to argue any thematic significance for these parallels.

However, Chudakova goes on to argue a rather more controversial case for another way in which Bulgakov's affinity with Gogol is reflected in *The Master and Margarita*.[148] She points out that the period when Bulgakov was working on his adaptations of Gogol was also a crucial phase in the writing of *The Master and Margarita*. In August 1933 Bulgakov had written to Veresayev to compliment him on his *Gogol' v zhizni* (*Gogol in his Lifetime*), an analogous work to his *Pushkin in his Lifetime*:

I sat up two nights over your Gogol. My God! What a figure! What a
personality![149]

In the same letter he reported to Veresayev that he had recently
been working on his novel, which he had left untouched for three
years. The main innovation introduced to the novel at this stage
was the character of the writer–hero, who was gradually to assume
the central position in the work, which had hitherto had the Biblical
themes as its main focus of interest. And when in August 1934
Bulgakov completed his cycle of work on Gogol with the film
scenario of *The Government Inspector* he was simultaneously
concluding the third – and first full – draft of *The Master and
Margarita*. Chudakova draws the following conclusions:

The parallel work on Gogol's writings and on his own project produced
some very significant results. In the notebook of additions to the novel
begun on 30 October 1934, a strangely familiar hero appeared: into
Ivanushka's room in the psychiatric clinic, *from the balcony*, 'treading on
tiptoes, there came a man of about thirty-five, thin and cleanshaven, with a
hanging lock of fair hair and a sharp bird nose'. And this last feature
compels us to recognize in the nocturnal guest the same man who had
already been standing on the balcony since 1930, and for whom, to
Bulgakov's sorrow, it seemed impossible to find a place in the adaptations
which he had created.[150]

She omits to add that this description of the Master, which she is
certainly justified in relating to the figure of Gogol, does not survive
in this exact form in the published version of the novel, where the
Master is described in slightly different terms:

A cleanshaven, darkhaired man of about thirty-eight, with a sharp nose,
troubled eyes, and a lock of hair hanging down over his forehead, peered
hesitantly from the balcony into the room.   (547)

Our privileged knowledge of the draft version suggests that Bulgakov may well have had an image of Gogol in mind as he wrote these
lines; but the changes between the two versions all diminish, rather
than reinforce, the likeness with Gogol, and it seems that Bulgakov
eventually decided not to encourage the reader to make any such
precise identification. Chudakova goes on to find other evidence
for a partial identification of the Master with Gogol: his obsession
with writing his great novel, his early career as a historian, his
illness and possible hypochondria, and, most importantly, the
burning of his novel. Here Chudakova sees verbal reminiscences

between Bulgakov's description in *The Master and Margarita* and the account of Gogol's actions provided by Pogodin; and she argues that Bulgakov's own burning of the draft of his novel, which took place during the writing of his letter to Stalin in March 1930, was much less likely to have inspired this episode in the novel because it took place in such different circumstances. But the episode could actually have derived from a very wide range of sources, not least the burning of their own works by both Molière and Pushkin, of which Bulgakov would have been just as aware.[151] We can but concur with Chudakova's own warning to her readers:

I would like to caution the reader against reading the fate of Gogol directly into the Master's story.[152]

There is a strong element of self-identification between Bulgakov and Gogol, just as there are elements in the figure of the Master which are obviously autobiographical, and Chudakova is correct in suggesting that there was, at least in its inception, a hint of Gogol in the portrayal of the Master, but as Yanovskaya has demonstrated, the Master became both less autobiographical and less like Gogol as successive drafts of *The Master and Margarita* were written.[153]

Bulgakov's own devotion to Gogol was sustained to the very end of his life. Chudakova cites a description of Bulgakov's last days:

In 1940, a few months after Bulgakov's death, his friend P. S. Popov wrote: 'Clinging to life, susceptible to attacks of profound melancholy at the thought of the end which soon awaited him, already deprived of his sight, he fearlessly asked that they should read to him about Gogol's last dreadful days and hours.'[154]

These may well have been the descriptions contained in Veresayev's *Gogol in his Lifetime* which, as we have seen, he had owned since 1933. Once again, one is struck by the depth of Bulgakov's personal involvement with Gogol, and the way in which he comes to terms with his own experiences through the medium of Gogol's words. It was especially fitting, therefore, that Yelena Sergeyevna was able in the 1950s to obtain the headstone which Aksakov had brought from the Crimea to lay on Gogol's grave; it had lain there until the 1930s, when Gogol's body was removed to the Novodevichy cemetery. Yelena Sergeyevna came across it many years afterwards, and was able to use it for Bulgakov's grave, a more than appropriate monument to the affinity which, as all Bulgakov's friends recognized, he had felt for his predecessor's work.[155]

It will perhaps not ever be possible to determine the exact reasons why Bulgakov did not write *about* Gogol as he wrote about Molière and Pushkin. It may be that the rebuffs he met with in his endeavours to bring Gogol onto the stage in his adaptations made him reluctant to attempt an independent work about him; and it may be that at the back of his mind during the writing of *The Master and Margarita* was the idea that he might invest the Master with some Gogolian characteristics, although this receded into the background as the writing progressed. Another hypothesis would be that the image of Gogol in Rome, so cherished by Bulgakov, had a significance beyond its association with the writing of *Dead Souls*; for if it represents the peak of Gogol's achievement, it also represents the moment of Gogol's greatest commitment to his art. Molière and Pushkin retained to the end of their lives a belief in the supreme importance of art, whereas in Gogol this came to be overshadowed by political and religious preoccupations. Perhaps Bulgakov could not bring himself to portray an artist who effectively renounces his vocation, as Gogol was to do after his writing of *Dead Souls* in Rome. This is a major theme which Bulgakov was to pursue only in *The Master and Margarita*, where the artist who abandons his art can be allowed final redemption within the compass of the fiction.

4

The Master and Margarita – 'Manuscripts don't burn'

'At that point his guest clasped his hands together, as though in prayer, and said in a whisper: "Oh, it's just as I guessed it! It's all just as I guessed!"'

(550)

Bulgakov's *The Master and Margarita* has a quality of rich complexity, the veins of which are still being explored. Both the novel's form and its themes mark it out as a unique masterpiece; parallels are hard to find either in Russian literature or in any West European traditions. This need not cause the critic to despair about finding the right slot in which to fit the work; it may be, indeed, that such an undertaking is doomed to prove unproductive. As one recent commentator on the novel has remarked:

Bulgakov's novel is indeed innovative to the highest degree ... When you come to try on the garb of Menippean satire it covers some parts very well, but leaves others exposed; Propp's criteria for magical fairy-tales are applicable only to certain events, and relatively humble ones at that, leaving almost all the novel and its main heroes stranded; the fantastic stumbles over blatant realism; myth comes up against scrupulous historical accuracy; theosophy confronts demonism; romanticism meets with buffoonery.[1]

While the work proclaims its individuality and resists attempts to find for it ancestors in earlier writings or siblings in contemporary texts, its thematic intricacy raises so many urgent questions demanding analysis and interpretation that the problem of genre recedes to a position of secondary importance. What is more, we cannot expect to understand what an innovative genre the book represents until we feel confident about the text's essential meanings and purposes. It is an indication of the contentiousness of these fundamental questions that in the years which have elapsed since the novel's publication, despite the number of studies which have been published, no single analysis of the work has succeeded in encompassing the text in its entirety.

The present study cannot aspire to comprehensiveness either. A number of ways of approaching the novel have already been suggested, and it will not be my principal purpose to examine them here. These include differences of interpretation which have prompted claims that the text deserves primarily to be investigated for its autobiographical, its political, its religious, or its philosophical significance, or for the interest of the text's formal aspects. The poetics of *The Master and Margarita* are only just beginning to receive due critical attention, as readers come to appreciate the wealth and resonant power of Bulgakov's language. Other approaches will be frustrated for as long as we are denied access to Bulgakov's archives and drafts, which would serve to shed light on his working methods. Here the intention will be to offer an approach which is at once more specifically textual and more broadly biographical: first, to discuss some of the structural complexities of the work and to indicate their importance for the theme of the artist's commitment to truth; and secondly, to show how the theme of the artist's destiny provides the cornerstone of the novel, a binding and supporting element which guarantees the strength, the coherence and the durability of the entire edifice. The portrayal of the fictional writer–hero in *The Master and Margarita* grew and developed alongside Bulgakov's work on Molière, Pushkin and Gogol (his handling of sources in all cases show interesting similarities), and above all the figure of the Master afforded Bulgakov the opportunity to draw together reflections on his own experiences as well as more general meditations on the nature and significance of the artistic vocation.

Bulgakov began work on the first draft of what would become *The Master and Margarita* towards the end of 1928, a full year before he started work on *The Cabal of Hypocrites*. If chronological order had been observed, the novel should therefore have occupied the first section of this study. It would not, however, be accurate to identify that particular moment as the beginning of Bulgakov's interest in the theme of the writer, since the erudite scholar Fesya who figures as the probable hero of the first draft is not a writer, strictly speaking, but a historian; he is concerned principally with mediaeval history, and in particular with demonology and aesthetics.[2] It is only in the third draft, which dates from 1932–3 and was composed simultaneously with Bulgakov's prose biography of Molière and *The Follies of Jourdain*, that it is finally determined

that the hero shall be a writer: he appears as a first-person narrator
with autobiographical overtones, he is described as a poet, and he is
sometimes even referred to as Faust, before at last acquiring the
name of Master in 1934.[3] As the novel was being reworked over the
course of the twelve years from 1928 until the author's final illness
caused him to abandon work on it early in 1940, the theme of the
writer gradually came to assume a more prominent and central
place in the work. The conversation between the two characters
who were to become Berlioz and Ivan, like the scenes at Griboyedov House, were present even in the first draft; in other words, the
main setting for the events in Moscow had always been the literary
world. But the focus on the individual artist appears not to have
formed part of the original conception.[4]

Any satisfactory critical interpretation of the novel must base
itself on a close reading of the text; but two problems complicate
the task. The first is the allusiveness of certain details in the text, a
discretion which can doubtless be traced to political considerations.
At one stage Bulgakov did expect to publish the novel, and in May
1929 he approached the Nedra publishing house with one of the
four chapters he had completed, the one about Griboyedov House.
But Nedra, even though they had published his work before,
declined on this occasion to take any risks.[5] As work on the novel
progressed its subversive messages became more apparent, and it is
difficult to believe that the author ever again had any serious
expectation that it would be published in his lifetime. As the typing
of the sixth (second complete) draft drew to an end in June 1938, he
wrote to Yelena Sergeyevna about the work's probable fate:

'What will come of it?', you ask. I don't know. You will probably pack it
away into the writing-desk or the cupboard . . . and from time to time you
will remember about it. But we can't tell our futures. I have already formed
my opinion of this thing, and if I can succeed in lifting the ending a little
more, then I will consider that it is worth correcting and packing away into
the darkness of a drawer.[6]

Sinyavsky has since argued that if Stalin had suspected the existence of the novel it would undoubtedly have been destroyed, while
its author would have risked being shot.[7] That Bulgakov was aware
of the danger is indicated by the fact that, even in a typescript which
might not see the light of day, he maintained a caution which has
misled some critics. In the chapter where the Master recounts to
Ivan the events of the previous year, his narrative is interrupted by

activity in the corridors of the psychiatric clinic as other patients are
delivered there. This compels the Master in a somewhat artificial
device to continue his story in a whisper inaudible to the reader,
just as he is telling Ivan about the culmination of the crisis over his
book: his growing alarm, the knocking at the windows, his disappearance for three months, and his reappearance in a coat from
which the buttons have been torn (565). These details confirm that
the knock on the window in fact signalled the Master's arrest and
imprisonment, which is corroborated in the 1973 edition of the
novel, where details are given of the denunciation written by Aloizy
Mogarych which is the immediate cause of the Master's arrest.[8]
This crucial fact appears to have been overlooked by a number of
critics, and it seriously distorts their view of the Master's motives
for turning his back on the world.[9]

The second and more problematic factor, however, is the 'unfinished' status of the text. Yelena Sergeyevna's testimony that the
revisions dictated to her by her husband were interrupted half-way
through the novel by his worsening condition is apparently corroborated by the annotations on the final draft preserved in the
archive.[10] There are, moreover, a number of discrepancies in the
novel, particularly in the latter half, which cannot be resolved
within the overall logic of the work. Two different accounts, for
instance, are given of the way the bodies of the Master and of
Margarita are disposed of (785–6, 790–1, 804–5); Margarita's flight
outside Moscow before the ball seems to promise some significant
adventure which never quite materializes; Iyeshua is variously
described as coming from the towns of Gamala and En-Sarid (438,
735); and there is some confusion over the wine which Pilate and
Afranius actually drink, and the one which is used to poison the
Master and Margarita (718, 785). Other slight inconsistencies,
inaccuracies and contradictions occur throughout the text. A
particular difficulty is presented by the Epilogue, which was only
written in May 1939, since there is some doubt as to whether it
belongs in the final version of the text or not.[11] Since it contradicts
some of the details of the main text (the fate of the heroes' bodies),
as well as pessimistically undermining the reader's faith in Ivan's
spiritual transformation, it is tempting to regard certain aspects of
the Epilogue as provisional; and the relatively unpolished style
which distinguishes it from the main text lends further weight to this
view.

These slight textual flaws do not, however, amount to serious defects in a work which has occasionally suffered from being considered incomplete or not ultimately cohesive; an argument which will be examined again below. The work is balanced, its structure finely wrought; and, perhaps paradoxically, it is the novel's most elusive character, the Master, who provides the work with its cohesion. This was identified as early as 1967, after the partial publication of the novel in the journal *Moskva*, by a Soviet critic named Skobelev:

The novel *The Master and Margarita* is a book above all about the destiny of the artist, about the grandeur of creative work … In *The Master and Margarita* this theme is not just one of the layers of the plot and the action, but the pivot of the work as a whole.[12]

This view has received surprisingly little elaboration in critical accounts of the text written since then.

The present study of *The Master and Margarita* has been divided into sections according to the following pattern: in the first part I will be discussing the structure of the work, and in particular the problems of the relationship between the 'Moscow' and the 'Yershalaim' chapters, looking both at how the two parts interlock with one another, and at the question of what parallels can be traced between the two. Each setting will then be examined separately: the Yershalaim story, the Master's novel about Pilate, will be considered in the light of the claims of authenticity made for it in the text. This will lead on to a discussion of the sources Bulgakov actually used for these chapters, and an examination of his interpretations of the figures of Pilate and Iyeshua. The Moscow scene will be surveyed for the portrait it offers of the Soviet literary establishment, a subject which is by no means incidental to the main theme of the work, but serves to highlight that false approach to art to which the Master's own dedication is opposed. The following section considers the crucial role played by Woland, a strikingly original variation on Goethe's Mephistopheles who, by the part he plays in determining the Master's final reward, reveals his own benevolent status as a supranatural being and confirms the value of the artist. The Master himself is the subject of the final section; the weighing of his limitations against his achievements does nothing to refute the view that it is through his role above all that we are enabled to meet the challenge posed by the text's complexity. In including within *The Master and Margarita* a sample of his writer–hero's work, a portrait of the artist himself, and an exposure of the literary establishment, Bulgakov raises a wealth of questions about his own view of the nature of inspiration and about the artist's role in society.

A tale of two cities

If there is one undertaking which lies, almost by definition, beyond the grasp of the literary critic, then that must be the endeavour to recapture the impressions derived from a single, first reading of a given text. Our reception of a novel involves us without fail in an acceptance of suspense; uncertainties and confusions arise, or questions remain unanswered, and to some extent we place our trust in the author and rely on him not to tantalize us in vain, but so to construct the dénouement of his narrative that we will close the book with the feeling that most of the perplexities have been resolved. No subsequent reading can recall that innocence; fore-knowledge of the unfolding of a plot imposes procedures of interpretation on us, however reluctant or even unconscious of them we may be.

Many readers of *The Master and Margarita*, if they were asked to give an account of the impact of the novel immediately after a first reading, would undoubtedly single out the brilliance of its comedy as its principal merit. But many would also find it necessary to acknowledge that this particular aspect was not sufficient to explain the grip that the work had had on their attention. The Yershalaim narrative, constituting as it does a distinct and yet clearly integral part of the whole, exerts a different hold on the reader. This dual impact is created in the very opening pages of the novel, specifically in the breathtaking transition between chapters 1 and 2, where a comic encounter between two pompous writers and an enigmatic stranger is succeeded by a realistic and beautiful account of the occasion when a Christ figure is brought before Pilate; and in the bathetic return to reality in Moscow which is represented by the transition between chapters 2 and 3. The insertion of the Pilate story into the Moscow narrative is explained in immediate terms by the fact that Woland, the stranger, undertakes to recount these events to his sceptical audience. But the conventional device of story-telling will not be sufficient, even for the first-time reader, to account for the astonishing divergence in narrative tone and power between the two chapters. Nothing in the character of Woland, in his language, or in the nature of his playful conversation with Berlioz and Ivan has prepared us for what ensues. And when the Yershalaim narrative is taken up again later, in Ivan's dream, the reader begins to realize that the function of this narrative within the frame story must indeed be more complex than the simple story-telling device in chapter 1 had tried to suggest. But the reader waits in vain for an explanation to the mystery; the ending of the novel does not include any comment on its own structure, and it seems that Bulgakov was determined to require of his readers that they should make the effort to go beyond the primary reading and return to the text with the benefit of hindsight if they were really seeking to understand its intricacies. The fact that almost the earliest problem raised in the novel is one of structure, and that it is left apparently unresolved by the author, is what justifies us here in according this question the most urgent priority. Our understanding of the novel's themes can only be complete when we have grasped the purposes of the interplay between the two *loci* of the action, which takes place separately either in Moscow or in Yershalaim, except at the very end of the novel when characters from each city are brought together in chapter 32.

A second element of suspense in this novel is that neither of its eponymous heroes makes an appearance in the first half of the work; but when do we finally meet the Master, and learn that he is a writer who is also preoccupied with the story of Pilate, we begin to sense that the solution to the structural problem posed by the Yershalaim chapters will be found through the Master. The solution is, however, clearly not a straightforward one, for the four Yershalaim chapters are presented to the reader as originating from a number of different sources. The first chapter consists of Woland's account, and his authoritative stature is such that we feel bound to believe in his omniscience; we are compelled to accept his statement that he was actually present during the events he describes to Berlioz and Ivan. We do not, however, need at the same time to accept Proffer's semi-serious suggestion that Woland figures in Yershalaim as the swallow which flies around Pilate's palace, nor Gasparov's view that he was there in the disguise of Afranius, the captain of the secret police.[13] Ivan's dream in Stravinsky's asylum, which constitutes the second Yershalaim chapter, accords precisely in content with Woland's account. The last two Yershalaim chapters are what Margarita reads to herself from the Master's manuscript after it has been resurrected from the flames. These in turn correspond to – and carry on neatly from – Ivan's dream. Margarita's reading therefore confirms the internal unity of the four Yershalaim chapters, and at the same time identifies this version of the events with what appears to be the whole of the Master's novel. The puzzle of how something which is a literary text written by the Master can coincide exactly with a story narrated by Woland and a vision dreamed by Ivan is a question which will be examined below when we come to consider the Yershalaim narrative as such. Meanwhile, recognizing that the Yershalaim chapters form a single text, and that the Master, on one level at least, is the author of that text, enables us to move on to a consideration of the ways in which the Yershalaim narrative and the Moscow narrative complement one another within *The Master and Margarita* as a whole.

Although the two sections of the novel, as defined by their settings, are clearly distinct from one another, there are also a number of ways in which the reader is invited to juxtapose them; several parallels and echoes can be traced in the chronology, the imagery, and the characterizations of each part. It will be my intention to argue that, on the whole, critical opinion has tended to exaggerate the links and similarities between Moscow and Yershalaim, and that this has led to a balanced perspective of the work getting lost in attempts to mould the novel into too compact a form.[14] The function of the internal echoes in *The Master and Margarita* is much more to give the work a fertile unity and to knit the inner novel to the outer framework, than to provide the basis for what can turn out to be rather limited and unproductive analogies. The echoes that we will consider operate in chronological, verbal, perhaps ideological and structural dimensions, but Bulgakov takes pains to restrict, rather than broaden out their significance.

The chronological structure of the novel is certainly complex, although it scarcely justifies the diagrams and percentage studies some investigators have seen fit to adduce in their endeavours to clarify the 'temporal articulation' of the work.[15] From time to time the chronology becomes confused, sometimes intentionally and sometimes not. Intentional confusions can arise from the supernatural powers of those who bring them about. Woland's ball ('It is called the spring ball of the full moon, or the ball of the hundred kings' (667)) seems to last for several hours, although it both begins and ends at midnight on the Friday night. Another magical distortion takes place at the very end of the novel and highlights the triumphant moment when the Master and Margarita are accorded their final reward:

The Master and Margarita saw the promised dawn. It began immediately, directly after the midnight moon. (799)

Elsewhere there are unintentional confusions which presumably derive from the fact that the work was not fully revised before Bulgakov's death: Pilate tells Caiaphas that it is almost midday when he sets out to announce the verdicts on Iyeshua and the others (454, confirmed again on pages 588 and 589), after which the narrator perplexes us by announcing that it is still only ten o'clock in the morning (458); and in Moscow the full moon which provides a mysterious backdrop to the supernatural events is allowed to stretch over several days, and is described as appearing on Wednesday (459), Friday (645, 667) and Saturday (794).

In fact a fundamental parallel is established in the device of having the principal events in both Moscow and Yershalaim take place over the latter half of a week, from Wednesday to Saturday in Moscow and from Friday to Saturday in Yershalaim. The full moon also figures in both cities. This inclines us to infer that events in Moscow are set in the Orthodox Holy Week, which can very occasionally fall in May in the Gregorian calendar if Easter is very late in the Julian calendar (which is still adhered to in the Russian Orthodox Church). This would imply that Woland's sabbath ball takes place on the anniversary of the Crucifixion; but, as we shall see when we come to analyse Woland's function in the novel, we should be wary of taking this to mean that Woland's ball should be interpreted as an aggressively blasphemous ritual. Bulgakov precisely subverts the expectations which he has apparently set up in establishing the chronological echo between the two occasions.

Perhaps we should make a distinction, then, between the notion of chronological parallels, which might suggest that Bulgakov was asking us to identify certain similarities between the two cities, and the notion of chronological echoing, which he deploys to less deterministic purpose. Such echoes are used very effectively, for example, as a bridging device at the beginning of chapter 27, when Margarita finishes reading about how Pilate meets the dawn on the fifteenth of nisan (Saturday) just as she herself meets the dawn on Saturday in Moscow. A more powerful image used to bind the two parts together in this manner is that of the impending storm. There are actually three storms in the novel: the first in Moscow on the Thursday evening as Ivan lies in the asylum (530ff.); the second in Yershalaim on Friday evening, which hastens the end of Iyeshua's sufferings (595ff.); and the final one in Moscow as the Master and Margarita bid farewell to Ivan on the Saturday evening (790). Much of the action of the novel, therefore, can be said to unfold in a pre-apocalyptic atmosphere.

Echoing is used, however, not just in chronological details, but also in language. The difference between the measured, elegant, intense and emotionally expressive writing of the Yershalaim chapters and the more varied style of the Moscow chapters, which draws on a more prosaic range of rhythms and vocabulary, would seem to establish a wide gulf between the two parts. Nevertheless, Bulgakov does sometimes use echoes or leitmotifs from the Yershalaim chapters in the Moscow chapters in order to lend the novel a greater coherence. The critic David Bethea, for example, has shown how images of horses and riders are threaded into the Moscow chapters when we would expect them (not least on historical grounds) to be confined to the Yershalaim chapters.[16] Boris Gasparov sees this sort of device as the novel's most distinctive stylistic characteristic:

The fundamental device which determines the whole structure of meaning in *The Master and Margarita*, and which has at the same time a broader general significance, appears to us to be the principle of *leitmotif construction* in the narrative ... All the links turn out to be only partial.[17]

Regrettably, he goes on to argue that, as a consequence of this otherwise persuasively defined principle, we should refrain from attempts to provide any all-embracing explanations of *The Master and Margarita*; it should only be approached through investigations of various patterns of associations from which no overall interpretations can be derived. He, for instance, endeavours to find some sort of significance in the fact that J. S. Bach's initials in Russian would be I. S. B., which Bulgakov uses in an anagram, 302 *bis*, the address of Styopa's flat, as well as in his selection of composers' names – (*Igor'*) Stravinsky and *Berlioz* – for some of his characters; this all being part of an attempt to demonstrate that Bulgakov based himself on Bach's St Matthew and St John Passions in his work on the Yershalaim chapters, an attempt which leaves the actual text far behind. A further example of Gasparov's endeavours to discover through leitmotif a coherence he believes the novel otherwise to lack is his drawing together of the images of the three sponges (actually two sponges and a loofah); one thrown at Ivan by the naked lady standing in her bath (468); one offered to Iyeshua on the tip of a lance (597), and one used to soothe Margarita's throbbing knee during the ball (685).[18]

Clearly this is a case where the novel's supposed shapelessness is compensated for by over-interpretation. Other echoes, however, do reach out from the Yershalaim chapters into Moscow. Sometimes these arise quite straightforwardly: when, for instance, Ivan compares Stravinsky to Pilate (504), or Margarita equates her failure to return in time to save the Master to Matvey's failure to spare Iyeshua the torments of crucifixion (633), these can naturally be explained by their knowledge (Ivan through his dream, Margarita through her reading) of the original story. A different effect is achieved when the narrator compares the shop-assistant's knife in the Torgsin shop to Matvey's (764), as this suggests the more removed omniscience of the author of *The Master and Margarita*.

Many of the interpretations which lay most stress on the analogies between the two settings have based themselves on the pronounced similarities between the description of Yershalaim which we associate with Margarita's reading of the Master's novel, and one of the descriptions of Moscow itself.[19] The passage in question is the one which Margarita reads to herself after the Master's mysterious disappearance, the only remaining fragment of the novel which he had thrust into the flames at the height of his despair:

She sat for almost an hour, holding on her knees the notebook damaged in the fire, leafing through it and reading over that which, after the burning, had no beginning and no end: '. . . the darkness which had spread from the Mediterranean sea came down over the city the procurator so detested. The hanging bridges joining the temple to the fearsome Antonia fortress disappeared, an abyss opened out from the sky and flooded the winged gods over the hippodrome, the Hasmonaean palace with its embrasures, bazaars, caravanserais, alleyways and ponds . . . Yershalaim, the great city, vanished as though it had never existed . . .' (635)

Azazello then recites part of this passage back to her as proof that
he has knowledge of the Master (641), and certain parts of it are
repeated like a refrain as Margarita finally settles down to read the
entire chapter while the Master, restored to her at last, sleeps
(714). But Bulgakov then draws on the Master's description of
Yershalaim for his own description of Moscow when Woland and
his suite are preparing to leave the city before the storm breaks:

> This darkness which had spread from the West came down over the
> gigantic city. The bridges and palaces disappeared. Everything vanished,
> as though none of it had ever existed.   (779)

Once again the temptation here is to read this as an emphatic
identification of the two cities, suggesting that what occurs in
Yershalaim should be seen as a direct prefiguration of what
happens in Moscow. But the device of reusing the phrases here is
much more an exercise in consolidating the themes and language of
the novel than a somewhat crude 'key' to the complexities of its
structure. On this occasion Gasparov has provided perhaps the best
general observation on the nature of the echoing of images as such
between the two sections with his suggestion that many specific
images, such as the burning sun which oppresses Pilate, reappear in
the Moscow chapters in fragmented, fractured forms: references to
the 'broken' sun reflected in a number of windows are to be found
in both the first and the last chapters of *The Master and Margarita*
(427 and 798).[20] But this is a consciously poetic use of language on
Bulgakov's part, and it does not follow that we should attribute to
the elaboration of a verbal image any *necessary* refinement of
meaning. Bulgakov's poetic use of reminiscence more often than
not involves a concern for the visual or aural reverberations of a
single word or object taken out of context; this is a method which
clearly accords with his similarly discriminating use of source
materials during his work on the Molière works and on Pushkin,
and indeed in his approach to his materials for the Yershalaim
chapters in *The Master and Margarita* itself.

It should be added that the device of carrying a sentence over
from the end of one chapter to the beginning of the next is used by
Bulgakov to cover all the transitions from Moscow to Yershalaim,
the first transition from Yershalaim back to Moscow, and to bridge
several other chapters as well. In other words, Bulgakov's decision
to reuse the sentence about darkness coming down over the city is

at least in part a feature in a broader device of emphatic repetition, which is used to invoke the dream-like state in which the visions of Yershalaim are perceived. This is underscored at the end of the first Yershalaim chapter, where Ivan's impression of Woland's narration is so vivid that he feels he has been dreaming, rather than simply listening to a story (459).

One further example of verbal echoing in the form of whole sentences raises a structural problem concerning the relationship between the Master's novel, which is made up of the Yershalaim chapters, and the outer novel represented not just by the Moscow chapters, but by Bulgakov's entire text of *The Master and Margarita*. It arises from the remark made by the Master to Ivan as he relates to him the story of his past:

> Pilate was flying, flying to a close, and I already knew what the last words of my novel would be: '. . . the fifth procurator of Judaea, the knight Pontius Pilate' ('. . . pyaty prokurator Iyudeyi, vsadnik Pontiy Pilat'). (554)

Chapter 26, the last of the Yershalaim chapters which make up the Master's novel, does indeed end with these words, except that the word 'knight' ('vsadnik') is omitted. But confusion arises when we reach the end of chapter 32, which also ends with these words in their exact original form, while the Epilogue which immediately follows introduces yet another variant, since it ends with the words 'Pontiy*skiy* Pilat'. This has prompted a number of hypotheses: Proffer concludes that the fact that the phrase only reappears in its exact form at the end of chapter 32, the original ending of the work, is an indication that the reader should equate the Master's novel with the whole of *The Master and Margarita*.[21] Milne, on the other hand, sees the novel about Pontius Pilate as a *figura* for *The Master and Margarita* itself, on the basis that Bulgakov is evoking his own experiences in the literary world in his description of the Master's trials. She argues that, since chapter 32 ends with the correct formulation, then:

> The 'novel within the novel' is suddenly revealed as occupying the same space as the 'outer novel' minus Epilogue; the Epilogue re-establishes the separate identity of Bulgakov's *The Master and Margarita* from the Master's 'novel about Pontius Pilate'.[22]

One regrettably unverifiable source in Moscow has reported that when Bulgakov began to read the novel to his friends *with* the

Epilogue in 1939, he used to omit the last paragraph of chapter 32 from the work, and that it was Yelena Sergeyevna who preferred the earlier version and insisted that it should be put back for the publication of the novel in the 1960s. The whole issue is beset with textual uncertainties, both about the author's final intentions, and about the possible importance of the slight variations in the phrasing of the controversial sentence. It sometimes goes unnoticed that a first variation of the phrase occurs even before the Master has identified it as having a special significance, for the very first sentence of the Master's novel ends in chapter 2 with the words 'the procurator of Judaea, Pontius Pilate' ('prokurator Iyudeyi Pontiy Pilat') (435). The emphatic positioning of this phrase at the end of the hypnotically melodious opening sentence of the story of Pilate sets the Master's narrative in a dignified and symmetrical frame. But to equate the Master's novel with *The Master and Margarita*, whether one includes the Epilogue or not, is to introduce an unnecessary and misleading blurring of distinctions.

The Master's sense of alienation from his surroundings surely guarantees that he cannot even fictionally be supposed to have chosen to write about them; we have only to recall his adamant refusal when Woland suggests that he should write about Aloizy Mogarych (708). The craftsmanship of the writing of the Yershalaim chapters is absolutely incompatible within the bounds of the fictional character with the relaxed and ironical style of the Moscow chapters. We should be satisfied that the phrase which closes chapter 26 does indeed fulfil the terms of the Master's remark to Ivan, and look to the reuse of the phrase at the end of *The Master and Margarita* for an additional significance. One interpretation would be that Bulgakov, who throughout the novel has chosen to invest the Master with a number of autobiographical traits without reducing him to a self-portrait, reinforces the reader's awareness of the author's sympathy for his hero through all his tribulations by consciously adapting a fictional moment and lending it an autobiographical significance. Bulgakov pays tribute to his writer–hero and asserts his solidarity with him by echoing his words in the closing passages of his own novel. The Master cannot be seen as the 'author' of *The Master and Margarita*; his concern is with Pontius Pilate alone.[23]

Not only has it proved possible to identify internal echoes in *The Master and Margarita* in the form of chronological patterns, imagery and phrasing, but it has also been suggested that certain parallels exist in the presentation of character; these are focussed particularly on the figure of the Master, with some critics finding points of identification between him and Pilate, while others prefer to see the Master as a modern Iyeshua. The case for the first view is the less convincing, for all the Master's obvious personal sympathy towards Pilate, the central subject of his labour of love, and for all the sensitive tracing in the novel of the difficulties of Pilate's situation. Much has been made of the fact that both are guilty of cowardice, but the extent and nature of this cowardice are surely of a different order. Pilate will forever regret a moment of physical and political fear, a retreat into his role as an Imperial official which leads him into a betrayal of human values. The Master's weakness is less specific, and its consequences carry a less universal significance; he is cowardly in that he fails to defend his art, his love, and himself when persecuted by the small-minded. But while in the terms of the novel the sacrifice of artistic integrity and the sacrifice of human values may be weighed one against the other, the spheres of the artist and of the political man of action nevertheless remain distinct.

More attention has been paid to the similarities between the Master and Iyeshua, although it is difficult to accept Skorino's view that the two are virtually interchangeable:

In the novel *The Master and Margarita* there is one image which emphatically doubles and coincides with the image of Iyeshua Ga-Notsri. That is the image of the Master.[24]

This approach simply disregards the whole matter of the Master's authorship of the novel within the novel. Certainly, some links can be established between the two figures, primarily in their shared experience of persecution for their ideas, their awareness of a higher reality, and their human naiveté. Around them stand parallel figures in the persons firstly of Judas and Aloizy Mogarych, both betrayers of trust, and in Matvey and Ivan, the imperfect disciples. Iyeshua shares with the Master the gift of a vision, and is comparable to the artist inasmuch as he perishes through society's contempt for his values. Indeed, not only is Iyeshua the bearer of the Word, but as a man of words he even brings about his downfall directly through his use of imagery:

Hegemon, never in my life have I planned to destroy the building of the temple, nor have I incited anyone else to such a senseless action . . . I was

speaking, hegemon, about the fact that the temple of the old faith will
collapse and a new temple of truth will be created. I said it like that so that
it would be more clearly understood.   (439, 441)

It is the literalism of certain of his listeners, who take his words at
their face value, which helps to instigate his arrest and sentence.
But rather than arguing about the extent to which Iyeshua can be
considered an artist figure, it is more fruitful to invert the comparison, and to see the artist as possessing many qualities in
common with the visionary and prophet. It is the Master who gains
in moral stature through the implicit reference back to Iyeshua.

This survey of the various ways in which Bulgakov establishes
echoes and parallels between the Moscow chapters and the Yershalaim chapters in *The Master and Margarita* is in the final count
notable for its limited results. The two cities are not set alongside
one another in order to mirror each other; the degree of echoing
between the two amounts to pleasing reminiscence rather than
meaningful identification. Bulgakov has no need of pedestrian
parallels to blend two different plots together; and in many ways it
is the lack of obvious parallels between the two parts which assures
the text its intricate richness. We cannot afford to gloss over the
complexity of the structural relationships binding the two parts
together in favour of a simplification which consists in assuming
that the Yershalaim narrative is introduced into the novel primarily
in order to shed greater light on the Moscow scene. This privileging
of the modern setting over the ancient world is indeed associated
with another critical tendency which was particularly prevalent in
the years immediately following the publication of *The Master and
Margarita*, and which argued that the reader needed to bring a
whole range of extrinsic information to bear upon the novel if it was
to be persuaded to yield up its secrets. One of Bulgakov's earliest
Western critics, Elena Mahlow, has assumed that the work is
written entirely in Aesopian language and consists of a ciphered
and allegorical account of the Stalinist period in Soviet history:
Iyeshua's old chiton and sandals reflect the economic hardships of
the Soviet proletariat in the 1930s, Matvey's dirty breadknife
becomes a symbol of the unresolved problem of freedom and
necessity, and the fourteenth of nisan is translated through peculiar
mathematics to become 27 February 1917 in this astonishing
study.[25] Piper and Rzhevsky agree that *The Master and Margarita* is
basically a cryptographical novel containing not-so-transparent

references to political personalities and events in the Soviet period.[26] But all of these approaches fail to get to grips with the novel's structural intricacy and seem almost to assume that the two settings are virtually interchangeable. In fact the two great cities of Yershalaim and Moscow are the homes of entirely separate ideologies, and the presence of two independent settings serves not so much to bind two distant historical periods together, but above all to confirm the significance of the Master's achievement as a writer.

What is truth?

The question 'What is truth?', which Pilate addresses to Iyeshua in the second chapter of *The Master and Margarita* (441), has a significance for Bulgakov's work beyond the obvious one of identifying the speaker with the Pilate of the Gospels, where these words are attributed to him (John, 18.37). In their responses to this question, and in demonstrating the extent of their faith in the truth, the major characters of the novel reveal their moral standing. Bulgakov enables this to happen by presenting his characters not with some nebulous notion of 'the truth', but with 'a truth', the account of what actually took place when Pilate was confronted with the task of passing a judgement on Iyeshua, Bulgakov's Christ-figure. The description of the arrest and death of Iyeshua, a description which untraditionally takes the figure of Pontius Pilate as its principal subject, provides the key to the structure of *The Master and Margarita*; for if we are to be convinced of the work's unity, then we must above all accept that the four chapters set in Yershalaim claim to represent an absolute truth. In the course of this section we will be considering first of all what is meant by this fictional 'absolute authenticity', and later going on to explore the faithfulness of Bulgakov's use of historical materials towards the Yershalaim chapters, before examining the ways in which he diverges from the received version of the story as contained in the Gospels.

We have already commented on the authoritativeness of Woland's narration, its compatibility with Ivan's subsequent dream, and the way in which both of these chapters evidently also form the first half of the Master's novel about Pilate. Chudakova is almost the only critic to have developed these facts into a convincing theory about the novel:

This unity of the text begun by Woland and subsequently identified with the Master's manuscripts means that the Master's novel takes on the status of some sort of 'fore-text', which has existed since primordial times and has only been drawn from the darkness of oblivion into the 'bright field' of modern consciousness by the genius of the artist. 'Oh, it's just as I guessed it!' exclaims the Master as he listens to Ivanushka's narration, and behind that exclamation lies the entire aesthetic position of Bulgakov himself.[27]

Chudakova characterizes the Master's inspiration in terms of guessing or 'divining' the truth, not as the result of scholarly investigation, but simply in the form of a vision. Earlier drafts of the novel made this even more explicit: in the third version of the text, dating from 1932–3, the Master was described as 'the author of a novel coinciding with Woland's Gospel';[28] and in the sixth version there is an exchange which Bulgakov eventually crossed out, where Woland himself confirmed the truth of what the Master had written:

'Listen to me, Master,' Woland began to speak, 'in your novel you guessed (wrote) the truth. Everything happened precisely as you described it.'[29]

The Master, too, is fully aware of the authenticity of his vision; towards the end of *The Master and Margarita*, as he begins to regain some of his confidence, his manner as he talks to Margarita makes this apparent:

He raised his head and appeared to her as he had when he was composing that which he had never seen, but which he knew for sure had been so.

(782)

The Master's assurance is confirmed for the reader by the fact that Woland tells the story in the Master's exact terms. Although Woland at first seems to Berlioz and Ivan to be a foreigner, his accent 'for some reason' disappears when he speaks of Pilate (435). In other words, the Russianness of the narrative is emphasized, as though Woland were recounting the truth in the only possible Russian words in which it can be rendered; that is to say, in the precise words used by the Master. Further confirmation of the absolute authenticity of his text is provided in the reactions of Woland and Iyeshua when they are confronted with the Master's novel. Woland, at first amused and astonished at the Master's choice of theme, falls solemn when presented with the actual text, for he immediately appreciates its significance (702–3). Iyeshua's request to Woland that the Master should be granted peace equally arises as a direct consequence of his reading of the novel (776). This visionary conception of the Master's inspiration aligns Bulgakov's approach with a neo-Platonic Romantic tradition, where ultimate truth is held to exist on a higher plane occasionally accessible only to the artist through the power of his genius.

Bulgakov offers his 'true' account of these events as a counterweight to the traditional versions embodied in the Gospels. Woland dismisses these out of hand:

'Nothing whatsoever of what is written in the Gospels ever actually happened, and if we were to start referring back to the Gospels as a historical source . . .' he smiled again. (459)

One of the major principles which appears to have governed Bulgakov's handling of material for the Yershalaim chapters is the determination to demonstrate the untrustworthiness of the Gospels. He does not just provide us with an alternative version of the facts, but also displays the stages at which, even given their relative proximity to the real events, distortions entered the records. His specific concern is to show how this affects the writing of Matvey's account; this Leviy Matvey corresponds to the tax-collector referred to as Matthew in the Gospel according to Matthew (9.9), and as Levi in Mark (2.13–14) and Luke (5.27–8), and he is the only Evangelist to figure in Bulgakov's portrayal. Bulgakov may have chosen Matvey precisely because the story of the writing of Matthew's Gospel is so confused, which would serve his intentions here. There exists one school of thought according to which the text now accepted as canonical is in fact a Greek version which is only based on – and adds to – an original Aramaic text by Matthew.[30] Bulgakov naturally makes no direct reference to this complication. But while the discrepancies between Matvey's version – of which we see only fragments – and the canonical version do not necessarily correspond to the differences between Matthew Aramaic and Matthew Greek, it is worth bearing in mind the fact that Matvey's version should not be *expected* to correspond to the canonical text.

However, Bulgakov suggests further layers of distortion which occur right at the beginning of the history of the writing of the Gospels; even the original notes taken by Matvey are discredited by Iyeshua, who complains of it to Pilate:

They haven't learnt anything, and they've muddled everything that I have
said. Altogether I'm beginning to fear that this confusion is going to persist
for a very long time. And all because of the fact that he takes inaccurate
notes of what I say . . . I once glanced at his parchment, and I was horrified.
I hadn't said a single thing of what was written there. I begged him: for
God's sake, burn your parchment!   (439)

Matvey's motives remain obscure, for he is shown in Bulgakov's
version to have had every opportunity to write an accurate account;
he follows Iyeshua around before his arrest, witnesses his death,
and also knows the true story of the death of Judas, since Pilate
makes quite explicit to him his responsibility for the murder, a fact
which he had carefully disguised in his inverted instructions to
Afranius. In suggesting that the historical truth then gets lost,
Bulgakov underlines his view of the Gospels as being themselves
works of fiction.

A further source of distortion is Afranius, whose report to Pilate
on the death of Iyeshua does not correspond to the events as earlier
described; he pretends that Iyeshua refused to drink, and that he
exonerated everyone from responsibility for his death (721).
Although we do not hear in the earlier description Iyeshua's words
about cowardice being the gravest of human sins, these are then
corroborated in Matvey's notes, which we are therefore on this
occasion inclined to believe (745). The reasons for Afranius's
mysterious and misleading behaviour have been explored at some
length by Richard Pope, with somewhat inconclusive results.[31] The
real explanation is presumably that Afranius, who is at least Pilate's
equal in perspicacity and psychological sensitivity, is exploiting the
situation in order to consolidate his power over Pilate, whom he
knows to be sympathetic to Iyeshua. The way that Afranius
occasionally glances at Pilate certainly suggests that his loyalty is
not wholly to be relied upon:

The procurator's guest opened his eyes wide and glanced at his interlocutor
suddenly and directly, as though his aim were swiftly to make out some
kind of insignificant speck on his interlocutor's nose. This lasted a flash,
after which his eyelids dropped again, the slits of his eyes narrowed, and
they began to gleam again good-naturedly and with a sharp intelligence.
                                                                        (718)

Afranius distorts the events in order to gratify Pilate's hope that
Iyeshua's death was noble (spurning the water and forgiving his
persecutors), not out of a spirit of generosity, but because Pilate in

his reactions will give himself away and place himself even more deeply in the secret policeman's grasp.

So the reader, privileged through the Master's narrative to have a description of what did actually take place, is at the same time invited to reflect on the significance of the misleading nature of Matvey's notes and of Afranius's words. When Pilate foils Matvey's bitter anger by confessing to the murder of Judas, Matvey is sufficiently mollified to accept a gift from him: 'Tell them to give me a piece of clean parchment' (746). The implication is that it is only at this stage that Matvey's notes begin to be written up into a coherent text, which will possibly be what we know as Matthew Aramaic, and which still therefore represents only a source on the road towards the canonical Gospel. But Matvey, who anyway seems to have a natural propensity for mythologizing the truth, apparently will ignore what Pilate has told him about Judas, just as he earlier misrepresented what Iyeshua had spoken. Again Bulgakov undermines our confidence in the trustworthiness of the Gospels as a historical source.

In offering the reader a kind of fifth Gospel – Hayward has described it as Bulgakov's 'own splendid neo-apocryphal version' of the Passion[32] – the author adopts an entirely unorthodox approach to the sacred story. But he is ultimately less concerned with the nature of the Master's heterodoxy or heresy, although this is naturally of some significance, than he is with the artist's duty to follow his own inspiration. Bulgakov undertakes the fantastic project of rewriting the Gospels not because he wishes to contribute to some sort of theological debate, but because this will fulfil an essential function in his portrayal of the figure of the artist.

One of the works which we know Bulgakov to have read during the composition of *The Master and Margarita* may have helped clarify his ideas about the justification for such an enterprise. This book, which Bulgakov apparently annotated in great detail, was Father Pavel Florensky's *Mnimosti v geometrii (Concepts of the Imaginary in Geometry*, Moscow, 1920).[33] Inspired by recent controversy over the theory of relativity, this study took the 600th anniversary of Dante's death as an occasion to investigate the innovative geometrical features of the non-Euclidean perspectives employed by Dante in his vision of the structure of Hell in *The Divine Comedy*.[34] In the first part of his study Florensky uses an analogy from literature to illuminate his thesis about geometry,

which may conversely shed some light on Bulgakov's attitude to the
canonical texts:

We know ... that, just as several translations of a single poetic work into
another language or languages do not obstruct one another, but actually
complement one another, even though none of them wholly substitutes for
the original, so scientific diagrams of some reality or other can and should
be multiplied; and truth will not thereby suffer in the least.[35]

Not only should a single reality be capable of being represented in
several aspects or interpretations but, as Florensky goes on to
argue, any one interpretation ceases to be valid as soon as it starts
to claim for itself a monopoly of authenticity. This view underpins
the argument implicit in Bulgakov's handling of the Biblical story:
that the authenticity of the Gospels can be questioned without this
obliging us to discard them, while the artist is nevertheless fully
justified in offering an entirely new, personal interpretation of the
story.

The suggestion that Bulgakov may have derived some inspiration
from Florensky towards the overall concept of *The Master and
Margarita* leads us on to the more specific problem of Bulgakov's
use of sources for the Yershalaim chapters, which has attracted
increasing attention in recent years. At the same time that he was
confronting the question of how to approach a 'historical' task in his
work on Molière and then on Pushkin, Bulgakov also had to decide
how to create a picture of Yershalaim which would similarly blend
historical verisimilitude with creative licence. Perhaps the most
reliable and sober summary of the facts is provided by Yanovskaya,
and we shall have to rely on her account until we are granted access
to Bulgakov's manuscripts and notebooks.[36] As the child of a
Professor of Comparative Religion in Kiev, Bulgakov had plentiful
opportunities to acquaint himself with the scriptures and apocryphal writings which form the basis for his subject. As Yanovskaya's
account makes clear, he was also thoroughly versed in the debates
which swept the theological world as a rationalistic nineteenth
century attempted to confront the problems of logic and of history
which the Biblical texts pose. But it is very misguided to assume on
Bulgakov's behalf an erudition which might suggest that he pursued
the more abstruse niceties of Christology in order to argue a highly
specialized case about the 'real' story of the Passion. A number of
studies of Bulgakov, such as those by El'baum and Zerkalov, have,
with scant regard for the available archival information about

Bulgakov's sources, made minute analyses of his interpretations in order to present him at the very least in the role of an acute Talmudic scholar, and certainly as a profound religious philosopher.[37] This not only disregards the problem of the function of the Yershalaim chapters in *The Master and Margarita* as a whole, but also scarcely fits in with anything else we know about Bulgakov's intellectual preoccupations. Zerkalov in fact eventually undercuts his own exhaustive account of the possible sources for Berlioz's survey of atheistic arguments by pointing out that Bulgakov in reality seems to have extracted all the points he needed from a convenient anthology, the fourth edition of *Antireligioznaya khrestomatiya* (*An Antireligious Anthology*, Moscow, 1930), edited by A. Gurev and published by the 'Bezbozhnik' ('Godless') publishing house.[38]

We can be more confident about asserting that four major works provided Bulgakov with the bulk of his material for the Yershalaim chapters, all of them contributions to the great nineteenth-century debate about how literally we can take the Bible. The first of these was D. F. Strauss's *Life of Jesus*, a work arguing the case that the Gospels should be viewed as myth, even if some credence could be given to the idea of the historical existence of Jesus. Bulgakov also made notes on A. Drews's book *The Myth About Christ*, where even the existence of Christ was deemed a myth. Both of these texts are somewhat dry, and Bulgakov seems not to have drawn on them very much for specific realia in the way that he certainly drew on F. W. Farrar's *The Life of Jesus Christ*, which he read, like the others, in Russian translation. This fascinating text was intended to present the Church's case in the debate, which it does by amassing an enormous amount of archaeological, historical, textual and geographical evidence in support of the traditional religious view. Almost every page of the text is embellished with footnotes on points of fact, with illustrations, including views of Jerusalem and of the surrounding area, and with pictures of coins, costumes, vegetation, the five-pointed 'Colossal lamp', architectural plans of important buildings, furniture, architectural features, maps, and works of art. It is this work above all which contributed to the astonishingly tangible realism of Bulgakov's writing in the Yershalaim chapters, even though Bulgakov is not concerned with Farrar's principal aim of demonstrating the plausibility of the Gospel narrations.

It emerges from Yanovskaya's account of the sources that
Bulgakov drew on a fourth text in particular as the starting-point
for his analysis of the significance of Christ; this was Ernest Renan's
Life of Jesus (as well as, to a lesser extent, the same author's
Antichrist). When, for example, he drew up columns in which to jot
down details about Christ from a number of sources, the first was
headed 'According to Ernest Renan', the second 'According to
F. W. Farrar', while the third was headed 'According to other
sources', and remained empty.[39] Renan's work, which by its very
title emphasized that the author viewed Jesus as a human rather
than a divine or supernatural figure, sought to investigate the text
of the Gospels as a historical document. This was not done, as he
hastened to make clear in his prefatory words, out of a spirit of
irreverence, but in order to cleanse religion of its, to him, abhorrent accretions of dogma and superstition. Renan hoped to serve
religion by his writing, where Bulgakov, by contrast, could scarcely
be described as religious except in a very loose sense of the word.
But certain points made by Renan, especially in his concluding
chapter, seem to have found distant reflection in the whole conception of *The Master and Margarita*. Fundamental among these is
Renan's view that the very story of the Passion is itself seditious;
that by presiding over this tragedy the State struck a terrible blow
against itself, since all the subsequent renderings of the story would
stress the appalling role of the Roman authorities, and would be
used and understood to undermine the position of the Empire.[40]
Bulgakov, in offering his version of the Passion in the modern era,
may of course similarly have been implying a challenge to the
notion of State power. Renan's view that the sublime figure of
Christ symbolizes the pinnacle of man's striving towards the noble
and the good is also important to the portrayal of Iyeshua in *The
Master and Margarita*.

   The identification of certain points of contact between Renan's
arguments and some of the interpretations offered in *The Master
and Margarita* still does not imply that Bulgakov was promoting a
specific school of thought within the theological debate, and we
must concur with Yanovskaya's concluding remarks:

Bulgakov sought what he needed in the extensive resources of Evangelical
studies, and he took from them what he needed. He worked on his sources
not as a researcher, but as an artist, looking for the truth of an image, not
the truth of the events.[41]

As ever, Bulgakov was seeking the striking detail and the small item which would lend his text an air of historical verisimilitude without committing either him or the reader to an acceptance of the historical reality of the events he describes, any more than he identifies himself through such a detail with the stance adopted by an author on a given issue. Bulgakov offers the reader in the Master's novel a version of the Gospels which in irrational – that is, fictional – terms is demonstrated to be some absolute, truly 'authorized' version. But at the same time he does not appear to argue any right of exclusivity for this text, for its significance relates more to the moral standing of its creator than to any effect it might be hoped that it would have on an audience. While the Master's novel, like the Biblical texts themselves, springs from and perhaps seeks to inspire what we might loosely term spirituality, it must be borne in mind that there is never the slightest suggestion that the Master is in a conventional sense religious, any more than Bulgakov was himself. The Master's novel is not primarily a polemic with the Canon; first and foremost it is an act of justification for the Master as an artist.

We move on finally to a consideration of the specific ways in which the Gospel stories are reinterpreted in *The Master and Margarita*. Bulgakov names the city in which the Master's novel is set Yershalaim, a rendering which closely resembles the Hebrew form, Yerushalaim. This represents one of the instances where he departs from the traditional Russian rendering of a name – which here would normally be Iyerusalim – in order to indicate that he is, on one level, consciously engaged in the creation of a fiction. It becomes a means of laying claim to objects, places or people as his own creations; but the act of renaming the town so that the name sounds more as it would have done 2000 years ago also enhances the immediacy of his narrative, and stresses that he is avoiding any suggestion of hindsight in his presentation of events. At the same time, the city undoubtedly remains the Jerusalem we associate with the birth of the Christian legend.

Bulgakov's interpretations of the figures of Pilate and Iyeshua are, similarly, more than straightforward reworkings of familiar Biblical subjects. He presents them in an unfamiliar mode, with the effect both of suggesting new insights into traditional images and myths, and of creating an entirely new 'myth', with repercussions for the larger world of his novel. The stylistic ploys adopted by

Bulgakov underpin this technique: El'baum's work shows convincingly how Bulgakov selects his language in order to keep the reader poised between the familiarity of realistic detail and the strangeness which appertains principally to the Greek or Hebrew vocabulary used where a Russian reader would expect to find the Russianized terms he knows from the Bible (hence 'igemon', 'Yershalaim', 'Iyeshua Ga-Notsri', 'tetradrakhma', and so on).[42] Over and above this technique of 'making strange' people or objects with traditional Biblical appellations, Bulgakov also goes to considerable lengths to avoid such words as 'raspyatiye' ('Crucifixion') or 'krest' ('Cross'), whose symbolic and emotive power could distract from the individuality of the rendering.[43] All these devices have the effect of drawing attention to the freshness and idiosyncrasy of the Master's vision.

The overriding difference of emphasis in the Master's text lies in the central significance of Pilate in the story, rather than the traditional weight given to Christ. The text abjures the relative distance of the Gospels in order to create a tautly constructed psychological study of Pilate, while Iyeshua recedes into secondary importance. Stylistically, this effect is achieved through the concentrated use of atmospheric imagery (light, colour, sounds, the sun, the moon, the gathering storm) to evoke Pilate's heightened emotional sensitivity, his sense of foreboding, and his premonition of personal and universal tragedy. Bulgakov appears to have leaned particularly heavily on Farrar's *The Life of Jesus Christ* for the portrait of Pilate; the following example indicates the way he drew on it for chapter 25 of *The Master and Margarita*:

Such was Pontius Pilate, whom the pomps and perils of the great yearly festival had summoned from his usual residence at Caesarea Philippi to the capital of the nation which he detested and the headquarters of a fanaticism which he despised. At Jerusalem he occupied one of the two gorgeous palaces which had been erected there by the lavish architectural extravagance of the first Herod. It was situated in the Upper City to the south-west of the Temple Hill ... It was one of those luxurious abodes 'surpassing all description' ... Between its colossal wings of white marble ... was an open space commanding a noble view of Jerusalem, adorned with sculptured porticoes and columns of many-coloured marble, paved with rich mosaics, varied with fountains and reservoirs, and green promenades which furnished a delightful asylum to flocks of doves ... A magnificent abode for a mere Roman knight! and yet the furious fanaticism of the populace at Jerusalem made it a house so little desirable, that neither Pilate nor his predecessors seem to have cared to enjoy its luxuries for more than a few weeks in the whole year. They were forced to be present in the Jewish capital during those crowded festivals which were always liable to be disturbed by some outburst of inflammable patriotism.[44]

Although the settings shift to Golgotha and to the city, away from Pilate in his monstrous and claustrophobic palace, nothing is described in the Yershalaim chapters which has not been at least ordained by him or does not relate to his frame of mind. Even the swallow which flies in and out of the balcony, considering whether to build a nest there (445, 449), must be interpreted as a reflection of Pilate's fleeting and joyous hope of securing spiritual peace, a hope dashed by the secretary's regretful announcement that there are still serious charges of political subversion outstanding against Iyeshua.

The tension is heightened by the unity of narrative perspective in the Yershalaim chapters, which fluctuates between an objective narrator and the thoughts of Pilate. Only once does this appear to be broken, and to powerful effect. A subjective narratorial interjection seems to be inserted into the account of Pilate's dream of the conversation he would like to have with Iyeshua:

And cowardice, undoubtedly, is one of the most terrible vices. So said Iyeshua Ga-Notsri. No, philosopher, I will gainsay you: it is the most terrible vice. (735)

The use of the personal pronoun here could simply indicate that Pilate is addressing Iyeshua in his dream; but it appears in such an ambiguous position that it could constitute a genuine external intervention. Whatever the exact identity of the speaker, the phrase throws into relief the theme of cowardice, which is brought through Pilate's voice to that of the presumed narrator, the Master. This sheds light on the Master's feelings about his own actions in the Moscow sections of *The Master and Margarita*; and the very imprecision of the speaker's identity can also be held to suggest that the phrase carries some sort of autobiographical significance for Bulgakov himself. The hero's regret about a failure of nerve is a recurrent theme in many of his works, and evidently became for Bulgakov something of a personal preoccupation:

He liked to repeat how much he detested cowardice. He used to say that all human baseness derived from cowardice.[45]

In the context of the Yershalaim chapters, it reinforces our sense of Pilate's story as a tragedy of irresolution in a man sensitive enough to recognize a higher force and a higher truth, yet who fails to safeguard it. Bulgakov's description in the first part of the book lays the foundations for the later theme of Pilate's repentance, which he inflates even beyond the traditionally sympathetic view of Pilate held in the Eastern Church and in the Apocrypha. His Pilate bears the burden of suffering we would normally associate with a tragic hero.

Bulgakov's portrayal of Iyeshua has aroused controversy on the grounds that it diminishes our traditional veneration for the figure of Christ by emphasizing all his most human traits. Iyeshua fears pain, hopes to evade death, and emerges in his own description of the events leading up to his arrest merely as a naive, rather than as a supremely wise victim. While the Gospels allow Christ certain mortal weaknesses, notably in the Gethsemane narratives, Bulgakov draws attention to them by stripping his portrait of most of its mystical features. In particular, there is no anticipation of a resurrection, and the Messianic aspect is entirely absent. However, if Iyeshua is only discreetly invested with an aura of the supernatural, his healing of Pilate's headache is perceived by the latter at least as a miracle; the presence of a compassionate God is hinted at in the storm which breaks as an apparent response to Matvey's despairing blasphemy; and Iyeshua's intervention on the Master's behalf at the end of *The Master and Margarita* confirms both that he has an existence in a supernatural dimension, and that he has supreme power.

One consequence of the presentation of Iyeshua as a particularly human Christ-figure is that the political significance of his actions is brought out more pointedly. Iyeshua's views on the transitoriness of earthly power finally seal his fate when he expounds them to Pilate:

Amongst other things I said ... that all power signifies the coercion of the people, and that there will come a time when there will no longer be the power of the Caesars, nor any other power. Man will pass into the kingdom of truth and justice, where no power of any kind will exist at all. (447)

Bulgakov may be harking back here to Renan who, as we have seen, was especially struck by the revolutionary impact of Iyeshua's actions and by his function as a champion of the poor and the weak.

The challenge to secular power which Iyeshua conceives as perfectly natural carries telling overtones for the twentieth century if the reign of Stalin is to be compared with that of Tiberius. But Iyeshua should not be reduced solely to a symbol of democratic freedom struggling against oppression and tyranny. For he is above all the bearer of a truth, a visionary whose destiny it is to be betrayed.

The 'truth' which the Master perceives is both a highly personal interpretation of the Passion on Bulgakov's part, and is also presented as an absolute, authentic vision of what occurred. The Master alone can offer the modern world this supreme insight into the reality and poignancy of an ancient truth, and *The Master and Margarita* acquires a particular richness from this confrontation between a truth of the ancient world and the ideology of the new, a conflict which is anticipated in the Yershalaim chapters themselves, where Iyeshua's vision is pitted against the prejudices of the old religion led by Caiaphas. This conflict is renewed in the modern world as the Master confronts the new philistinism of the literary establishment.

Moscow: the cultural establishment

Bulgakov turned on several occasions during his literary career to the subject of his own experiences in the cultural environment of Soviet Russia, but in his later works he treated the shortcomings of the theatrical and literary worlds in notably different terms. His most extensive attempt to write an autobiographical novel which would chart his experiences in the theatrical world came in the late 1930s. The topic naturally lent itself to satire, and this was the tone he adopted even in his early sketch towards the novel, the fragment *For my Secret Friend* written for Yelena Sergeyevna in 1929. The project continued to attract him, and in 1936–7 he wrote a good half of the novel which we know in its unfinished form as *A Theatrical Novel*. It takes as its subject the author's experiences as his first novel is transformed into a play for the 'Independent' Theatre, and Bulgakov makes little attempt to conceal the fact that the aim of the work is to expose the pretensions and pomposity of the Moscow Arts Theatre (MKhAT) under Stanislavsky's autocratic rule. As in *The Crimson Island* (1927), he bitterly mocks the theatre's notorious highhandedness with regard to the rights of the author. In the various dealings he had with MKhAT over the plays he wrote for them, he had had to battle continuously to defend the integrity of his text and the subtlety of his interpretations, contending with artistic objections as well as explicit political censorship. But no defeat had equalled the fiasco over his Molière play, which came to a head early in 1936. *A Theatrical Novel* blends the relatively happier story of how Bulgakov had in the mid-1920s converted *The White Guard* into his play *The Days of the Turbins* with an account of his dismay over the difficulties he encountered with *The Cabal of Hypocrites* in the 1930s. The fact that he envisaged the novel culminating in the hero's suicide is a measure of his desperate mood in 1936–7.

A Theatrical Novel has a caustic appeal if the reader is familiar with the full story of Bulgakov's relationship with MKhAT and with the nature and reputation of Stanislavsky's work; almost every character and episode in the novel has its prototype, and Bulgakov's friends from the theatre acknowledged it a masterly caricature when they came to hear him read it.[46] But the autobiographical focus of the plot and the work's very topicality hinder it from reaching depths of profundity. To the modern reader its value is that of a curiosity, and it scarcely ranks with the more enduring portions of Bulgakov's oeuvre. The personal satire on historical figures is rather narrow, and the work cannot very usefully be set alongside Bulgakov's other studies of the writer, where the theme acquires more universal dimensions. Maksudov, the hero of *A Theatrical Novel*, is capable of describing the disasters that befall him with a self-irony that Bulgakov's other writer–heroes lack; for them, creation is always a matter of the utmost earnestness. Molière, whose concern is rather with the theatre than with literature, brings to his profession a sober and considered dedication. Molière also has the advantage that he is at once a playwright and the manager of his theatre, so that the whole theatre is at one with his intentions and wishes; Bulgakov, himself a talented actor and producer as well as a playwright, must often have yearned for Molière's authority. In *A Theatrical Novel* Maksudov is merely a small cog in the elaborate bureaucracy which has arrogated to itself the right to control the entire process of staging a play. While Molière stands as the supreme model of integrated theatre (bearing in mind, of course, the importance of royal patronage), Maksudov figures as a pawn in a cultural world adulterated by political and administrative intervention.

This autobiographical context of Bulgakov's theatrical satire encourages us to draw a distinction between the literary setting on the one hand and the theatrical setting on the other, within the Moscow chapters of *The Master and Margarita*. The former continues to concentrate Bulgakov's most heartfelt observations about art and society, while the latter, like *A Theatrical Novel* itself, provides an opportunity for malice about a world of pretension and cynicism upon which Bulgakov took exuberant revenge. The havoc the demons wreak on the Variety Theatre and the genuine suffering they visit upon its administrators provide the novel with some of its finest black comedy; but the victims suffer this punishment for offences which are unspecified, the implication being that the kind of people who engage in theatrical administration are by definition hypocritical, greedy and inefficient, and that they simply deserve to be shaken out of their complacency. Neither Rimsky nor Varenukha, nor even Styopa Likhodeyev have any direct connection with the Master, and the blows that are dealt to them are largely delivered by Woland's assistants. Woland himself is much more actively concerned about the literary scene, clearly reflecting Bulgakov's own anxieties about the directions in which its ideology was moving in the late 1920s and early 1930s.

The theme of literature is crucial to the Moscow section of *The Master and Margarita*, the grotesque behaviour of the official literary world only highlighting the significance of the Master's achievement by suggesting how certain writers have opted for the 'false' choices of compromise and conformism. Amongst the reasons given by Woland for visiting Moscow is his wish to observe the moeurs of the inhabitants. This he succeeds in doing during the first part of the performance at the Variety Theatre, which culminates in Begemot ripping the compère Bengal'sky's head off. Woland is impressed by the plea of a woman who intercedes on his behalf 'for God's sake' (541), and his overall conclusions about the populace are not too severe:

'Well ...' he replied pensively, 'they're just like other people. They're fond of money, but then that was always so ... Mankind loves money, whatever it's made of; leather, paper, bronze or gold. They're unthinking, but what of that ... and compassion does occasionally knock at their hearts ... they're just ordinary people, and on the whole they remind me of the previous ones ... it's just that the housing problem has affected them ...' and he gave a loud order: 'Put his head back on.'   (541)

However, this constitutes only a small part of the investigations conducted by Woland and his band into the state of mind of the people of Moscow, and the task assumes rather more serious dimensions when the group of people under discussion are representatives of the literary establishment. After all, Woland times his first appearance in Moscow in order to intervene in a literary conversation between Berlioz and Ivan, and from then on his attention is largely focussed on the people associated with Berlioz's circle of power and influence. Woland may be worried about Moscow under the Soviet régime, but it is above all to the literary world that he looks in order to discover an explanation for this state of affairs, and it is they who suffer the brunt of his terrifying but salutary tricks.

Two of the novel's most prominent themes, the position of the writer in contemporary society and the problem of 'truth', are introduced in the discussion between Berlioz and Ivan. The two littérateurs are first presented to the reader with considerable irony:

The former was none other than Mikhail Aleksandrovich Berlioz, chairman of the board of one of Moscow's most prominent literary associations (which was known as Massolit for short), and editor of a literary magazine; his young companion was the poet Ivan Nikolayevich Ponyryov, who wrote under the pseudonym Bezdomny.   (423)

Bulgakov's choice of names here is typical of the shifting autobiographical references with which he invests the work, sometimes as a wry joke, elsewhere to identify himself with the trials of his heroes. Berlioz shares Bulgakov's initials M. A. B. and even his Christian name; Bulgakov's fondness for the sequence *MA* is perhaps reflected elsewhere in the choices of the names *Ma*ksudov, the *Ma*ster, and *Ma*rgarita (as well as *Ma*dlen and even *Mol'*yer?). Ivan's pseudonym Bezdomny ('homeless'), while obviously intended to sound affected, had in fact been used by Bulgakov himself for his story *Kuda delis'? (Where Did they Get to?)* in 1923.[47] We need not attribute much weight here to his mocking self-identification with the two characters; he may be recalling his own youthful pretensions in Ivan's pseudonym, but Berlioz, as a bureaucrat and chairman of the sardonically named Massolit, represents all that Bulgakov found most distasteful about the new arbiters of culture. He sets their discussion in a context where irrational forces seem to be conspiring to undermine their dignity (the heat, the apricot juice which makes them hiccup); but this is just a prelude to the more serious ways in which Berlioz's rationalist and materialist complacency is about to be subverted.

Their conversation serves to define some of the ideological precepts on which the Soviet literary establishment is founded:

The thing was that the editor had commissioned the poet to write an important anti-religious epic poem for the next volume of his journal . . . Bezdomny had delineated the main hero of his poem, Jesus, in very black tones, but nevertheless, in the editor's view, the whole poem would have to be rewritten. And so at the moment the editor was giving the poet something of a lecture about Jesus, in order to underline the poet's basic error. It is difficult to say what had led Ivan Nikolayevich astray – whether it was the imaginative strength of his talent, or his complete ignorance of the subject on which he proposed to write – but in his depiction Jesus had emerged just like a living character, albeit rather an unattractive one. What Berlioz wanted to demonstrate to the poet was that the main point was not what sort of a person Jesus was, whether he was good or bad, but that this Jesus, as such, had never actually existed, and that all the stories about him were simply made up, a perfectly ordinary myth. (425)

Berlioz's arguments identify him as a representative of the 'mythological' school of thought represented in Bulgakov's sources by the writings of A. Drews, which in its concern to prove that the Christian Canon belongs to a long tradition of mythological writing seems to denigrate by implication the value of myth itself; Berlioz refers sneeringly to 'perfectly ordinary myth'. The modern implication of this view is surely that imaginative fiction, the heir to myth, is equally dispensable; we have only to recall the Futurist slogan 'Fiction is the opium of the people!'[48] The narrator suggests, however, that imagination is not so easily suppressed, and puts forward the hypothesis that Ivan may unwittingly have succumbed to the 'imaginative strength of his talent'. This grievous ideological error sets an immediate distance between Ivan and Berlioz; it also indicates where Ivan stands in Bulgakov's estimation.

In the passage quoted above, Bulgakov seems to broaden the scope of his arguments by calling his characters 'the editor' and 'the poet' more frequently than he uses their proper names; the conflict between the artist and the social forces which endeavour to guide and circumscribe his activities is thus neatly invoked as a backdrop to the conversation. Berlioz will all too soon suffer the fate he has called down upon himself by refusing to acknowledge the existence of Christ, of God, or even of the devil, and by indoctrinating others

with the same view. Ivan, however, is a far more complex personality, whose evolution is perhaps the most striking development
in the plot of the Moscow chapters. But for the moment he shows
little inclination to rebel against Berlioz's strictures, or to question
the way in which the editor seeks to impose on him a 'sotsial'ny
zakaz' or 'socialist commission' in art, to use the phrase eventually
taken over by the language of socialist realism.[49] He is, however,
deeply moved by the beauty and interest of Woland's story; and
after Berlioz's death he begins to reveal his capacity for believing in
the supernatural, which had been heralded in his poem about
Christ. During his pursuit of Woland around Moscow he suddenly
steals an icon: a subconscious acknowledgement of the fact that he
is up against the devil, which is converted into conscious knowledge after his conversation in Stravinsky's asylum with the Master.
His new sensitivity, what is more, is not confined to the realm of
the supernatural; more importantly for the main themes of the
book, his new honesty and clarity of perception oblige him to start
looking critically at his art:

For the first time he suddenly experienced an inexplicable revulsion
against poetry, and for some reason his own verses, which immediately
came to mind, gave him disagreeable feelings ... No, I shan't write any
more verse ... The poems that I wrote are bad poems, and I realize that
now.

(505, 753)

When he meets the Master Ivan is, in other words, already ripe to
become the disciple of a man dedicated to a different and higher
form of art. As a reward for his willingness to recognize the
supernatural, he is granted a dream in which he learns the continuation of Woland's story about Pilate and Iyeshua; if only briefly, he
too is granted access to a portion of that higher truth which is the
Master's vision.

Milne has argued that this comprises the utmost of his reward,
and that in the Epilogue his turning away from literature towards
history indicates that his dream about Iyeshua's execution should
be seen as 'his last "creative" act'.[50] This is true of his waking life,
certainly, but in his dreams he does succeed in pursuing his fascination with Pilate a little further. In chapter 27, when the detective
arrives at last to question Ivan about Berlioz's death, Ivan has just
been asleep and dreaming; he has had not only a vision of Yershalaim, which he could be remembering from Woland's description,

and of the crosses on Golgotha after Matvey has cut down the
bodies – which he saw in his own earlier dream – but he also has a
new vision of Pilate:

As Ivan slept there appeared before him a man sitting motionless on a seat;
he was clean-shaven, with a strained, yellow face – a man in a white cloak
lined in red, gazing with hatred into the luxuriant, alien garden.   (752)

This image actually belongs to chapter 26 (726), and since that
chapter and the previous one purport to be what Margarita reads,
Ivan could not know of it except in a *further* vision. Similarly,
although Ivan has effectively been brainwashed back into conformity in the Epilogue, he is still haunted by dreams of Pilate on the
anniversary of Woland's visit, at the time of the vernal full moon. In
that recurring dream he not only sees again the details of the
crucifixion, but also hears Pilate's conversation with Iyeshua as
they walk at last together up the moonbeam:

'O gods, ye gods,' said the man in the cloak, turning his haughty face
towards his companion, 'what a crude execution! But tell me, I beg you,'
and here the haughty face became pleading, 'it didn't really happen, did it?
I implore you, tell me that it didn't happen!'
    'Well of course not,' replied his companion in a hoarse voice, 'you
imagined it.'   (811)

Although this episode was foreseen in Pilate's dream in chapter 26
(735), the actual conversation takes place only after the Master's
destiny has been resolved, and does not, strictly speaking, even
belong to the Master's novel. To this extent we may argue that Ivan
has not been entirely lost back to the Establishment, that he still has
some creative capacities, and that there is still therefore some hope
of redemption for him. When the Master comes to bid him farewell
as he leaves Moscow, he names him as his disciple (790), and even
entrusts the sacred theme of Pilate to him:

You'll write the continuation of his story!   (789)

In the event, Ivan abandons this task as he is sucked back into
contemporary life, and he never writes anything about Pilate; but at
least he does discover, not just the sequel, but even the ending,
unforeseen by the Master himself, to Pilate's story. This is confirmed in the reassurances he receives at the end of his yearly
dreams from the Master and Margarita:

'And so that's how it ended, then?'
'That's how it ended, my disciple,' answers number one hundred and eighteen, and the woman comes close to Ivan and says:
'Of course that's how. Everything came to an end, everything comes to an end ... And I will kiss you on the forehead, and everything will be as it should for you.'   (811)

This assertion of what Milne has aptly termed Woland's 'sense of poetic justice'[51] provides a muted but powerful counterbalance to the pessimism which pervades the closing pages of the novel; it betokens the fact that Ivan too will eventually be released from his sufferings and judged with compassion. The pressure of circumstances obliges Ivan in the end to renounce his faith in a higher reality, just as the Master renounced his art; but for both even the temporary attainment of what we might call a state of grace serves as a guarantee of some reward after death.

A rather more limited transformation takes place in the figure of Ryukhin, the poet who becomes the scapegoat for Ivan's newly discovered contempt for Establishment literature:

'He's a typical little kulak in his psychology,' burst out Ivan Nikolayevich, who was evidently dying to unmask Ryukhin, 'and, what's more, a little kulak carefully masquerading as a proletarian. Just look at his sanctimonious physiognomy, and compare it with those resounding verses he composed for the first of May! Ha, ha ... "Rise, banners, and unfurl!" but you just take a look inside him to find out what he's really thinking ... you'll be horrified!'   (484)

The virulence of this attack of course derives from the fact that Ivan can see himself in Ryukhin, so that his aggression is prompted partly by self-disgust. Ryukhin is eventually brought to reflect upon his work, and he has to admit, like Ivan, that his poetry is bad and that he does not even believe in it himself. This absence of conviction is a fault shared by the critics who write so scathingly about the Master's novel, and it becomes, therefore, a hallmark of Establishment art:

There was something uncommonly false and hesitant that could be felt literally in every line of those articles, despite their menacing and confident tone. I kept feeling – and I couldn't rid myself of this impression – that the authors of these articles were not saying what they wanted, and that their frenzy was aroused precisely because of this.   (561-2)

The crime of insincerity is pointedly set against the Master's virtue of integrity. As Ryukhin is driven past the statue of Pushkin, his resentment overflows in a burst of invective against the acknowledged genius; but this is already symptomatic of the fact that Ryukhin is undergoing a traumatic experience of self-discovery. The suggestion is that one hack at least has been lost to the Establishment as he comes to a realization of his shortcomings. As the night comes to an end, the poet faces the stark light of day and the knowledge that his insincerity has been unmasked:

The poet had wasted his night while the others were carousing, and he now realized that he couldn't summon it back again. He had only to lift his head from the lamp to the sky to understand that the night had gone irrevocably ... Day fell implacably on the poet. (490)

Ivan's expostulations have not been in vain, if only because he has achieved his purpose of turning Ryukhin away from his false art. There is no indication, however, that Ryukhin will learn to create a true art in its place.[52]

The Master is seen as a lone hero on the literary horizon, with Ivan as someone who has the potential to free himself from the mould into which he has been cast, and Ryukhin a much lesser version of Ivan. But these are rare individuals in a world of hypocrisy and debased values, and even Woland and his suite cannot be sure of achieving any transformations in it. Woland's first act on arriving in Moscow is to attack the head of the literary establishment, Berlioz. But the survival of the status quo is scarcely threatened by his death, since literature has been so institutionalized that the death of one individual changes nothing. As Bulgakov describes the opulence of Griboyedov House, the innumerable doors besieged by applicants for better housing, 'creative travel', and other privileges, and as he dwells on the splendours of the best restaurant in Moscow, a grotesque portrait of the materialistic aspirations motivating the world of culture emerges all too clearly.

During an evening at Griboyedov House, Bulgakov shows the ludicrously named poets Pavianov, Bogokhul'sky, Sladky, Shpichkin and Adel'fina Buzdyak dancing the night away with their fellow-writers to the sound of the renowned Dom Griboyedova jazz band, with the singer shrieking out his 'Hallelujah!'. In a curious digression the narrator notes the sudden appearance of the piratical Archibal'd Archibal'dovich, the restaurant's handsome maître d'hôtel, and indulges in a fantasy about the pirate's deeds in the Caribbean; he then brings himself up short, reproving himself

for getting carried away, and reminds himself that in fact there is
nothing at all beyond banal reality. Contemplating the horrors of
mediocrity and vulgarity before his eyes, he echoes Pilate's words:

And it's terrifying ... O gods, ye gods, bring me poison, poison!   (477)

It is striking that the narrator should see fit to adduce Pilate's words
about a momentous disaster in the context of this satire on a literary
club; it suggests that we are being asked to interpret it as a
genuinely catastrophic state of affairs, that the power of philistines
and pharisees is a crucial indicator of a nation's cultural decline.
The scene is summed up in the conclusion: 'In a word, it was hell'
(477). Other incongruous details contribute to a parody of hell
which gains in impact from the fact that in the novel the devil
himself is associated with rather less debauched and horrendous
scenes. Even Woland's spring ball, where the jazz band also plays
'Hallelujah!' has a curiously salubrious character: the guests'
enjoyment is more genuine, the evening culminates in a
judgement-scene with Berlioz being despatched to the oblivion he
deserves, and the company of murderers and criminals behaves
with perfect grace. The paradox implied is that the devil encounters
in Griboyedov House a hell far worse than anything he could
himself devise.

In a subsequent comic encounter Woland's minions Korov'yev
and Begemot have difficulties in getting in to Griboyedov House
because they do not possess membership cards. Korov'yev remon-
strates with the woman who bars their way:

'But surely, in order to be certain that Dostoyevsky is a writer, you don't
have to ask him for a pass? Just take any five pages from any one of his
novels, and you won't need his pass to be confident that you're dealing with
a writer.' ...
'Dostoyevsky is dead,' said the young lady, although she didn't sound too
sure.
'I protest!' cried Begemot heatedly. 'Dostoyevsky is immortal!'   (769)

While this exchange suggests in a mortal dimension Bulgakov's
resistance to the idea of the bureaucratization of literature and the
imposition upon it of exclusive constraints – which is presumably
how he would have interpreted the formation of the Union of
Writers in 1932 – Begemot's clichéd remark about Dostoyevsky's
immortality takes on a new significance when we consider that the
Master is indeed about to be granted immortality because of his

work. The choice of Dostoyevsky as an example here is of course not without relevance in view of the proscription under which he was increasingly placed during the Stalinist period.

The visit of Korov'yev and Begemot to Griboyedov House culminates, inevitably, in that august institution being engulfed in flames. Woland later reproves the rascally pair for their behaviour, but a serious note can be detected in their banter:

'And what was Korov'yev up to while you were marauding about?' asked Woland.

'I was helping the firemen, messire,' answered Korov'yev, pointing to his torn trousers.

'Ah, well in that case, of course, it will be necessary to rebuild the whole building.'

'It will be built, messire,' replied Korov'yev, 'allow me to assure you of that.'

'Then it only remains for me to hope that it will be better than the previous one,' commented Woland.

'And so it will, messire,' said Korov'yev.

'Just as you trust me,' added the cat, 'I am a true prophet.'   (778)

The devils' campaign against the literary establishment, which began with the murder of Berlioz, now ends in the destruction of the building in which it is housed. The comic way in which Korov'yev and Begemot assure Woland that it will be rebuilt in fact leaves us in some doubt as to whether the literary establishment really will make use of this opportunity to reconstruct their institution in a new and better form. All the evidence of the Epilogue suggests that, just as they remain impervious to the truth of the Master's novel, now lost to them, so they also ignore the message of Woland's visit. The image of the building ravaged by fire recalls Iyeshua's words when talking to the people of Yershalaim:

I was speaking, hegemon, about the fact that the temple of the old faith will collapse and a new temple of truth will be created.   (441)

As in ancient Yershalaim, so in modern Moscow there is a need for the prevalent corrupt ideology, symbolized in both cities by their temples, to give way to a new and purified truth. Woland with all his wisdom can do nothing to bring about any transformations in the cultural world of Moscow unless the protagonists themselves wish to escape their limitations; his first encounter in Moscow is with Ivan, who does take some steps to free himself from his environment, and the latter part of the novel is taken up with Woland's concern for the ultimate destiny of the Master, a figure who has never been part of the literary establishment in any case. Others, like Berlioz, are beyond hope, but the relationships Woland builds up with Ivan and the Master encourage us to believe that the sensitive man of art can be redeemed.

Woland

As will have become apparent, Woland is a key figure in the novel; his identity, status, aims and ethos are all crucial to a just understanding of the work, in which from first to last he operates as the mainspring of the action. Although he does not literally appear in the Yershalaim chapters, his claim to have witnessed the events which unfold in that city is perfectly acceptable, given his supernatural authority. He therefore provides an unproblematic element of direct continuity between the world of Pilate and modern Moscow, and his function as a linking figure extends also beyond the end of the plot of *The Master and Margarita* into a mysterious realm where Iyeshua, Pilate, the Master and Margarita, and he and his retinue all have different roles to perform. The very fact of his imperturbable ease within the three different settings makes it less startling that one novel should combine them with such boldness. What is remarkable about Woland is that (in company with other figures in the novel – notably of course the Master, but in different senses also Margarita and Ivan, and, in another dimension, Pilate) he gains in stature and certainly in seriousness of purpose as the novel develops.

Indeed, the very presence of the devil in *The Master and Margarita* elevates the issues raised in the novel to a universal level. For he is no mere demon or mischievous prankster; Woland, whom Matvey addresses as 'the spirit of evil and ruler of the shades' (775), may travel with a suite of minor demons, but he himself commands the dignity which comes with ultimate power over the forces of life and death. He treats with the utmost seriousness the moral standing of all the mortals with whom he comes into contact, and is portrayed together with Iyeshua as one of the final arbiters of human destiny.

Bulgakov drew on a number of sources to create the character of Woland. His second wife has suggested that A. V. Chayanov's anonymously published *Venediktov, ili dostopamyatnye sobytiya zhizni moyey* (*Venediktov, or the Memorable Events of My Life*), a book of which Bulgakov was especially fond, may have supplied the basic inspiration for a story about a devil's visit to Moscow.[53] But it is not easy to see any direct links between Chayanov's Hoffmannesque horror story, with its narrator, coincidentally named Bulgakov, struggling for the soul of his beloved against the devil Venediktov, and the benevolent function which Woland fulfils in the love story of the Master and Margarita.

The work which was clearly central to Bulgakov's conception of Woland was Goethe's *Faust*. As ever, when Bulgakov 'uses' a source his references to it remain allusive. In this case, the references to *Faust* considerably enrich the fabric of *The Master and Margarita*, but they fall short of constituting substantial thematic parallels; the reminiscences from *Faust* are left open-ended and suggestive, rather than correlative. The epigraph from Goethe's work, which Bulgakov added to his text only in 1938, may guide the better-read reader to the source of Woland's name, thereby establishing a connection between Woland and Mephistopheles long before the Master makes Woland's parentage explicit during his conversation with Ivan. But the choice of the name Woland itself remains a puzzle. Of all the names which the devil has been given, Bulgakov opts specifically for one which has been bestowed upon him in a literary text, but at the same time for one which appears to be deliberately obscure. Mephistopheles uses it of himself just once in *Faust*, and at an unimportant juncture; Bulgakov could just as well have called his devil Mephistopheles, but by giving Woland one of Mephistopheles's alternative names, he manages to establish a link between the two figures which is less binding than direct identification.[54] There is a further complication concerning Bulgakov's use of the name Woland, which is that when Ivan catches sight of his visiting card he sees a name beginning with 'W' (434), which is why it has been spelt that way in the present study. But Goethe himself spells the name *V*oland, and it is difficult to say what significance should be read into the alteration. Perhaps we should accept Yanovskaya's opinion, based on the fact that the name was spelt correctly in the first draft and only became *W*oland in 1937, that Bulgakov was again playing with associations of his own name, here through an inverted 'M'.[55] Alternatively, Bulgakov may have been insisting on a distinction between Goethe's

Voland and his Woland, although it is hard to see what purpose this would serve when the great majority of his readers could be relied upon not to recognize the source in the first place.[56] What is important, however, is that the problems of good and evil raised by the presence of the devil should have been addressed here through the eyes of an artist, through Goethe's vision of Mephistopheles/ Voland; Bulgakov is not entering into a religious debate as a theologian, but pursuing a literary tradition.

The text of *The Master and Margarita* contains numerous other concealed references to *Faust*. The black poodle head which appears as an adornment of Woland's cane (426), of Margarita's chain (677), and of her cushion (679), serves to recall the fact that when Mephistopheles first appears to Faust, it is in the incarnation of a black poodle; indeed, a larger role had been envisaged by Bulgakov for a black poodle in one of the early drafts of the novel, where it was to have been spotted by two nurses leaping out of the window of Stravinsky's asylum.[57] The name Margarita carries an association with *Faust*, since it is the usual Russian rendering of the name Gretchen. The latter's murder of her baby in *Faust* is echoed in Frieda's story. There is a further reminiscence of Gretchen as Goethe depicts her during the carousals on Walpurgis night in the scar which encircles the neck of Woland's assistant Gella. Woland makes what is in fact an inaccurate reference to Faust sitting over a retort fashioning a homunculus (799); in Goethe's text, it is Wagner who manufactures the homunculus. And in more general terms the story of a man who strives to break through the limitations of his mortality, finds himself dealing with the devil, and is finally redeemed, is common to the two works. But all these echoes precisely do not add up to a systematic response on Bulgakov's part to the content of *Faust*: Woland is not Mephistophelean, he is not mischievous, he is not a tempter, and he is not concerned to win the Master's soul; the self-assured Margarita is no twentieth-century wronged Gretchen; and the Master, unlike Faust, hungers neither for experience nor for power. As always, Bulgakov borrows suggestive images from a text, but then leaves them to acquire a new life of their own in a fresh context; a reading of the earlier work does little to illuminate the issues of the later one.

A study of Bulgakov's other works reminds us, too, that his appreciation of the Faust story was considerably affected by his knowledge of it through the medium of Gounod's opera of the same name. References to various parts of the music for the opera, and especially to the image of the operatic score standing open on the piano, a childhood memory of prime importance for Bulgakov, appear a good dozen times in his writings. That his familiarity with the opera influenced his use of the Faust motif in *The Master and Margarita* is specifically demonstrated by the fact that one of the early titles which he considered for the novel was Mephistopheles's opening line to Faust in the Russian libretto of the opera: 'Vot i ya!' ('Here I am!').[58] The words were in fact eventually used for Woland's opening remarks to Styopa Likhodeyev (494), and were taken up again in *A Theatrical Novel* to accompany the entrance of the Mephistophelean Rudol'fi as Maksudov prepares for the first time to commit suicide. Bulgakov may have rejected the line as a title for *The Master and Margarita* precisely because he did not wish to labour the association or constrain himself to what might seem a mere re-examination of the themes and problems earlier explored by Goethe and by Gounod's librettists, Jules Barbier and Michel Carré. He again does not invite specific identification, but invokes the operatic predecessor alongside the literary one in order to provide a second backdrop to his own plot.

Two further works provided Bulgakov with the traditional insignia with which he decks his devil. The first was the Brokgauz–Efron Encyclopaedia, where he took specific notes on one or two entries.[59] A second major source was M. A. Orlov's *Istoriya snosheniy cheloveka s d'yavolom* (*A History of Man's Relations with the Devil*, St Petersburg, 1904). This suggested details such as the rejuvenating cream which Margarita rubs on herself before the ball; Woland's unexpectedly shabby garb; and the money which the devil gives to the greedy and then transforms into something worthless, a detail which may also have been inspired by a comparable episode in *Faust* (Part 2).[60] In his introduction, moreover, Orlov makes some remarks about pagan views of good and evil deities which may shed some light on Bulgakov's portrayal of the relationship between the two forces:

The pagan not only believed in the existence of the malevolent spirit, but also served him. The evil deity was just as much a deity for him as the good spirit. What's more, there was no need for him to concern himself and make such special efforts with the good deity. Evil gods were another matter. They have to be persuaded to be well disposed towards you,

otherwise all you can expect from them is malice and harm. For this reason
the cult of the evil spirit in primitive society was elaborated far more
deeply, in much more detail, and more thoroughly than the cult of
benevolent gods ... Christianity, on the other hand, took up an entirely
different position with regard to the evil spirit. While formally recognizing
its existence, and without thinking of denying it, it turned this position into
a dogma and declared the evil spirit to be 'Satan' (that is, 'opponent'), the
enemy of the good deity, a sort of contrary to deity. God must be
worshipped, while Satan is worthy only of horror.[61]

Bulgakov seems to incline towards this pagan view, with the
virtuous deity Iyeshua playing a largely passive, muted role, and
the prince of evil having an ultimately moral purpose; indeed, he
needs to be propitiated if he is not to mete out stern punishment for
misdeeds. This notion that Woland should be understood as a
positive figure in the novel has been surprisingly widely dis-
regarded, which has led to the view sometimes being expressed,
particularly in certain émigré publications such as *Novy zhurnal*
and *Vestnik russkogo khristianskogo dvizheniya*, that Woland
should be interpreted strictly in the Christian tradition as the source
of all evil; it has even been maintained that Woland should be held
responsible for all the Master's trials and troubles.[62] But it is
virtually impossible to construct any sort of coherent interpretation
of the novel from this standpoint.

Bulgakov makes it perfectly clear that he does not view the role
of Woland in conventional religious terms, by deciding to borrow
Goethe's own unorthodox description in *Faust* for *The Master and
Margarita*: Bulgakov's epigraph is the passage where Mephistopheles gives Faust an account of his own identity which refers us
rather to the pagan than to the Christian view of his role:

'... Well, so who are you?'
'I am a part of that power which forever desires evil and forever
accomplishes good.'   (423)

Woland is likewise a dark power whose ultimate achievements are
far from evil; he is subservient to the forces of light, and contributes
by his very existence to the good presumably desired by Iyeshua
and by a God about whom we have no information. When Iyeshua
sends Woland his emissary Matvey, the latter is heeded even as he
is being scorned as an individual. Woland mocks him for his naiveté
in wishing for a world cleansed of the forces of darkness, and

echoes the epigraph as he points out the necessity of his own existence for that of goodness:

You pronounce your words as though you did not recognize shadows, nor evil either. Will you not be so kind as to consider the problem of what would become of your good if evil did not exist? And how the world would look if shadows were to disappear from its surface?　(776)

The taunting tone of Woland's remarks does nothing to detract from the force of his argument that virtue has to define itself through contrast with evil; in the same way, his ambition is to set the people of Moscow on the path towards virtue through procedures of torment and provocation.

So Woland figures in the novel as a kind of plenipotentiary ambassador from the supernatural realm; his task is to establish contact with mankind at a moment when it appears to have cut itself off from its spiritual heritage. Soviet man has ceased to see that upon his actions will hang consequences which may not even become apparent until the next life, that he is responsible for determining his own destiny through the choices he makes. In this existentialist vision of the dilemmas of choice confronting the individual, Woland is not empowered to influence the decisions that each person takes. By meting out punishments and allocating rewards, he can only hope to give modern man a salutary reminder of his own responsibilities in the spiritual domain, responsibilities which have not been swept away with the setting-up of a materialist state power.

As for Iyeshua, he withdraws after the striking portrayal of him in the Yershalaim chapters as an all-too-human deity, to a distant and awesome majesty; his activities are largely cloaked in mystery. Woland makes no attempt to challenge his supreme authority, especially since it becomes clear at the end of the novel, where Woland and his retinue of demons are transformed and elevated, that his own authority is almost as considerable. There is a gradual movement throughout *The Master and Margarita* towards this transfiguration; Woland, who operates at first in a somewhat comic guise, becomes increasingly sober and darkly imposing as the story unfolds. The hocus-pocus gives way to the sombre meting-out of justice; and the aggrieved hurt with which he initially responds to the information that the inhabitants of Moscow do not believe in his existence, any more than they do in God's, is gradually replaced by

a graver appreciation of the situation. Shortly before their departure from Moscow, Azazello comments to Woland that he finds
Rome the more attractive city (775). This mention of Rome seems
somewhat irrelevant to the rest of the conversation, unless we are
to understand it as a means of juxtaposing the two great cities in a
way which reminds us of the threads of similarity which bind
together all the great cities of Bulgakov's prose: Jerusalem, Rome
and Kiev as three well-springs of Christianity triumphant, while
modern Moscow has succumbed to an alienation from Christianity
which seems likely to guarantee its decline.

Woland is more a prophet than an agent of the destruction which
threatens to overwhelm Moscow. It would appear that the culmination to his visit for which the atmospherics and the details of the
gathering storm were preparing us throughout the second half of
The Master and Margarita was going to be an apocalyptic destruction of the godless city. One critic at least has described the ending
as though these expectations were in fact realized:

The devils become the four horsemen of the Apocalypse, who on the Day
of Judgement lead away the souls of those who have suffered greatly during
their earthly lives and reward them with peace, before wreaking vengeance
over the earth for those martyred in Christ's service.[63]

But the anticipated scenes of destruction do not then materialize.
The passage during which the supposed apocalyptic catastrophes
take place is somewhat unclear, but the whistles which Leatherbarrow goes on to compare to the trumpeting of the Angels of the
Apocalypse are both spontaneous and unserious, and Woland
insists that Korov'yev's should be 'without any tricks which might
cause damage to life or limb!' (793). The damage inflicted on the
city amounts to no more than a landslide, and even this brings
about no loss of life:

Margarita didn't even hear this whistle, but she observed it while she and
her fiery horse were being flung some thirty yards to one side. Near to her
an oaktree was entirely uprooted, and the earth was covered in cracks right
down to the river's edge. An enormous section of the bank, together with
the landing-stage and the restaurant, slid into the river. The water in the
river seethed and flew up, and an entire river bus, its passengers wholly
unharmed, was thrown on to the low green bank on the other side. (793)

At this point in particular the text reads as though it were still
provisional, but it does seem as though Bulgakov, having originally

intended to finish the novel with an apocalyptic scene – which would have been in keeping with his earlier fascination with apocalyptic motifs in *The White Guard* – then changed his mind. The Epilogue certainly makes no mention of any untoward destruction having taken place. It would appear that Bulgakov decided to focus attention in the end exclusively on the literary themes of the novel, so that Woland's punishments and cleansing fires are ultimately visited not upon the entire populace of Moscow, but above all on the denizens of the literary establishment. Were his anger directed more widely, at society in general, it might be possible to view Woland's function in the novel as being comparable to that of a satirist, as has occasionally been suggested.[64] But Woland does not operate through books or words, not least because his powers are so much greater; his task is not the creation of art, but its rescue. The literary establishment is more guilty than the rest of the people of Moscow because they persecute the Master and reject his work, a novel which might have offered the means for Soviet society to rediscover its spiritual concerns; Woland's increasing involvement with the Master's destiny, like his wrath against Berlioz and Massolit, bears testimony to the profound significance he attaches to art as the repository of spiritual values.

The *theme* of the Passion is introduced by Woland to the narrative because it has an acute relevance in the modern world as the story of a sacrifice performed by one man for the sake of an ideal, a story which has laid the foundations for our understanding of the concepts of good and evil ever since. Bulgakov focusses primarily on the figure of Pilate because his is, surely, the primordial sin of cowardice; however, he is anxious to demonstrate that even this, the most terrible example of the most terrible sin, is eventually pardonable in his ideal world, where the mere capacity to desire the good can prove finally redemptive. The whole Biblical tradition represents a concern for values which Bulgakov believes to be missing in the new Soviet State with its materialist intolerance and absolutism. It is perhaps of no small relevance that one of the lectures given by the Master's prototype in the first draft of the novel was on the secularization of ethics;[65] an anxiety about the status of ethics in a society aggressively devoted to secularity can be said to lie right at the heart of *The Master and Margarita*. As the bearer in the novel of a message of truth, the Master offers his contemporaries an opportunity to ponder these issues; their rejection of the opportunity does not, as we shall see below, diminish the moral stature of the bearer.

The Master

> ,,Я один, всё тонет в фарисействе.''
> ('I am alone, while everything drowns in pharisaism.')
> Boris Pasternak[66]

The mysterious figure who acquires the name of Master in 1934 (some two years after Bulgakov had used it of Molière in his biography), and who only gives the novel its title in the autumn of 1937,[67] retains a somewhat enigmatic aura in the completed text. The expectations concerning the novel's hero which are aroused in the reader by the title are satisfied only after an unusually long delay; the hero appears in chapter 11, and then only fleetingly, before being properly introduced in chapter 13. He goes on to occupy a relatively small proportion of the novel, and initiates virtually none of the action. When he does enter the scene, it is to declare that he has renounced his name and his past:

'I no longer have a name,' replied the strange visitor with sombre contempt, 'I have forsworn it as I have forsworn everything else in life. Let us forget about it.' (553)

His story, however, is of considerable interest, and as he recounts to Ivan the events which brought him to the asylum, we begin to gain some sense of the qualities which will justify the respect in which he is to be held by Woland and Iyeshua, and the love which Margarita bears him. We are afforded glimpses of a character which does not accord with the pitiful circumstances in which we have met him. Although he has turned his back on human society, he nevertheless still possesses a concern for human values. He engages immediately with Ivan in an intimate relationship which contains a certain pedagogic element, for the Master is a scholar, capable of recognizing – to the discredit of the well-read Berlioz – not only that the strange man they have met is the devil, but even that he is specifically Woland. This is already an indication of his almost supernatural intuition, because while it might be possible for him to recognize that the particular features with which the devil has chosen to deck himself identify him with Goethe's creation Mephistopheles, there is no conceivable way that he could know that he had adopted the name Woland, which Mephistopheles uses only once of himself in the whole of Goethe's *Faust*. Further evidence of this propensity for 'higher' intuitions is given later in the novel, when the Master addresses Margarita as Margot (705), at a time when he could not know that Korov'yev calls her Queen Margot as a mark of her royal ancestry (677).

The Master is also perceptive on an ordinary, social level: he instantly identifies Ivan as a hack writer who churns out poor verse, and promptly urges him to abandon this career. The distinction he draws between true and false art emerges in the climax to this scene, when Ivan asks him if he too is a writer. He dismisses a title which represents mere membership of a profession, and asserts instead his individual vocation; donning his cap in a gesture which Bulgakov describes with a hint of affectionate irony, he declares: 'I am a master' (553). Margarita's gift of love is here transformed into the poet's wreath.

The most striking aspect of the Master's account of himself is that he makes no attempt to explain how he wrote his novel, or even how he gained his inspiration for it. There is no indication that he has earned his inspiration through virtuous deeds, and certainly no indication that it has anything to do with religious faith. The creative process is taken for granted, it is neither analysed, nor made to seem a painstaking process of construction, but rather the reception and transcription of a vision which, as we have seen, embodies a higher truth. His writing is described as an entirely private, individual pursuit, which takes place within the confines of the book-lined basement in which he isolates himself from his past and from the outside world. The Master's only comment on this period is expressed in typically Romantic terms: 'Ah, that was a golden age' (554). But this was a solitary bliss: even Margarita, who in many respects fulfils the role of the ideal Romantic companion, is scarcely involved in the composition of the novel. She is his devoted lover, the creator of his earthly happiness, but she is not his muse. It is universally recognized that Bulgakov invested his heroine with the traits of his third wife and great love, Yelena Sergeyevna, who gave him considerable practical as well as moral support in his writing. But the Master's relationship with Margarita does not define his identity as a writer; his work carries a value above and beyond the limitations of his personal history and destiny.

Once the novel is finished and the inspired creative mood has passed, the Master comes back down from the realms of the imagination and goes out to offer his art to the real world:

And the time finally came for me to relinquish my secret refuge and to emerge into the world.
   And I came out into the real world bearing the book in my arms, and at that point my life ended . . .
   I found myself for the first time in the literary world, and even now, when it's all over and my destruction stares me in the face, I remember it with horror!   (558)

His encounter with the world of literature is significantly evoked here in terms of a death; it is as though his creative life could only have meaning when it was a private activity communicated to his beloved alone. The creative act is not validated by the reception of the work, but by the author's own experience of and belief in his creation.

The Master's confrontation with the literary world is a tragic one. He is greeted at first with amazement, and later, after the publication of a portion of the novel, with articles insinuating that his work is dangerously reactionary. These directly recall the language and tone of the reviews with which some critics had denounced Bulgakov's own works, and he describes their absurdities with a certain relish. The attacks affect even the Master's relationship with Margarita, as we learn from the 1973 edition of the novel: she, who had declared that her life was bound up in the novel, and who had encouraged him to publish a part of it, now seems slightly to drift away from him (558, 560). The real world has sullied ideal love as it rejects pure art. The Master is driven into a state of depression, and his paranoid fears take the form of nightmares about a tentacular octopus, clearly symbolizing the long arms of the State, which is poised to arrest him. Eventually the prospect of persecution brings him to the point where he turns away from his creation: he abandons his art by burning the novel, thereby renouncing his highest achievement and destroying his only literary work. His explanation to Margarita is touchingly helpless:

I have come to hate the novel, and I am afraid. I am ill. I am terrified.
                                                                (564)

It is a gesture of despair about his artistic vocation. His rejection of self is reinforced by the trauma of prison, whence he emerges lacking faith not just in his art, but even in the nature of Margarita's devotion to him. He enters the clinic voluntarily to seek refuge from a hostile world, but also from his entire past. He feels he has no alternative: 'I have nowhere to escape to' (548). But Ivan irrupts into his sanctuary, and the conversation between them which serves as our first introduction to the Master marks the beginning of a process of rebirth which can be completed only after his death. In the end the Master is to be reconciled to his art, and although his contemporary world can find no place for him, it is through his art that he will find 'somewhere to go'.

For the moment, however, he continues to deny his past. He refuses to tell Ivan the continuation of Woland's story about Pilate and Iyeshua, although he is evidently capable of doing so; indeed, nowhere in the novel does the Master himself actually narrate the story he has written. His indifference towards it lasts even beyond his reunion with Margarita, and Woland himself is incapable of rekindling his interest: the Master's only response is to reiterate that:

It's hateful to me, that novel . . . I have suffered too much because of it . . . I have no more dreams, and no more inspiration either.   (708)

He also declines whatever it is Margarita offers him in a whisper – presumably publication and worldly success.

The fact that Woland is the first to recite a chapter of Pilate's story could mislead us into thinking that he is immediately preoccupied with the Master's fate. Belza, for instance, asserts that Woland

one way or another will concern himself with the destiny of the Master, for whose sake, as is clear from the whole conception of the novel, he has in fact come to Moscow.[68]

In reality, his presence in Moscow bears no relation to the Master's novel, and we may recall his surprise and interest when he learns that its theme is coincidentally that of his own conversation of three evenings before. Woland gives Berlioz and Ivan one explanation for his visit, which is that he has come to do some research on Gerbert Aurillac, the scholar and mathematician who as Pope Silvester the Second reputedly combined his religious duties with an active interest in the arts of necromancy.[69] But Korov'yev later gives Margarita a different explanation, which is that Woland has come to Moscow to observe its inhabitants and to celebrate his annual black sabbath. The hostess of the ball must by tradition be

named Margarita; the Master's lover is meanwhile in such a plight
that she unwittingly declares her readiness to serve the devil,
mournfully exclaiming:

Ah, truly, I would sell my soul to the devil just to know whether he is alive
or not!   (639)

As it turns out, this declaration is the structural lynch-pin of the
novel, as it enables the Yershalaim story, the modern world in
Moscow, and the supernatural forces in the work all to converge.
By doing her duty for Woland, Margarita regains the Master,
thereby incidentally drawing Woland's attention to the novel.
Woland, while able to foresee that the Master's literary career is
not completely over – 'your novel will still bring you some surprises'
(709) – is for the moment content to grant the pair their modest
wish to return to their basement idyll. It is only Iyeshua's intervention through his surly ambassador Matvey which brings about the
lovers' premature deaths, opening the way for the fulfilment of the
Master's destiny and the redemption of his art.

   The death itself is effected in a manner which adumbrates the
ultimate significance of the poet's achievement. To confirm the
importance of the link between the Master and Pilate, the poison is
administered with poetic appropriateness 'in the same Falernian
wine' (785) which Pilate had drunk in the Master's novel. The fact
that, presumably due to an oversight on Bulgakov's part, it is
actually a different wine – Pilate replied to Afranius's enquiry
about the wine's origin by saying that it was in fact wine from
Caecuba – scarcely diminishes the force of this gesture. When the
Master comes round, he believes that he has been killed, but
Azazello protests:

After all, your lover is still calling you Master, your mind is still functioning, so how can you be dead? Surely, in order to consider yourself alive, it's
not strictly necessary to sit in a basement wearing a shirt and hospital
underpants? That's ridiculous!   (787)

This argument may once again reflect Bulgakov's reading of the
work of Father Pavel Florensky, who considers at some length the
idea that a physical body can effect a transition through death,
passing from one level of reality to another without losing its mass
or shape, by penetrating to a realm where these become notional:

The illusoriness of the body's parameters must be understood not as an
indication of its unreality, but merely as evidence of its transition to a

different reality. The realm of illusoriness is concrete and attainable, and in the language of Dante it is called the Empyrean ... The transition from a surface of reality to one of illusion is possible only if space is *shattered* and the body is *turned inside out* through itself.[70]

One of Bulgakov's friends recalled a conversation with him when he was already close to death, during which he expressed his belief that some such transformation was perhaps conceivable:

It sometimes appears to me that death is an extension of life. We simply can't picture to ourselves how it happens. But somehow or other it does happen ... I'm not talking about the afterlife, of course, I'm not a clergyman or a theosophist, heaven forbid ... No, I think I must really be in a bad way to start talking about such unfathomable matters.[71]

These imprecise reflections encourage us to feel that it is in just such a non-religious sense that we should understand the Master and Margarita's elevation to an Empyrean realm, where they retain a notional physical reality even though they have left their bodies behind. The transition also involves a ceremonial of purification. Milne has suggested that Margarita's image is 'left as one of ambiguous witchery',[72] but Bulgakov does in fact mark her release from her pact with the devil; she is freed from her harsher witch-like traits before being woken by Azazello to her life in the other world:

With his iron hands Azazello turned her over as lightly as a doll to face him and began to gaze at her. The poisoned woman's face changed before his very eyes. Even in the gathering twilight of the storm it was possible to see how her temporary witch's squint and the harshness and exuberance of her features began to fade. The dead woman's face became suffused with light and eventually softened; and her expression ceased to look predatory, and turned simply into a feminine grimace of suffering. (786)

In a first act of faith the Master now becomes reconciled to his hitherto wavering belief in the existence of the supernatural, and accepts that he and his lover have been transported to some kind of extra-terrestrial dimension. At this point is it Margarita, who until now had had greater understanding of the supernatural world, who falters. When she and the Master were returned to the basement it was she who stayed up all night to read through the novel, while the Master remained indifferent. Now she is anxious that the text of the novel so recently restored to the Master will be lost if he does not carry the manuscript away with him:

'It's not necessary,' replied the Master, 'I remember it off by heart.'
'But you won't forget a word, a single word of it?' asked Margarita,
nestling close to her lover and wiping the blood from the cut on his brow.
'Don't worry! Now I shall never forget anything again!' he answered.

(787)

We hear now the voice of a different man; for with these words the
Master demonstrates that he has at last regained faith in himself,
and above all in his writing. His sufferings are over.

The immortal destiny to which the Master accedes is not,
however, entirely triumphant; there is some degree of reservation
implied in Iyeshua's judgement on the artist, as conveyed to
Woland by Matvey:

He hasn't earned light, he has earned peace.   (776)

Yanovskaya has pointed out that as early as 1931, even before the
writer was confirmed as the central figure in the work, the hero of
Bulgakov's manuscript was already described as not attaining the
highest reward, although Proffer points out that this exact formulation was only hit upon very late in the writing of the novel, in May
1939.[73] Beyond Matvey's words we hear Bulgakov invoking all the
themes of hesitation, failure and regret which pervade his oeuvre
from the earliest days of his literary career. If the phrase is also to
be construed as Bulgakov's final judgement on himself, we are
invited to sympathize with his weary hopelessness about the
possibility of gaining either worldly renown, or any triumphant
reward in the next world to compensate for his tribulations; he can
envisage no happier prospect than release from persecution, a
marvellous final peace.

The notion that, like Bulgakov, the Master can envisage nothing
further for himself than peace, identifies the judgement passed on
him as being in accordance with the principle earlier enunciated by
Woland:

All theories are equally valid. There is among them one, according to
which each shall be rewarded according to his faith. So be it!   (689)

In other words, the Master's destiny is in a sense defined by the
limitations of his own imagination and aspirations. He has doubted
Margarita's love, as well as renouncing his vision in fainthearted
fashion; Margarita, by contrast, achieves all that she does in the
novel through the strength of her faith. Her first words on waking

on the fateful Friday when she meets Azazello are: 'I believe it! . . . I believe it!' (663). If the Master does not achieve the supreme reward of light, it is because he has not desired it, and not only because he has lacked faith and courage. And so his redemption cannot be compared with the supreme elevation of Goethe's Faust, of whom the Angels can say:

He who strives and ever strives, him we can redeem.[74]

The Master long ago abandoned the struggle to defend his art; his longing for peace is an expression of defeat in that particular battle. But before being despatched to the quiet destiny for which he has yearned, the Master has still to be rewarded for his initial integrity in following the dictates of his inspiration. This will mark the peak of his achievement.

The two lovers are brought to some indeterminate location to observe the torments of Pilate. The significance of this fusion of the Master's fiction with his actual experience is explained when the Master is permitted to redeem his hero and free him to run up the moonbeam, towards the destiny which Pilate had foreseen for himself in his prophetic dream some two millennia earlier:

No sooner had the procurator lost contact with surrounding reality, than he set off immediately along a glittering road and went right up it towards the moon. He even burst out laughing with happiness in his dream, for everything was working out so excellently and freshly on the limpid blue road. He was accompanied by Banga, and by his side walked the wandering philosopher. They were arguing about something very complex and important, and what's more neither of them could convince the other. They couldn't agree about anything, and as a result their discussion was particularly interesting and interminable. Naturally, today's execution turned out to be a pure misunderstanding; after all, here was the philosopher, who had dreamed up the incredibly absurd notion that all people were good, walking alongside him, so consequently he was alive . . . There had been no execution!   (734–5)

The fact that Pilate's happy fulfilment does not bind him to an immediate acceptance of the authenticity of all Iyeshua's views underlines the extent to which Bulgakov was concerned that the 'truth' he offers his readers is not to be understood as a dogmatic text excluding all other versions of the same story.

This act of liberation closes the main chronological span of the novel, which in stretching from the time of the Crucifixion to the date of the Master's death marks the length of Pilate's sentence to isolation and remorse as punishment for his cowardice; a kind of Purgatory, though it should be remembered that such a notion is entirely foreign to the precepts of the Orthodox Church.[75] Here again a slight chronological oversight appears to have crept into the text, for Margarita calculates his sufferings as having lasted a mere 12,000 moons (797), which she feels to be excessive enough, when in fact he has been sitting there almost twice as long. But on this night, 'the sort of night when accounts are settled' (795), the kingdom of truth predicted by Iyeshua in his conversation with Pilate (448) finally comes to pass, and justice is meted out to the sinners according to their just deserts. The Master, who has been worthy of a great vision, takes an active part in shaping Pilate's fate, and his vision is validated by being demonstrated to be an historical, if extra-terrestrial truth. In a sense, the Master is actively contributing to 'Christian' legend by providing an ending to Pilate's story; his action suggests that the Christian myth is still in the process of being created, and that its essential truths therefore still have an active validity for the modern world. The Master enables the final act of a drama controlled by supreme destiny to be played out. When Pilate is reassured that the Crucifixion did not take place, this is not a denial of historical truth, but the expression of a higher truth, which is that Pilate is now free to obliterate from his memory a deed that is no longer being held against him.

Bulgakov is, incidentally, at pains to emphasize here that the Master is acting specifically in his capacity as an artist. Margarita, not sensing the limitations of her own powers, at first attempts to release Pilate herself, as she had earlier absolved Frieda from further punishment. But in this case the compassion which she had succeeded in introducing to Woland's domain is not adequate. The release of Pilate is a matter of artistic truth, and the Master at last crowns his labours with the actual final words to his novel, which he could not himself have anticipated:

You are free! You are free! He is waiting for you!   (797)

The Master's sympathetic portrayal of a universally detested figure is brought to its logical conclusion in the form of forgiveness, a resolution which for Bulgakov had always held a particular attraction. As early as 1928, the critic Gorbachov had noted the significance of the theme of forgiveness for Bulgakov's first novel,

The White Guard, which Gorbachov scorned for its apparent political ambivalence:

> It is typical of Bulgakov that he should bring about some sort of all-forgiveness, allowing that both of the sides heroically struggling in the civil war, the Bolsheviks and the Whites, should enjoy ultimate moral righteousness, self-sacrifice, heroism, and the right to 'glory and eternal rest'.[76]

While Bulgakov offered forgiveness in *The White Guard* as a way towards political reconciliation, in *The Master and Margarita* he suggests that it is an acceptable response to moral weakness as represented either by Pilate's crime or by the Master's lack of heroism. He seeks always to avoid condemnation; we are reminded of his conclusions in *The Cabal of Hypocrites* and *The Last Days* that it is fate which in the end brings about the suffering visited upon the individual. Moral absolutism evidently repels him; and it is perhaps typical that one of the books in his library should have been Spasovich's textbook of criminal law, which includes an important section dealing with the various forms of absolution and amnesty that can be granted to a criminal.[77] His attention may well have been drawn to a particular passage dealing with the notion of 'abolitio', the removal of guilt, where it is pointed out that liberal constitutions allow for a concept of 'abolitio' more generous than the one enshrined in Roman law, for in modern times 'it is based on the imagined (fictitious) proposition that the crime never took place, that as a fact it is excluded from reality'.[78] Hence perhaps Pilate's obsession with the idea, not that he should justify his crime or be forgiven for it, but that it should be erased from the record; and it is Bulgakov's decision that he should be granted this wish.

The Master is now allotted his Romantic destiny. This takes the form of a cosy home, domestic peace and security in the company of his beloved, and a life furnished with all the appurtenances of cultured society in the late eighteenth and early nineteenth centuries, including music, goosequills for his lucubrations, Goethean scientific investigation, and the harmonious beauties of domesticated nature. Here the Master will live as a poet, with no fear of the recriminations or exactions of an authoritarian society. An essential feature of the idyll is that the Master, like Pilate, and like Ivan in the closing lines of the novel, should in turn be freed from his tormenting memories. Pilate's story ends with an evocation of their shared sense of relief:

The Master's memory, his restless, troubled memory, began to fade. Someone had released the Master into freedom, just as he himself, a moment before, had released the hero he had created. After being pardoned on that Saturday night, there departed forever into boundless space his hero, the son of the astrologer–king, the cruel fifth procurator of Judaea, the knight Pontius Pilate.   (799)

While the Master's insight and inspiration have served to redeem both his hero and himself, they have not proved sufficient to convince those who are incapable of perceiving the truth for themselves. The writer's insights alienate him from his modern surroundings. The Master is fully aware of the distance which separates his work from that of his contemporaries, so that his doubts about the possibility of envisaging a realistic future for himself and Margarita after their return to the basement seem wholly justified. After he burns the novel in a futile endeavour to evade the danger which threatens him, Woland returns the text to him with the words 'manuscripts don't burn' (703), a statement mildly mocking the Master's incredulity, but which carries within it the full force of Bulgakov's deeply held belief in the ultimate integrity – and durability – of art. Milne has concluded that *The Master and Margarita*

is, like its ancestor the mediaeval mystery play, a comedy of spiritual victory over the material world and death.[79]

The Master may have achieved a personal spiritual triumph, but it is arguable whether there is any sense in which either the material world or death itself have been defeated. Towards the end of the novel the narrator comes forward to pronounce some reflections on death which suggest at most a resigned acceptance of it rather than any exultation:

O gods, ye gods! How sad the earth is at evening! And how mysterious the mists are over the marshes. Anyone who has wandered in such mists, anyone who has suffered a great deal before death, anyone who has winged his way over this earth bearing an impossible burden on his back, such a man knows it. The weary man also knows. And he will quit without regret the earth's mists, its marshes and rivers, and he will deliver himself with a light heart into the arms of death, knowing that she alone* can soothe him*.   (794)[80]

Here the voice of the author himself can be clearly heard, in sentiments which convey his own longing for welcome oblivion as his last illness took its course. All the comedy of the novel recedes as the Master and his creator go forward to confront death, for the real world has nothing of value left for them. In the final fire which consumes the basement after the deaths of the Master and of Margarita, the manuscript of the novel is once again destroyed. Although it will take on a new existence in the next world, the real world has lost it forever. The pessimism which we associate with the closing pages of *The Master and Margarita* derives partly from the fact that Moscow has proved itself utterly indifferent to the Master's creation. He and his novel vanish without trace, and nobody will even remember his true name:

And so he disappeared, known only by the lifeless label 'Number one hundred and eighteen from number one block'. (805)

The world is as yet too corrupt and unfeeling to benefit from the work's message or appreciate its creator, so both are removed from it; only death and an after-life can offer the Master and his lover a future. The only remedy, as the author sees it, might be to prize the faculty of creativity which, in the Romantic tradition, Bulgakov sets up as the highest manifestation of the human spirit, the repository of ethical values. Of the writer he demands the faith, the love, the integrity, and above all the concern for truth which we might associate with a religious vocation.

5

A Romantic vision

,,Придётся поминать того, кто, полный сил,
И светлых замыслов, и воли,
Как будто бы вчера со мною говорил,
Скрывая дрожь предсмертной боли.''

('I have now to recall a man who, filled with strengths, and bright
inventions, and willpower, was speaking to me, it seems, only yesterday,
concealing the tremor of the pain that ushers in death.')

Anna Akhmatova[1]

It is the intention of this concluding chapter to put Bulgakov's
achievement into perspective through two different approaches. In
a series of statements made in the late 1930s as he looked back over
his career, Bulgakov confirmed the pessimistic view of the writer's
position which he had voiced in the various studies of the writer he
had undertaken since 1929. These will be set alongside some
conclusions concerning his work formulated by his friends and
contemporaries, in an attempt to sum up Bulgakov's role in and
impact on the literary world of his day. But before that his writings
will be considered in relation to a larger literary context, for while
the individuality of his work continues to frustrate endeavours to
relate Bulgakov to any of the literary groupings of his day, his debt
to the nineteenth century has yet to receive a thorough investigation. My concern here is to undertake a preliminary exploration
of Bulgakov's relationship to the views on the artist and his work
disseminated by the European Romantic movement, a subject
which would certainly merit a more detailed study.

A twentieth-century Romantic

After 1917 every literary group in the Soviet Union found itself
exercised by the essential question of how to relate to the literature
and culture of the past. The Futurist call in 1912 for Pushkin,
Dostoyevsky and Tolstoy to be 'thrown overboard from the

steamship of modernity'[2] was to pose a fundamental challenge to the arbiters of cultural affairs in the new régime, since it argued that a truly radical power would be unable to avoid the distasteful necessity of destroying the cultural heritage along with the political, social and economic structures of the previous age. One of the first Communist decrees called for the removal of all Tsarist monuments, although this was revoked and followed by a series of decrees relating to the preservation of monuments after Gor'ky had protested about it.[3] Proletkul't and LEF went on to call for the elimination of bourgeois art, in a manner which made the issue into a yardstick of political orthodoxy, so that attempts by the Party to curb the extremism of the iconoclasts could only appear reactionary. Mayakovsky continued to express his agitation over the question in *Klop* (*The Bedbug*, 1928–9), where just a drunkard and a bedbug resurrected from the past are sufficient to undermine the rational morality of an ideal future society. It was a debate which only really came to an end in 1932, when the Party clamped down on the authority of the RAPP group and imposed its own relatively conservative tastes on the cultural world.

In his book *Lot's Wife and the Venus of Milo*, Boris Thomson has explored this issue in particular relation to those writers and literary groups who made explicit their determination to reject the culture of the past; he is less concerned with the other writers of the period:

The majority of artists, of course (e.g. Akhmatova, Mandel'shtam and Pasternak), and most Soviet writers (e.g. Chukovsky, Erenburg, Fedin, Paustovsky and the majority of the 'fellow-travellers' of the 1920s) saw no problem at all ... the continuity of the cultural heritage is an unspoken premiss behind their work.[4]

In certain cases, nevertheless, acceptance of the cultural heritage was more conscious and purposeful than a mere 'unspoken premiss', and constituted in effect an aggressive gesture of rejection of the new culture. As early as 1922, Zamyatin in *My* (*We*) was invoking the music of Scriabin and the poetry of Pushkin as forces capable of destabilizing the rational Utopia, and Bulgakov's responses to the increasing restrictions imposed in cultural affairs should also be regarded in this light. But rather than becoming involved in any way in the public literary debates of the period, he soon withdrew and adopted a detached stance. The attitudes which we can then read into his works concerning the significance of literature, the nature of the creative process, and the role of the artist are all significantly informed by the heritage of Romantic thought.

In relating Bulgakov to a trend in European intellectual history as elusive and as broad as Romanticism, which was at the same time so profoundly influential and far-reaching in its effects on the cultural profile of the nineteenth century, I am not suggesting that he particularly modelled himself on any one of its exponents, nor that he conducted any sort of a systematic investigation of the subject. The kinship between his views and what are generally held to constitute the essence of Romantic ideas about the artistic calling is nevertheless striking. Furthermore, his response differs considerably from those of most twentieth-century post-Romantic writers, amongst whom the foremost are recognized to be the Symbolists. Bulgakov shares with the Symbolists a high esteem for the person of the artist and for the value of art; but he lacks their emotional mysticism, their early self-indulgent aestheticism, and their overriding concern with beauty. The inevitable gulf set between them by the poetic form, which Bulgakov found so uncongenial, is made deeper by the Symbolist fascination with the resonance of words and their delight in indeterminacies of meaning. The Symbolists' prose works bring them no closer to Bulgakov; there is an enormous distance between the inward-looking structure and language of, say, Bely's *Peterburg* (*Petersburg*) and the shifting patterns and multivalent scope of *The Master and Margarita*. If anything, Bulgakov is more in sympathy with the quieter pretensions of the Acmeists, and of Mandel'shtam in particular, although of course when the latter looks back and yearns for world culture, it is to the classical world or to Dante that he turns, rather than to the nineteenth century. But where the Symbolists are inclined to elevate the figure of the poet in hubristic self-aggrandizement, Mandel'shtam, and Bulgakov after him, see him in more sober terms, though with no less a sense of the dignity of the poetic vocation. In the Pushkinian tradition, they place a high value on physical reality, while Symbolist thought is prone to considering reality a mere and contemptible stopping-place on the way towards a mystical realm to which only they, the chosen, will accede. The way that Pushkin's more unpretentious conviction that the poet has a vital spiritual role to play is passed down to Mandel'shtam's generation together with a belief in the poet's ethical responsibilities has been commented on by Max Hayward:

It was thanks to Pushkin that the Word, embodied in poetry, became almost sacrosanct in the literal sense, evoking a feeling akin to religious awe: the poet is high priest ... For this reason, in the Soviet period one or two poets were able to survive as the repositories of alternative values. It would have been impossible without Pushkin, the supreme legislator even in death: he laid it down that the spirit, whose voice he was, is *absolutely free*.[5]

While Bulgakov is clearly not one of the 'poets' Hayward has in mind here, there are nevertheless important ways in which he shares in this tradition; and his personal Romantic inspiration overlaps in many respects with the Symbolist and Acmeist view of their craft.

Apart from the Symbolists, to whom the label neo-Romantic is sometimes attached, Soviet criticism has seen a number of other writers as representatives of a new Romantic school. Some Soviet interpretations of the Symbolist aesthetic have considered their fascination with Romantic ideas a decadent obsession with the grotesque, the occult and the absurd, which leads to an excessive preoccupation with the individual and with morbidly mystical philosophies; and they refer instead to a healthier branch of Romanticism epitomized in the earlier works of Gor'ky. And it is indeed from Gor'ky himself that we can date the equation which is so often made in Soviet criticism between Romanticism and idealism (in the non-philosophical sense of the word). This arises in an important distinction enunciated by Gor'ky in 1928 in his essay *O tom, kak ya uchilsya pisat'* (*How I Learned to Write*):

In Romanticism it is vital to distinguish ... two sharply differing tendencies: passive Romanticism, which either attempts to reconcile man with reality by embellishing it, or to distract him from reality towards a sterile absorption in his internal world, towards reflections about the 'fateful riddles of life', about love and about death; towards riddles which cannot be resolved by means of 'speculation' and contemplation, but can only be solved by science. Active Romanticism, on the other hand, strives to strengthen man's will for life, to provoke in him a rebelliousness towards reality and against its every oppression.[6]

This distinction may originally have derived from Schiller, who in his discussion of naive and sentimental poetry divided 'sentimental' poets into two categories, those who mourn the lost world of nature and become elegiac poets, and those who criticize the defects of the real world and become satirists.[7] This notion was later taken up by

Belinsky, who differentiated what he called 'Romanticism in the spirit of the Middle Ages' from 'the new Romanticism'. In the first category he placed works describing an attitude where the here and now is detested and rejected in favour of an unattainable ideal; while in the second, creative use is made of hatred of the status quo, and a real possibility of improving the world is posited.[8] In the Soviet period the division of Romanticism into two categories has informed a long process, which is still continuing, whereby what Gor'ky termed 'passive' Romanticism is heavily attacked, while 'active' Romanticism is shown to form part of that circle of ideas which have furthered the development of socialism.

Initially the response to Gor'ky's ideas, which had had the intention of making the term Romanticism acceptable, was unequivocally hostile; Fadeyev, in a virulent speech entitled *Doloy Shillera!* (*Down with Schiller!*) given to a meeting of RAPP in 1929, argued that by definition all forms of Romanticism were reactionary.[9] In the course of time, however, this fundamentalist view came to be modified when idealism and imagination gained more respectability as components of socialist art, and 'revolutionary Romanticism' came to be acknowledged as a basic ingredient of socialist realism, a means of accommodating the dream of the goal within the strict realism of literary description. By the mid-1940s, Fadeyev himself was to be one of the most ardent exponents of 'revolutionary Romanticism'. In recent years, the study of Romanticism in the Soviet Union has seen a long-overdue reassessment of the Russian Romantic movement itself; but there seems to be an increasing tendency to subsume the term Romanticism in its twentieth-century manifestations into the notion of socialist realism as a *stylistic* tendency, and to disregard the movement's potential significance as a set of radical ideas. What is more, so many different 'Romanticisms' seem to have been invented in order to include writers as varied as Grin, Olesha, Babel', Paustovsky and even Chekhov under the somewhat indiscriminate heading of Romantics, that the term becomes pointlessly vague and loses its usefulness as a definition. And I shall hope to demonstrate that Bulgakov's Romanticism is altogether of a different nature to the Romanticism of these writers, who in certain cases earn the title through what might rather be called their sentimentality.

Bulgakov remains firmly entrenched in a traditional form of Romanticism, almost to the point of anachronism, at a time when those around him, whether Symbolists or revolutionary Romantics, were all seeking redefinitions of the term. In its original form in the nineteenth century, Romanticism had represented a step forwards, a liberation from the stultifying yoke of neoclassicism; but now, in the twentieth century, neoclassical attitudes were reasserting themselves in the guise of socialist realism, which had inherited its proscriptive and prescriptive tenets. If Romanticism had originally represented the rejection of a past, for Bulgakov the assumption of Romantic attitudes indicated the rejection of a future.

But what precise elements of the Romantic tradition can be said most to have inspired Bulgakov's presentation of the writer and of his craft? The first notion that we typically associate with Romanticism is subjectivity; the author retreats from claims to impartiality and asserts, on the contrary, the individuality of his vision. He makes the reader aware of the author's presence, whether as a supposedly real self (Maksudov in *A Theatrical Novel*), as a narrator whose personality is meant to be perceived as separate from that of the real author (the intermittent voice of the dog Sharik, for instance, in *The Heart of a Dog*), or as a character in the work (the narrator with his goosequill in *The Life of Monsieur de Molière*). This self-awareness of the writer in his works is an aspect of the complex notion of 'Romantic irony'. One striking form which this subjectivism can assume is the inclusion in the work of a character, himself a writer, whose opinions and experiences we are seemingly invited to identify with those of the author; a characteristic instance of this kind of ambiguity is to be found in the quite evidently implausible disclaimers of responsibility for the work which open Bulgakov's *A Theatrical Novel* (273). And one of the last critics in the Soviet Union to approach Romanticism in the spirit of the European critical tradition, A. I. Beletsky, sums up the problem as follows:

It is typical of Romantic heroes that they are all to a greater or lesser degree self-portraits, and the reader perceives them as such despite the semi-serious excuses authors make in their prefaces and the provisos made in the very text of the works.[10]

Whatever the ultimate distinctions which, as critics, we may feel bound to draw between artist, hero, and artist–hero, it is entirely characteristic of Romantic writing that these distinctions should deliberately be blurred by the author himself.

The Romantic interest in the individual, held to have been initiated with the writing by Rousseau of his *Confessions* (1765–70), has important implications for the writer's choice of genre. While the supreme Romantic genre remains the lyric poem, the general shift in interest towards the personality of the author fostered the development of all kinds of biographical and autobiographical writing, both of which are strongly represented in Bulgakov's oeuvre. Romantic irony, in drawing our attention to the fictionality of a work, is creatively used by Bulgakov to heighten the tension between historicity and fiction in his portrayal of a historical figure in the biography of Molière.

The French Revolution of 1789 heralded the arrival of a vital new concern in European thought with the notion of freedom, which was to become one of the banners of the Romantic movement. This had implications for the aesthetic position of the writer, but also for his political stance. In the latter case, the desire for freedom might either tempt the individual to opt for revolutionary commitment or, on the contrary, to an assertion of his right to determine his fate without regard for the needs of society, an option which laid a number of Romantic thinkers open to charges of social indifference or escapism. In Romantic writing the importance of the hero relative to the society in which he belongs is almost invariably magnified as, consequently, is the distance – of hostility and incomprehension – which separates them. Bulgakov's heroes are by no means Byronic, asserting their superiority in arrogant defiance of society's conventions; nevertheless, they act in an essentially egocentric and anti-democratic manner, much to the fury of Bulgakov's Establishment critics. His writer–hero shows no interest whatsoever in social issues, but rather, as one critic has said of Baudelaire, 'remains true to a central Romantic tradition in abstaining from any attempt to alter the social order'.[11] This type of Romantic is no reformer, he is a dreamer; society responds by viewing him with suspicion, and it is rare for a hope of reconciliation to be posited. Authority invariably interprets such indifference to its majesty as inherently subversive. The vital Romantic theme of the relations between the artist and authority is ushered in by Goethe in his play *Torquato Tasso* (final version 1789), where he gives a portrayal of Tasso as he comes to a realization of his need to shrug off the constraints of patronage. But Goethe was dealing with a delicate issue of etiquette and honour; in

Bulgakov's hands, the theme was to take on a more acute significance, since Molière and Pushkin, like Bulgakov himself, could
incur very serious penalties when they jeopardized the favour of
their patrons. In the Soviet period Bulgakov is one of the first prose
writers to deal at length with these problems of artistic freedom.
The other way in which the Romantic artist expresses his
freedom and independence is by disregarding the requirements of
aesthetic conventions. Where Pope in his *Essay on Criticism* had
addressed himself to the critic rather than to the poet, and had
sought to establish extrinsic criteria for the evaluation of a work,
where Boileau had insisted on the need for adherence to the
Aristotelian unities, the Romantic movement proclaimed the
freedom of the artist to create as he pleased. As Bulgakov puts it in
his biography of Molière:

Even by summoning Aristotle to his assistance, no-one will ever succeed
in proving that a successful work which is written in good verse, has an
interesting plot, and contains effective and well-delineated parts, is not a
play.   (102)

The Romantic emphasis was always on the intrinsic qualities of the
work, rather than on the extrinsic criteria of morality, utility, or
conformity to aesthetic standards. Poe's pronouncement to the
effect that the concern of poetry was neither truth, nor duty, but
beauty alone, was seized upon by Baudelaire and became a
cornerstone of Symbolist aesthetics.[12] And although Bulgakov
certainly prized integrity even above beauty, he nevertheless aligns
himself with the Romantic outlook on aesthetic regulations in his
stance against censorship and in his disregard for the tenets of
socialist realism. The rich allusiveness of his style, which implies a
refusal to accommodate himself to the lack of education of the new
mass audiences, is a further mark of his refusal to submit to external
requirements. This exclusivity, which need not be equated with the
arrogant pose of some of the Symbolist poets, can in fact lead to
tragic loneliness for the poet, as described by Gogol:

Alas! it is an incontrovertible truth: that the more a poet becomes a poet,
the more he depicts feelings familiar only to poets, the more noticeably the
crowd surrounding him thins out, until finally it becomes so restricted that
he can count all the true appreciators of his work on his two hands.[13]

So the Romantic image of the artist contains elements both of the
exalted genius and of the alienated victim. He may be surrounded

by such a mystique that we are invited to draw a parallel between his creative powers and those of a god, or at the very least those of a prophet or visionary. In Russia the elevated view of the poet's status had always been very potent, both before and after 1917; and Soviet criticism has continued to the present day to allow the poet an exalted position, remaining unmoved either by the Proletkul't and RAPP attempts in the 1920s to challenge this prestige accorded to the writer, or by the formalists' exclusion of the personality of the writer from the scope of their investigations on theoretical grounds. It is a continuing paradox of the reality of socialist–realist practices that the writer should be singled out so much for honour. The Romantic artist, however, is also frequently portrayed as the victim of an uncomprehending society, persecuted in the idealistic pursuit of his vision, and doomed for the sake of his art. His sacred ideal is often in the end unattainable, which is why so many portrayals of Romantic heroes seem to verge on the ironic. The Romantic concern is with noble failures rather than heroic successes.

The paradoxical relationship between nobility and failure becomes the specific object of Bulgakov's concern in his 1937–8 adaptation of *Don Quixote*, a task undertaken when he was already conscious that his career was drawing to a close. Peter Doyle has analysed the way in which succeeding generations have accorded the tale of Don Quixote a varying reception: initially seen as a mocking satire on the fantastical behaviour induced in Don Quixote by excessive indulgence in reading tales of chivalry, it was interpreted in the nineteenth century as a tragedy depicting the failure of idealism. The modern view treats *Don Quixote* as a work of ambivalence evoking the uncertainties of truth and morality. The Russian tradition, perhaps predictably, has always leaned towards the second view of the work, and Bulgakov is no exception.[14] The actor Cherkasov, whose career largely grew out of his portrayal of Quixote in a number of different adaptations of the novel, commented in his memoirs that of all the interpretations he had performed, Bulgakov's was the most tragic.[15] For although it recounts a selection of Quixote's adventures very much in the spirit of Cervantes's text, Bulgakov's adaptation gains its real power from the lyrical impact of its opening and closing scenes, where he frames the main story in an atmosphere of melancholic pessimism. And in a key moment in the play Don Quixote brings together the functions of the poet and of the knight when he upbraids Sancho for his obstinacy in seeing Quixote's Dulcinea as the flesh-and-blood Aldonza:

The poet and the knight praise and love not the woman who is made of flesh and blood, but the woman who has been created by his inexhaustible fantasy! I love her as she figured in my dreams! Oh, Sancho, I love my ideal![16]

The poignancy of the moment derives from Quixote's near-awareness that he is pursuing a chimera. But in the original, as in Bulgakov's interpretation, he retains his honour precisely because he remains faithful to his fantasy. The artists in Bulgakov's other works similarly gain in stature by remaining faithful to their inspiration. When Quixote at the end of Bulgakov's play admits to his friends that he has been allowing his delusions to get the better of his reason, this is not a moment of triumph, with the madman restored at last to sanity; it is a tragic realization of the prosaic nature of reality as the dreamer sinks towards death.

In the opening scene of this adaptation, Bulgakov not only shows that Quixote has culled all his ideas on honour from his reading of tales of chivalry, but even that he has come so to confuse fiction with reality that when he wants to describe to Aldonza what he hopes will be his future, he does so by reading *verbatim* from a written text (8–9). The way that he embraces unquestioningly and in its entirety a literary evocation of a chivalric ideal constitutes a Romantic visionary experience, in that it offers an escape from an alien present into other worlds. Sometimes this is an escape into the past as evoked by the nostalgic notion of 'the golden age'; or the Romantic artist's vision may lead him into the future, or indeed beyond the bounds of the physical world altogether. In their understanding of the nature of the poetic vision, the Romantics took up the Platonic notion that beauty captures but a fraction of the marvels which exist in some higher reality. Poe, for example, in his lecture on *The Poetic Principle*, described the artistic endeavour as follows:

Inspired by an ecstatic prescience of the glories beyond the grave, we struggle, by multiform combinations among the things and thoughts of Time, to attain a portion of that Loveliness, whose very elements, perhaps, appertain to eternity alone.[17]

The artist does not have permanent access to the 'glories beyond the grave', although he is privileged briefly to enter the higher

reality in moments of inspiration; perhaps after death he may hope
to enter into full enjoyment of those glories, but meanwhile his
inspiration can serve as a bridge between the temporal and the
eternal, with art, as William Blake suggests, partaking rather of the
higher realm than of dull, mortal reality:

This world of Imagination is the world of Eternity; it is the divine bosom
into which we shall all go after the death of the Vegetated body ... There
exists in that Eternal world the Permanent Realities of Every Thing which
we see reflected in this Vegetable Glass of Nature.[18]

Art is here seen as a means – perhaps the only means – of
penetrating to some sort of universal truth.[19]

The work of art which arises out of the artist's inspiration does
not have to correspond to or reproduce that universal truth; the
experience of inspiration above all illuminates and confirms the
artist's ideas, for he is not just a passive vessel. In a discussion of the
Romantics' attitudes to the relationship between truth and reality,
Isaiah Berlin has emphasized that

there runs through their writings a common notion, held with varying
degrees of consciousness and depth, that truth is not an objective structure,
independent of those who seek it, the hidden treasure waiting to be found,
but is itself in all its guises created by the seeker.[20]

In the Romantic view of inspiration the focus of interest is always
on the artist himself rather than on the product of his labours, so
that what matters is not necessarily that he has had a *particular*
vision, but that he has attained some sort of state of grace which
allows him to be granted that inspiration. The strict content of the
work of art is ultimately of lesser significance than the sincerity with
which it is executed. Bulgakov's portrayal of his 'thrice Romantic
Master' (798), and the latter's relationship to his work is difficult to
understand outside this Romantic tradition; in the Master's case, as
it happens, the truth *is* presented as an objective and independent
entity, but we have seen earlier that it is not offered as a dogma,
and is validated by the Master's integrity.

A different branch of Romanticism has a rather less rosy vision of
the world than the idealistic one described above, and insists on
ultimate irrationality, seeing no reason to assume that the forces
which govern the world are benevolent. These Romantics portray
mortals as being subject to the whims of the devil or of other evil
forces which erupt unpredictably into the world of normality. This

is far removed from the common sense of the neoclassical outlook
and even from that of the classical world, where malicious spirits
were at least usually nameable and the causes of their anger
identifiable. The works of Hoffmann and Poe evoke a nightmarish
world where sanity is always in doubt, a world of the fantastic and
the grotesque which was to provide inspiration for writers as
different as Gogol and Melville. Stories using horror, suspense and
mystery to achieve their effects often derive from this tradition;
these might be fairy-tales for adults where supernatural experience
forms part of the logic of the work; detective stories, where the
reader is eventually reassured of the rational explanation for a
mystery; or science fiction, which as a mixed genre can culminate in
either a rational or an irrational explanation. Bulgakov's reading of
these genres, as described in Chapter 1, introduced him to a darker
vision which is particularly reflected in his work of the early 1920s.

One author in this tradition whose works held a special fascination for Bulgakov was E. T. A. Hoffmann, who had been redis-
covered and translated by the Symbolists at the turn of the
century.[21] In the summer of 1938 Bulgakov wrote an excited letter
to Yelena Sergeyevna, who was having a holiday in Lebedyan'
while Bulgakov, during what was virtually the only separation of
their entire married life, dictated the last draft of *The Master and
Margarita*:

Dear friend Lyusya!
  By chance I have come across an article about the fantastic in Hoffmann.
I am keeping it for you, since I know that it will stun you as much as it has
me. I am right in *The Master and Margarita*! You will understand what this
discovery means to me; I am right![22]

The article in question was I. Mirimsky's 'Sotsial'naya fantastika
Gofmana' ('Hoffmann's Social Fantasy'), an annotated copy of
which has survived in Bulgakov's archive to the present day.[23]
Yermolinsky recounts that Bulgakov subsequently used to read
extracts from it to his friends, without explaining that it was about
Hoffmann, and suggesting that it was in fact a contemporary
assessment of his own works.[24] His friends were certainly taken in
by the game, for the apparent relevance to Bulgakov of remarks
quoted from Hoffmann – and of Mirimsky's own commentaries on
him – is almost uncanny. The article includes a description of the
devil's visit to the city (Berlin), a discussion of the close relationship
between irony and tragedy and between the real and the fantastic

places in Hoffmann's works, and it continues with an examination
of Hoffmann's portrayal of the artist in terms which are undeniably
applicable to Bulgakov:

The genuine artist is doomed to tragic solitude in this world, where life and
true art are infinitely distant from one another ... The tragedy of Kreisler
is the tragedy of the helplessness of art in the face of a reality which is
inimical to art ... For Hoffmann, the artist is a man not of this world ...
[Kreisler] was evidently seeking in vain for a haven where he might at last
find clarity and calm, without which the artist cannot create ... The artist
rises at will above all that is finite, including his own art; in the incorporeal
realm which he creates, the artist's will can be regarded as a universal
means of liberation from the real world.[25]

Mirimsky goes on to comment on the multifaceted nature of the
character of Kater Murr, who is at once a philistine and a scholar, a
solid burgher and a moralist; a figure Bulgakov takes up parodically
in the character of Begemot. Yanovskaya, who has had access to
Bulgakov's copy of the article, gives an interesting account of
some of the passages which Bulgakov underlined, presumably as
being of particular relevance to himself and to his artistic outlook;
one section, where Mirimsky discusses the destiny of the artist in
Hoffmann's work, could serve equally well to sum up the Master's
plight in *The Master and Margarita*:

If the man of genius makes his peace with reality, it will lead him to the
morass of philistinism, to an 'honourable' official way of thinking; but if he
doesn't entirely give in to reality, then he will end in premature death or
madness.[26]

In the earlier part of his career, in works such as the *Diaboliad*
collection, Bulgakov had consciously modelled himself on Hoffmann and Gogol for his treatment of fantastical subjects; by his last
years, he found confirmation in this study of Hoffmann of the
'rightness' of his most cherished values concerning the artist's
destiny, blending together the story of Hoffmann's reception as a
writer and his accounts of the writer as a fictional hero, rather as he
saw the story of his own life blending into that of his heroes.

Another characteristic theme of the darker branch of Romantic
writing is the uncertainty of identity. Where Shakespeare, for
example, uses twins and mistaken identities as comic obstacles in
the way of the plot's progression towards a happy ending, the
device of the 'Doppelgänger' is used by Jean Paul and Hoffmann to

create a sinister atmosphere where reality is constantly elusive. This theme is directly taken up by Bulgakov in the title story of the *Diaboliad* collection, while Romantic atmospherics of horror pervade stories such as *The Fateful Eggs* and *The Heart of a Dog*. In Bulgakov's mature works, however, his sense of the irrational becomes contained within a more organized vision of the world, as expressed in Woland's words to Margarita concerning the ultimate 'rightness' of the way the world is organized (797). What unites both the darker and the more positive – if scarcely joyful – vision of Bulgakov's early and late works is the fundamental Romantic belief that there is more to the world than immediate reality.

This is not to suggest, of course, that the Romantic outlook embraces a conventional religious explanation of the world; the relationship between the Romantics and organized religion is subtle and complex. In his study of the English Romantics, Bowra makes the remark that

They were, too, in their own way, religious, in their sense of the holiness of reality and the awe which they felt in its presence. But, so far as their central beliefs were concerned, they were not orthodox . . . The Romantic movement was a prodigious attempt to discover the world of spirit through the unaided efforts of the solitary soul.[27]

The fundamentally subjective nature of Romanticism, always contemplating the world through the eyes of the individual, means that religion comes to be regarded almost as a symbolical or metaphorical system whose terminology and concepts can be freely borrowed and adapted in order to describe individual experience. The poet figures as a demon, or else as a god; his inspiration is seen in terms of possession; and the sum of his oeuvre comes to constitute the sum of his deeds, providing the evidence upon which he will be judged. This sacralization of literature is by no means hostile to or incompatible with a code of morality; but good and evil are seen as a dilemma of the individual, who has the freedom to make his own choices and decisions on the path towards salvation or damnation; Romanticism insists on individual responsibility. One consequence of the way that the Romantic takes over the language of religion is that his challenge to authority is evoked in terms of defiance of God, of blasphemy, or of a pact with the devil. Romanticism was indeed to foster an actual fascination with the occult which was subsequently to be of considerable significance to the Symbolists.

To sum up, then, Romanticism is a semi-mystical movement

which, without conforming to religious convention, arrogates its language in order to suggest art's penetration into a higher realm. It is particularly fascinated with the image of man standing at the threshold of death and therefore of judgement; this was to be an essential concern for Bulgakov, who portrays Molière, Pushkin and Don Quixote, as well as the Master, all as they approach death. Romanticism tries to suggest that the function of art is to bring to the world an adumbration of what lies above and beyond, thereby virtually claiming for art the status of a religion. Bulgakov's treatment of religious themes, notably in *The Master and Margarita*, has to be set against this context of Romantic thought in order to become fully comprehensible. The question of the exact nature of Bulgakov's religious beliefs remains as yet unclear, but his knowledge of and sensitivity to ritual and to Biblical scholarship do not seem to have been paralleled by any actual participation in religious observances. In his portraits of the artist, he always in the end refers, as we have seen, to the influence of fate rather than to that of a deity as the final authority determining the writer's destiny. In *The Master and Margarita*, Bulgakov's exploration of religious themes serves to reveal his preoccupation with the problem of the modern age's lack of spirituality, interweaving attitudes to both literature and religion as measures of the new philistinism.

Last days

As Bulgakov looked back in the last few years of his life over the setbacks and rejections which had characterized his literary career, his consciousness of failure combined with a prescience of approaching death to give rise to a series of statements of deep pessimism. The severe blow of the banning of *The Cabal of Hypocrites* in March 1936 marked the end of all his hopes of being able to survive in his chosen profession; it also, in the event, was to prove the destruction of his last attempt to speak about the plight of the writer in print or on stage. In June 1936 the composer Asaf'yev invited Bulgakov to write the libretto for his opera *Minin and Pozharsky*, and this offered the prospect of a solution to his disaffection with MKhAT; in September Bulgakov duly resigned from MKhAT and joined the Bol'shoy theatre, undertaking to write one libretto for them a year. But it was not a means of dispelling his deep depression, as we can

see from his letter of 5 October 1936 to his friend Yakov Leont'yevich Leont'yev:

Today is a day of celebration for me. Exactly ten years ago the première of
the 'Turbins' took place. It's the tenth anniversary.
    I sit by my inkwell and wait for the door to open and for a delegation
from Stanislavsky and Nemirovich to appear with a speech and some
expensive mark of tribute. All my ruined or maimed plays will be
enumerated in the speech, and a list will be drawn up of all the joys which
they, Stan. and Nem., have brought me in ten years at Arts Theatre Street.
The expensive tribute will take the form of a large saucepan made of some
kind of precious metal (copper, for example), filled with all the blood they
have sucked from me in ten years.[28]

And in a letter on the same day to Popov he describes how it was
that he finally took the decision to leave MKhAT:

I was in a state of terrible confusion, misery and brooding, which
culminated in my sending in my resignation to the Arts Theatre and
breaking off my contract for the Merry Wives.
    Enough! Everything has to have a limit . . .
    Give an order for a bottle of Clicquot to be brought up from your cellar,
and drink to the health of The Days of the Turbins; today the play
celebrates its tenth anniversary. I take off my greasy writer's skull-cap to
the old lady, my wife in turn congratulates me, and there's an end to the
anniversary.[29]

In November 1936 Bulgakov returned to the project he had
embarked on in September 1929 under the title For my Secret
Friend, feeling in this second 'year of catastrophe' a renewed urge
to give an autobiographical account of the vagaries of his writing
career. In her article on Bulgakov's archive Chudakova has provided us with a facsimile illustration of the first page of the
manuscript of what became A Theatrical Novel. It is dated 26
November 1936, and it is possible to see that although the original
title to the work was indeed 'Teatral'ny roman' ('A Theatrical
Novel'), Bulgakov later added above it the title which has been
used as a subtitle in the published version: 'Zapiski pokoynika'
('Notes of the Deceased').[30] The latter was underlined three times,
which might suggest that this was in the end his favoured title for
the work; it would certainly have been particularly appropriate,
since it can be taken not only to refer to Maksudov's suicide, which
is anticipated in the Foreword to the work, but also assumes a more
acerbic autobiographical relevance as an expression of Bulgakov's
feeling that he had already undergone his literary death.

The year 1937 was, as we know, no easier for Bulgakov, and a series of letters to Asaf'yev about *Minin and Pozharsky* traces the course of his unhappiness:

9.1.37 – Things are difficult for me, and I feel bad. The obsessive thought of my ruined literary life and of my hopeless future engenders other black thoughts . . . from my heart I wish you what is running out for me; strength.

24.3.37 – Do you know, despite all the hardships with which I am paying for my literary life, despite my weariness and gloom, I am following *Minin* very closely, and I am doing all that I can to get the opera on stage.

10.5.37 – I've been suffering for a month now from complete nervous exhaustion.

2.10.37 – Over the last seven years I have written sixteen things in various genres, and they have all perished. This is an impossible situation, and our home is filled with utter hopelessness and gloom.

18.12.37 – Your hypothesis that I have been recommended not to associate with you is entirely groundless. Absolutely no-one has recommended any such thing, and if anyone should think of doing so, then I'm the sort of person, let me tell you, who is capable of not obeying. And I was quite confident that you knew me well enough, that you knew that I wasn't like the others. I send you a reproach![31]

This last letter reminds us that the Stalinist terror was at its height in 1937 – the letter of 10 May mentions the arrest of the Bol'shoy director, Mutnykh – so that the apprehensions and anxieties these letters reveal are not unfounded imaginings. And in April 1937 he was writing to Veresayev in a similar vein:

I am very exhausted, and I am brooding. My recent attempts to write for the theatre were pure quixotry on my part. And I won't repeat them. You won't find me any more on the theatrical front. I've had experience, and I've suffered too much.[32]

By the autumn of 1937 Bulgakov's defeat was rendered complete as it became apparent that *Minin and Pozharsky* was going to be abandoned by the Bol'shoy in favour of a production of *Ivan Susanin*,[33] and as a fleeting hope that *Flight* might be staged if Bulgakov was prepared to make some alterations to it also vanished. At this point Bulgakov decided to give up *A Theatrical Novel* and devote his energies to completing *The Master and Margarita*, although it is difficult to credit Chudakova's view that he now imagined there would be some chance of getting it published.[34] His sense that this work would mark the end of his literary career is summed up in his description of it on 15 June 1938 as his 'last sunset novel'.[35]

When Bulgakov refers in his letter to Veresayev to the extent of his sufferings, we are reminded that in absolute terms, of course, his experiences were less devastating than the fate of so many others, including friends and acquaintances, during those traumatic years. At the time, the telephone calls he received from Stalin and the way in which Stalin appeared to take a personal interest in his career aroused a good deal of comment in literary circles.[36] His position was scarcely enviable, even if he was spared the horrors of trial and imprisonment; but the one act which has come close to tarnishing his reputation was the writing of his play *Batum*, a play about the young Stalin and his part in revolutionary circles in Batum prior to 1905.[37] One is particularly at a loss to understand why the initial conception of it should have dated back to 1936, just after a very successful dress rehearsal of *The Cabal of Hypocrites*, unless he was already having a premonition of the disaster that would soon strike.[38] When he returned to the *Batum* project in 1939, it was at the behest of friends from MKhAT concerned about his future and that of his family, and although the crisis over its cancellation precipitated the onset of his final illness, it is difficult to believe that the destruction of this particular theatrical project otherwise meant as much to him as his earlier failures.[39] All things considered, the text is not excessively eulogistic, and its very dullness seems to indicate that Bulgakov was by no means wholeheartedly involved in its writing. On the whole, Bulgakov can be said to have preserved his political integrity. A specific example of this is the letter he presumed to address to Stalin on 4 February 1938 on behalf of one of his close friends, the playwright Nikolay Erdman:

Permit me to turn to you with a request concerning the playwright Nikolay Robertovich Erdman, who has fully completed his three-year sentence of exile in the towns of Yeniseisk and Tomsk, and who is currently living in the town of Kalinin.

Confident in the fact that literary gifts are extremely highly prized in our fatherland, and knowing at the same time that the writer Nikolay Erdman is currently deprived of the opportunity to practise his skills as the result of the negative attitude which has developed towards him, and which has been sharply voiced in the press, I take the liberty of asking you to turn your attention to his fate.

In the hope that the lot of the writer N. Erdman might be relieved if you were to think it worthwhile considering this request, I ask wholeheartedly for N. Erdman to be given the possibility of returning to Moscow and of working in literature without hindrance, so that he might escape from his solitary state and his spiritual depression.[40]

It is not known whether this carefully worded letter, which was written as part of a concerted campaign by all Erdman's friends on his behalf, had any direct effect, but apparently Bulgakov himself believed that he had succeeded in alleviating his friend's situation with his appeal. Of the three friends, Zamyatin, Erdman and Bulgakov, who during the 1920s were classed among the extreme right wing of the 'fellow-travellers', Zamyatin eventually emigrated, Erdman returned to Moscow and was reconciled to the Establishment – he even found himself dragooned during the war into writing sketches for the NKVD song and dance ensemble – while Bulgakov established a rather more reserved *modus vivendi* with the régime after having been refused permission on several occasions to leave the country. Bulgakov preserved for himself a modicum of inner freedom throughout his experience of oppression in the secret composition of *The Master and Margarita*, a work of disaffection which undoubtedly ranks alongside *We*. Edwards has classed Zamyatin and Bulgakov together with Pil'nyak as writers who all, in the Dostoyevskian tradition, reject the technological Utopia, but he rightly concludes that this is achieved in *Goly god* (*The Naked Year*) and *We* using rather a different approach to that adopted in *The Master and Margarita*:

Bulgakov's novel more directly draws on the writing and thought of the pre-revolution and thereby constitutes an implicit and fundamental rejection of the Soviet present.[41]

Where Zamyatin's desire for continual change and suspicion of complacency suggests an alienation from the status quo, rather than from the present as such, Bulgakov turns so abruptly away from the culture and institutions of the present that it is difficult ever to imagine a reconciliation.

Bulgakov's strength of personality gave him the courage of his conviction that his determination to live by the cultural standards of the old world was legitimate, and it was underpinned by his absolute sense of vocation. To some, this appeared a somewhat exaggerated, self-important stance, as some rather malicious comments by Katayev make clear:

Blue-eyes ... was altogether a conservative; he deeply respected all the recognized pre-Revolutionary authorities, and couldn't stand the Commander [Mayakovsky], Meyerkhol'd, or Tatlin ... He liked to give instruction; there was something of the mentor in him. One got the impression that to him alone had been revealed the higher truths, not only of art, but of human life in general ... Blue-eyes slightly played up the role of the famous Russian writer, not to say classic, and went around at home in striped flannelette pyjamas gathered at the back with elastic, which didn't conceal his elegant figure, and, of course, in well-worn slippers.[42]

And Yermolinsky felt that he occasionally affected his conservatism in order to provoke his friends:

More than once he teased his interlocutors with his predilection for 'conservatism in art'. 'It's marvellous when the curtains don't open, but rise, and when the curtain is adorned with flying cupids,' he would say, 'but then these days they perform with no curtain at all.' ... 'It's utterly sickening,' Bulgakov would complain, 'all the mystery of the theatre vanishes ... But I dream of reintroducing an orchestra to play in theatres during the intervals, like they used to have in the provinces.'[43]

But there can be no doubt that his outlook was indeed largely formed by the past and by his cultural heritage; even by accepting the role of the suffering artist misjudged by the world he is fulfilling a familiar stereotype in Romantic thinking. Pavel Markov, one of Bulgakov's more sensitive critics and friends, has characterized his feelings about the writer's vocation as follows:

Bulgakov understood literature as a calling, as a duty, as an internal necessity; without it, life became meaningless for him.[44]

The poem which Akhmatova wrote in March 1940, immediately after Bulgakov's death, pays tribute to his moral courage in remaining faithful to his own ideals – a compliment indeed from one who had herself undergone so much, and who had only recently learned of the death of Mandel'shtam – and she offers it to him as a gift in the knowledge that even in his lifetime there was a great distance between the languages of their art:

Вот это я тебе, взамен могильных роз,
Взамен кадильного куренья;
Ты так сурово жил и до конца донёс
Великолепное презренье.
Ты пил вино, ты как никто шутил
И в душных стенах задыхался,
И гостью страшную ты сам к себе впустил
И с ней наедине остался.

(I offer this to you in place of graveside roses, instead of smoking incense; you lived so severely, and carried to the end your magnificent disdain. You drank wine, you were an incomparable jester, you gasped for breath in stifling walls, and you let in your awesome guest yourself, and remained with her alone.)[45]

But perhaps the most moving comment of all comes from Pavel Popov, who paid tribute to his friend in a letter written to him in December 1939, when the hopelessness of Bulgakov's condition had become apparent. It is a subjective, very loving assessment in a private letter between old friends; yet Popov, who had made it his business to study Bulgakov's art during his lifetime, and who had immediately been struck by the scale of his achievement, identifies some telling features of his art:

Reading the lines you have written, you know that there is a genuine literary culture: transported by fantasy to the places you describe, you understand that creative imagination has not dried up, that the lamp lit by the Romantics, Hoffmann, and so on, burns and gleams, and that altogether the art of words has not forsaken mankind ... Your every word, even if casually uttered, is a work of art, whatever it is that you are speaking about. Everything else relating to literature is shallow before you ... and I have always wanted, as I still want, to kiss the hand of the man who wrote Molière.[46]

Notes

I THE TEMPERING OF THE STEEL

1 From *Razgovor o Dante*, *Sobraniye sochineniy* (New York, 1971), vol. 2, 384.

2 The novel was first published in two parts in the journal *Moskva*, 11 (1966) and 1 (1967). The complete text is available in M. Bulgakov, *Romany* (Moscow, 1973), and in subsequent Soviet editions.

3 M. O. Chudakova, 'Arkhiv M. A. Bulgakova', in *Biblioteka SSSR imeni V. I. Lenina, Zapiski otdela rukopisey*, 37 (Moscow, 1976) (hereafter Chudakova, 'Arkhiv'); A. C. Wright, *Mikhail Bulgakov: Life and Interpretations* (Toronto, 1978) (hereafter Wright, *Mikhail Bulgakov*); L. Yanovskaya, *Tvorchesky put' Mikhaila Bulgakova* (Moscow, 1983) (hereafter Yanovskaya, *Tvorchesky put'*); E. Proffer, *Bulgakov – Life and Work* (Ann Arbor, 1984) (hereafter Proffer, *Bulgakov*).

4 The most rewarding of these are L. Milne, *'The Master and Margarita' – A Comedy of Victory* (Birmingham, 1977) (hereafter Milne, *'The Master and Margarita'*); H. El'baum, *Analiz iudeyskikh glav 'Mastera i Margarity' M. Bulgakova* (Ann Arbor, 1981) (hereafter El'baum); M. Kreps, *Bulgakov i Pasternak kak romanisty* (Ann Arbor, 1984) (hereafter Kreps); A. Zerkalov, *Yevangeliye Mikhaila Bulgakova* (Ann Arbor, 1984) (hereafter Zerkalov).

5 The story has been published in M. Bulgakov, *Rannjaja neizdannaja proza* (Munich, 1976), along with several of the available variants of the text. The dedication, omitted in M. A. Bulgakov, *Sobraniye sochineniy*, vol. 1 (Ann Arbor, 1982), is on p. 11.

6 *Rannjaja neizdannaja proza*, 201.

7 The story was first published in the newspaper *Nakanune*, 20 April 1924, p. 3, and is reprinted in *Rannjaja neizdannaja proza*, 158–73. The play *Bagrovy ostrov*, never published in the USSR, was first printed in M. Bulgakov, *P'esy* (Paris, 1971); further references will be given after quotations in the text.

8 For details of this letter see pp. 6 and 16 below.

9 See letter to K. P. Bulgakov of 16 February 1921, published by Ye. A. Zemskaya in 'M. A. Bulgakov: pis'ma k rodnym (1921–22g.)', *Izvestiya AN SSSR – seriya literatury i yazyka*, 35 (1976), no. 5, 451–64, p. 456 (hereafter Zemskaya).

10 I. Turkel'taub, 'Bagrovy ostrov v Moskovskom Kamernom Teatre', *Zhizn' iskusstva*, no. 52, 23 December 1928, 10–11 (p. 10).

11 A. Tairov, 'O bagrovom ostrove', *Sovremenny teatr*, no. 50, 11 November 1928, 803.

12 I. Bachelis, 'O belykh arapakh i krasnykh tuzemtsakh', *Molodaya gvardiya*, 1 (1929), 105–8 (p. 107).

13 P. Novitsky, 'Bagrovy ostrov', *Repertuarny byulleten'*, 12 (1928), 9–10 (p. 10).

14 Published in *Grani*, 66 (1967), 155–61 (pp. 157 and 158). This letter has provoked controversy which it will be impossible to resolve until access is granted to Bulgakov's archive (Fond 562) in the Lenin Library, Moscow. It appears that typed and signed copies of at least part of the letter exist in the archive, but the authenticity of the whole cannot be guaranteed.

15 M. Bulgakov, *Zhizn' gospodina de Mol'yera* (in the series 'Zhizn' zamechatel'nykh lyudey', Moscow, 1962), 108; further references will be given after quotations in the text.

16 *Teatral'ny roman*, published in *Romany* (Moscow, 1973), 287; further references will be given after quotations in the text.

17 For this information and what follows see L. Milne, 'K biografii M. A. Bulgakova', *Novy zhurnal*, 111 (June 1973), 151–74 (pp. 169–70) (hereafter Milne, 'K biografii'); also Yanovskaya, *Tvorchesky put'*, 193–5.

18 Quoted in Milne, 'K biografii', 169, note 3.

19 V. V. Mayakovsky, *Klop*, in *Sochineniya*, vol. 3 (Moscow, 1965), 506.

20 Milne, 'K biografii', 151 and 152–3; she points out that the letter may not actually have been sent in this form.

21 *Ibid.*, 153; although there is equally some doubt as to whether *this* letter was sent, the fact that some sort of letter was received is confirmed by the letter to Gor'ky cited immediately below.

22 *Ibid.*, 153.

23 *Ibid.*, 154; this letter is dated 28 September 1929.

24 Cited from Bulgakov's *Dni Turbinykh* album (no. 2), Pushkinsky Dom, F. 369, ed. khr. 77. He compiled these albums of cuttings and documents for several of his works.

25 Chudakova, 'Arkhiv', 56, note 73.

26 *Nedra*, 4 (Moscow, 1924), 221–57.

27 The story is reviewed in Zamyatin's essay 'O segodnyashnem i sov-remennom', first published in *Russky sovremennik*, 2 (1924), 263–72, and reprinted in his *Litsa* (New York, 1967), 211–30 (p. 217).

28 Letters of 3 August and 13 September 1928 (unpublished), Pushkinsky Dom, F. 369, ed. khr. 391.

29 *Ibid.*, and from further unpublished letters of 15 July 1929 and 23 October 1930.

30 *Ibid.*, letter of 15 July 1929; the play was taken on at the Vakhtangov theatre, and was performed in 1930–1 under the title *Sensatsiya*.

31 In *Neizdanny Bulgakov: teksty i materialy*, edited by E. Proffer (Ann Arbor, 1977), 25–7 (hereafter *Neizdanny Bulgakov*).
32 L. Ye. Belozerskaya-Bulgakova, *O, myod vospominaniy* (Ann Arbor, 1979) (hereafter *O, myod vospominaniy*), 82.
33 Quoted by A. M. Shane in *The Life and Works of Evgenij Zamjatin* (Berkeley and Los Angeles, 1968), 69.
34 *Ibid.*, 72.
35 Pushkinsky Dom, F. 369, ed. khr. 391; the letter is quoted in English in Proffer, *Bulgakov*, 332, where there is a misunderstanding of the word 'agasfery'. This is not a reference to 'the agasphere' (?), but a humorous plural of the name 'Agasfer' (Ahasuerus, the Wandering Jew).
36 Pushkinsky Dom, F. 369, ed. khr. 321, 322, 391 and 392.
37 *Ibid.*, ed. khr. 321.
38 Cited in Chudakova, 'Arkhiv', 81; some extracts from the manuscript have been published by L. Yanovskaya under the title 'Mne prisnilsya son' in *Nedelya*, 43 (1974), 10–11.
39 Chudakova, 'Arkhiv', 85.
40 M. O. Chudakova, 'K tvorcheskoy biografii M. A. Bulgakova, 1916–23' (hereafter Chudakova, 'K tvorcheskoy biografii'), in *Voprosy literatury*, 7 (1973), 231–55 (p. 232).
41 Published in *Grani*, 158–9; see note 14 above. Blyum's views on satire were contained in an article 'Vozroditsya li satira?' in *Literaturnaya gazeta*, 27 May 1929. They were extremely influential; Meyerkhol'd refers to them in a 1936 speech in which he cites Blyum's dictum that 'Satire is unnecessary in Soviet conditions' (see Meyerkhol'd's *Stat'i, pis'ma, rechi, besedy*, vol. 2 (Moscow, 1968), 355). In *O, myod vospominaniy* Bulgakov's second wife recalls that in the first production of *Bagrovy ostrov* the censor Savva Lukich was deliberately made up to look like Blyum, whom Bulgakov considered his explicit opponent (p. 59).
42 S. Yermolinsky, 'Mikhail Bulgakov (iz zapisok raznykh let)', published in his *Dramaticheskiye sochineniya* (Moscow, 1982), 583–700 (p. 604).
43 Horace, *Satires*, 1.1.25ff.: 'Praeterea. ne sic ut qui iocularia ridens percurram – quamquam *ridentem dicere verum quid vetat?*' ('But further, that I may not run over this in a laughing manner, like those who treat of ludicrous subjects – though what hinders one being merry while telling the truth?). I am indebted to the late Mr Tom Stinton, Wadham College, Oxford for this reference.
44 'Sovetskiye pisateli o Shchedrine', *Novy mir*, 1 (1976), 199–229 (p. 199).
45 *Ibid.*, 210.
46 Pushkinsky Dom, F. 369, ed. khr. 327.
47 For an account of the conversation see S. Lyandres, 'Russky pisatel' ne mozhet zhit' bez rodiny ...', *Voprosy literatury*, 9 (1966), 134–9, (p. 139). It is not known whether Bulgakov's relationship with Yelena Sergeyevna by now represented a significant factor in his decision.

48 Chudakova has broached the subject in a number of articles: 'Usloviye sushchestvovaniya', in *V mire knig*, 12 (1974), 79–81; 'Biblioteka M. Bulgakova i krug ego chteniya', in *Vstrechi s knigoy* (Moscow, 1979), 244–300; and 'M. A. Bulgakov-chitatel'', in *Kniga. Issledovaniya i materialy*, XL (Moscow, 1980), 164–84. See also the Appendix 'Bulgakov's library' in J. Curtis, 'Mikhail Bulgakov: Literature and the Writer (1929–40)' (unpublished D.Phil. Thesis, Oxford, 1982).

49 S. Yermolinsky, 'O Mikhaile Bulgakove. Glava iz knigi vospominaniy', in *Teatr*, 9 (1966), 79–97 (p. 91).

50 See pp. 355, 356, 366, 375, 420.

51 The story was originally published in *Nakanune*, 6 July 1923, 2–3; it is reprinted in *Rannjaja neizdannaja proza*, 98–107 (pp. 98–9).

52 See the letter to P. S. Popov, 26 October 1931, Pushkinsky Dom, F. 369, ed. khr. 334, published by V. Gudkova in *Teatr*, 5 (1981), 90–1; there is a reply from Popov on 30 October 1931, Pushkinsky Dom, F. 369, ed. khr. 466.

53 *O, myod vospominaniy*, 74.

54 Letter of 20 June 1934, published in *Neizdanny Bulgakov*, 90.

55 Unpublished letter of 14 March 1935, Pushkinsky Dom, F. 369, ed. khr. 334.

56 *O, myod vospominaniy*, 37–8.

57 See Chudakova, 'Arkhiv', 94–5.

58 Letter of 24 April 1932, Pushkinsky Dom, F. 369, ed. khr. 334; published in Milne, 'K biografii', 165–7.

59 M. O. Chudakova, 'Tvorcheskaya istoriya romana M. Bulgakova *Master i Margarita*' (hereafter Chudakova, 'Tvorcheskaya istoriya romana'), *Voprosy literatury*, 1 (1976), 218–53 (p. 236).

60 S. Yermolinsky, 'O Mikhaile Bulgakove', in *Teatr*, 9 (1966), 79–97 (p. 80).

61 See *Neizdanny Bulgakov*, 61.

62 *O, myod vospominaniy*, 37 and 50.

63 See Chudakova's works referred to in note 48 above, and in particular her 'Biblioteka M. Bulgakova i krug ego chteniya', 250–3.

64 N. Natov has argued that Bulgakov may also have been thinking of Katayev's clearly autobiographical story *Zimoy* (1923); see '*Theatrical Novel*: Bulgakov's Tragicomic Vision of his Theatrical Career', in *Canadian–American Slavic Studies*, XV, 2–3 (Summer–Fall 1981), 192–215 (p. 205). In the same journal E. Proffer states that it was the Katayev work *rather* than Slyozkin's novel that Bulgakov had in mind here; see 'Red-Bricked Moscow; 1921–23', 167–91 (p. 187).

65 See Bulgakov's letter on the subject to P. Ya. Zavolokin on 24 November 1922, published by A. S. Burmistrov in *Sovetskiye arkhivy*, 4 (1973), 101–2.

66 See the announcement concerning it in *Nakanune*, 7 December 1922, cited by V. Petelin in 'Vozvrashcheniye mastera – Zametki o tvorchestve Mikhaila Bulgakova', *Moskva*, 7 (1976), 193–209 (p. 194).

67 See Wright, *Mikhail Bulgakov*, 254, note 19; and S. Yermolinsky, 'O Mikhaile Bulgakove', in *Teatr*, 9 (1966), 79–97 (p. 97).

68 Quoted from an unpublished letter of 1 November 1967 from Yelena Sergeyevna Bulgakova to Dr D. G. B. Piper of Manchester University, to whom I am grateful for permission to use this material.

69 *O, myod vospominaniy*, 71.

70 M. O. Chudakova, 'Usloviye sushchestvovaniya', in *V mire knig*, 12 (1974), 79–81 (p. 79).

71 As note 68 above.

72 Chudakova, 'K tvorcheskoy biografii', 250; and 'Arkhiv', 28–31.

73 The play *Adam i Eva*, never published in the USSR, was first printed in M. Bulgakov, *P'esy* (Paris, 1971) (p. 7); further references to this edition will be given after quotations in the text.

2 BULGAKOV AND MOLIÈRE

1 From an unpublished letter to Dr D. G. B. Piper from Yelena Sergeyevna Bulgakova. See chapter 1, note 68 above.

2 T. Chambers, 'Bulgakov's Molieriana', *Essays in Poetics* (Keele, September 1977), vol. 2, 2, 1–26 (pp. 4–5).

3 Chudakova, 'Arkhiv', 85–93. The materials in the MKhAT Museum are poorly catalogued; we have endeavoured to give some indication of their holdings in A. C. Wright and J. Curtis, 'A Partial Check-list of Bulgakov Materials in Soviet Archives', *Canadian–American Slavic Studies*, XV, 2–3 (Summer–Fall 1981), 440–56.

4 The cast-list is contained in an unnumbered file in the 'Arkhiv postanovok' of the MKhAT Museum. Information about the rehearsals is drawn from the 'Protokol repetitsiy' (Books 1–5, reference Ch. R., 83–7).

5 A highly confused and unreliable account of both plot and production is to be found in N. Gorchakov, *Rezhissyorskiye uroki Stanislavskogo* (Moscow, 1950).

6 See letters from L. M. Leonidov to Stanislavsky on 28 January and 19 February 1930, published in L. M. Leonidov, *Vospominaniya, stat'i, besedy, perepiska, zapisnye knizhki* (Moscow, 1960), 323 and 333.

7 Chudakova, 'Arkhiv', 92, note 145.

8 The play has been published under the title *Kabala svyatosh (Mol'yer)* in M. Bulgakov, *P'esy* (Moscow, 1962; reprinted Letchworth, 1971). A different version, available in M. Bulgakov, *Dramy i komedii* (Moscow, 1965) has most of the details from the 1929 draft restored, except for the last line concerning the role of fate. All further references will be to the 1965 edition, and will be given after quotations in the text.

9 See letter to Gor'ky, 30 September 1931, in *Neizdanny Bulgakov*, 29.

10 Letter of 25 December 1931, Pushkinsky Dom, F. 369, ed. khr. 332; published almost in its entirety in *Neizdanny Bulgakov*, 31.

11 *Neizdanny Bulgakov*, 31.

12 See letter to Popov of 19 March 1932, Pushkinsky Dom, F. 369, ed. khr. 334; partially published in Milne, 'K biografii', 164–5.

13 V. Vishnevsky, 'Kto zhe vy?', *Krasnaya gazeta* (vech. vyp.), no. 266 (2933), 11 November 1931. P. S. Popov included a copy of the article in an unpublished letter to Bulgakov of 26 April 1932, Pushkinsky Dom, F. 369, ed. khr. 466.

14 MKhAT Museum, No. 1332. Most of them have been published in *Neizdanny Bulgakov*, 91–133, and further page references to these will be given after quotations in the text. The exception is the key rehearsal of 17 April 1935, of which Proffer has only an extract (134).

15 There were fourteen rehearsals with Stanislavsky: the first was on 31 October 1934, the second on 4 March 1935, and the last on 9 May 1935. Bulgakov attended those of 4 March, 5 March, 23 March and 14 April (the latter presumably only for the first part, since it is impossible to believe that comments made towards the end could have been made in his presence). There is no record for the first rehearsal.

16 N. Gorchakov, *Rezhissyorskiye uroki Stanislavskogo*, 359.

17 Unpublished letter, Pushkinsky Dom, F. 369, ed. khr. 334.

18 From the stenographic record of the rehearsal of 17 April 1935, MKhAT Museum, No. 1332.

19 *Ibid.*

20 Letter of 22 April 1935, published in *Neizdanny Bulgakov*, 135.

21 N. Gorchakov, *Rezhissyorskiye uroki Stanislavskogo*, 385.

22 'Sumbur vmesto muzyki – Ob opere *Ledi Makbet Mtsenskogo uyezda*' and 'Baletnaya fal'sh'', *Pravda*, 28 January and 6 February 1936.

23 Extracts from the diary are given in Yanovskaya, *Tvorchesky put'*, 220–1.

24 Unpublished letter, Pushkinsky Dom, F. 369, ed. khr. 334.

25 'Vneshny blesk i fal'shivoye soderzhaniye', *Pravda*, 9 March 1936, p. 3.

26 S. Yermolinsky, 'O Mikhaile Bulgakove', in *Teatr*, 9 (1966), 79–97 (p. 84).

27 See V. Ya. Vilenkin, *Vospominaniya s kommentariyami* (Moscow, 1982), 387.

28 See Yanovskaya, *Tvorchesky put'*, 222. It is, perhaps, scarcely surprising that, when Bulgakov in July 1936 for the first time fully wrote out the Master's final destiny, he portrayed him in almost Molierian guise, wearing a 'kaftan' and a powdered wig (Chudakova, 'Tvorcheskaya istoriya romana', 242).

29 See Proffer, *Bulgakov*, 410–11.

30 Eugène Despois, *Le Théâtre français sous Louis XIV* (Paris, 1874), 324; this was one of the sources used by Bulgakov; others will be discussed below in relation to his prose biography of Molière.

31 *Neizdanny Bulgakov*, 94.

32 Quoted in Peter Doyle's translation from his unpublished Ph.D. thesis 'M. A. Bulgakov (1891–1940). A Study of his Life and Works',

(Manchester, 1975), 385. I am grateful to him for permission to use this material.

33 T. Chambers, 'Bulgakov's Molieriana', *Essays in Poetics* (September 1977), vol. 2, 2, pp. 14, 17.

34 This information is largely drawn from two works: Jean Léonor Gallois, sieur de Grimarest, *Vie de Monsieur de Molière* (Paris 1705, reprinted 1930), 28–35; and *Registre de Lagrange (1658–1685)*, publ. Comédie Française (Paris, 1876). Grimarest's biography, the first to be written, was used extensively by Bulgakov, and will be discussed in further detail below.

35 These entries bear no relation to those made in actual fact by Lagrange (see his *Registre*, pp. 31, 41 and 140–1). Bulgakov is correct in suggesting that Lagrange decorated his text with hieroglyphics to mark important events, although the signs he describes (a lily and a black cross) are not among those Lagrange used. The date 17 February did have a certain significance in Molière's life: Madeleine Béjart died on 17 February 1672, and Molière himself died exactly one year later. The lack of any reference to Lagrange's *Registre* in Bulgakov's notes suggests, strangely enough, that he did not actually use it as a source.

36 Grimarest, *Vie de Monsieur de Molière*, 89.

37 'Kharakteristika deystvuyushchikh lits', MKhAT Museum, 'Arkhiv postanovok', unnumbered file, reference N4137, V. Zh., 12-a. This contains materials for the roles of Louis XIV, Armande, Lagrange and the cobbler, but not for Molière.

38 The prototype for this figure was Pierre Roullé, the curé of St Barthélemy. During the *Tartuffe* scandal in 1664 he denounced Molière in a pamphlet entitled *Le Roi Glorieux au Monde*, where he described Molière as a demon and impious libertine who should be consigned to the stake.

39 Chudakova, 'Arkhiv', 90.

40 The prototype for Charron was probably the Archbishop of Paris, Hardouin de Péréfixe. Péréfixe was a member of the notorious Compagnie du Saint Sacrement, more familiarly known as the 'cabale des dévots' – hence Bulgakov's title. The society was founded in May 1627 by the Duc de Vendatour; it was a secret religious masonry, regarded with suspicion by most of the bishops, parliament and Mazarin. This society was prepared to intervene in any question which affected the prestige of sacred subjects and institutions. On 17 April 1664 a secret meeting of the cabal took place at which the members undertook to procure the suppression of *Tartuffe* (John Palmer, *Molière* (New York, 1930), 332–3). Bulgakov uses these facts as the basis for a portrayal of the cabal as a much more fervent and vindictive body than the original.

41 The dated text was No. 44, a prompter's copy. The others are No. 82, a copy belonging to the assistant producer Shelonsky; No. 322, a further prompter's copy; and No. 327, a copy which was evidently scarcely used.

42 The song, dated 20 February 1935, is to be found in the 'Protokol repetitsiy', Book 2, in the MKhAT Museum (reference Ch. R. 84).

43 The cobbler's tirade is to be found in the MKhAT copies referred to in note 41.

44 Yanovskaya gives a different account of this question, suggesting that the idea of having Moirron actually tortured was only a passing whim of Stanislavsky's, and was only mentioned in April 1935 (*Tvorchesky put'*, 218–19). The evidence of the MKhAT texts does, however, argue that the idea was used in the final production.

45 It is the speech in *Dom Juan* where the hero speaks of his limitless desire for amorous adventures: 'j'ai, sur ce sujet, l'ambition des conquérans ... et, comme Alexandre, je souhaiterois qu'il y eût d'autres mondes, pour y pouvoir étendre mes conquêtes amoureuses.'

46 See note 8 above.

47 Chudakova, 'Arkhiv', 103.

48 Pushkinsky Dom, F. 369, ed. khr. 334. Partially quoted in Chudakova, 'Arkhiv', 103.

49 See Yanovskaya, *Tvorchesky put'*, 212.

50 Cited in G. Fayman, 'Na polyakh issledovaniya o Bulgakove', *Voprosy literatury*, 12 (1981), 195–211 (p. 211).

51 *Ibid.*, 209; see also Chudakova, 'Arkhiv', 105.

52 Pushkinsky Dom, F. 369, ed. khr. 334. Partially published in Milne, 'K biografii', 167. 'Ye. S.' is Yelena Sergeyevna Bulgakova; 'K.' is probably one of Bulgakov's friends, N. N. Lyamin.

53 Cited in Milne, 'K biografii', 174, note 48.

54 *O, myod vospominaniy*, 119.

55 The 1962 'Zhizn' zamechatel'nykh lyudey' edition of the biography describes the work as 'Vypusk 1(334)'. Since it also points out that the series was founded by Gor'ky in 1933, it seems conceivable that Bulgakov's work was intended as the first of the series – which might account for the freedom of his approach as well as for the qualms of the editors. After the rejection of his manuscript the commission was offered to S. S. Mokul'sky, who produced his conventional *Mol'yer* in 1935.

56 Chudakova, 'Biblioteka M. Bulgakova i krug ego chteniya', in *Vstrechi s knigoy*, (Moscow, 1979), 256.

57 Grimarest, *Vie de Monsieur de Molière*, 117.

58 *Ibid.*, 7.

59 Lagrange, *Registre*, 76.

60 Grimarest, *Vie de Monsieur de Molière*, 88.

61 Patouillet, 73, note 8; 74, note 12.

62 John Palmer, *Molière* (New York, 1930, reprinted 1970), 21, 489.

63 Gustave Michaut, *La Jeunesse de Molière* (Paris, 1922); *Les Débuts de Molière* (Paris, 1923); *Les Luttes de Molière* (Paris, 1925).

64 Palmer, *Molière*, 30–3.

65 For this quotation and the next see note 41 above.

66 Barro, *Mol'yer – ego zhizn' i literaturnaya deyatel'nost'*, 57–60.
67 Mantsius, *Mol'yer – teatry, publika, aktyory ego vremeni*, 104–5.
68 Grimarest, *Vie de Monsieur de Molière*, 11.
69 Palmer, *Molière*, 225–6.
70 *Ibid.*, 231.
71 *Zhizn' gospodina de Mol'yera* (notes), 234.
72 Alfred Simon, *Molière* (Paris, 1957), 34.
73 V. Kaverin, in his postscript to the 1962 edition of Bulgakov's biography (225–32), states that Bulgakov did use Lagrange (231); perhaps he was taken in by the inauthentic details Bulgakov introduces to his play.
74 *Zhizn' gospodina de Mol'yera* (prefatory note), 6.
75 K. Rudnitsky, 'Primechaniya', in M. Bulgakov, *P'esy* (Moscow, 1962), 473.
76 Chudakova, 'Arkhiv', 104. Bulgakov and Yelena Sergeyevna, having met and embarked on a relationship in 1929, had agreed on a separation for the sake of their families, which lasted from February 1931 to September 1932; they married on 4 October 1932.
77 Seminar paper given at St Antony's College, Oxford in 1978.
78 Palmer, *Molière*, 314–16.
79 P. Descaves, *Molière en U.R.S.S.* (Paris, 1954), 82–3.
80 K. Rudnitsky, 'Mol'yer, Tartyuf i Bulgakov', *Nauka i religiya*, 1 (1972), 84–90 (p. 87).
81 The play was first published in M. Bulgakov, *Dramy i komedii* (Moscow, 1965; reprinted Letchworth, 1971 as a separate play). References to the 1965 edition will be given after quotations in the text.
82 Lagrange, *Registre*, 111.
83 Bulgakov would have found out that Hubert might have resented what was becoming an outdated tradition from his reading of Despois, *Le Théâtre français sous Louis XIV*, 148: 'Il faut ajouter que les rôles de vieille femme pendant tout le XVIIe siècle étaient joués par des hommes. Hubert créa quelques-uns de ces rôles dans la troupe de Molière. Mais après lui tous ces rôles furent remplis par des femmes.'
84 B. Lyubimov, review of M. Bulgakov, *Dramy i komedii*, in *Teatr*, 4 (1966), 120.
85 K. Rudnitsky, 'Mol'yer, Tartyuf i Bulgakov', in *Nauka i religiya*, 1 (1972), 84–90 (p. 87).
86 Wright, *Mikhail Bulgakov*, 177.
87 Proffer, *Bulgakov*, 364.
88 Unpublished letter to V. Vol'f, Pushkinsky Dom, F. 369, ed. khr. 223.
89 Wright, *Bulgakov*, 186; the first publication of the translation was in *Mol'yer. Sobraniye sochineniy v 4 tomakh*, vol. 3 (Leningrad, 1939), 371–497. It was 'reprinted' in *Mol'yer. Izbrannye komedii* (Moscow–Leningrad, 1952).
90 Her translation is referred to by V. Lakshin in 'Eskizy k tryom portretam', *Druzhba narodov*, 9 (1978), 200–20 (p. 216).
91 V. Kaverin, *Zdravstvuy, brat, pisat' ochen' trudno* (Moscow, 1965), 90.

92 P. Markov, *O teatre*, vol. 4: *Dnevnik teatral'nogo kritika 1930–76* (Moscow, 1977), 352–3.

93 E. Proffer, 'The Major Works of Mikhail Bulgakov' (unpublished Ph.D. thesis, Indiana, 1971), p. 39, note 2.

94 Unpublished letter of 29 January 1937, Pushkinsky Dom, F. 369, ed. khr. 334.

3 PUSHKIN AND GOGOL – BULGAKOV'S RUSSIAN MASTERS?

1 M. Tsvetayeva, 'Moy Pushkin', in *Izbrannaya proza v dvukh tomakh*, vol. 2 (New York, 1979), 250. The essay dates from 1937.

2 *Dni Turbinykh* (Letchworth, 1970, reissued 1975), 70; *Master i Margarita*, 489; *V'yuga*, in *Zapiski yunogo vracha*, (Letchworth, 1970, reissued 1975); *Posledniye dni*, (Letchworth, 1970), 9, 41, 45, 49, 79. Further references to these editions will be given after quotations in the text.

3 In M. Bulgakov, *Rannjaja nesobrannaja proza* (Munich, 1978), 193.

4 The story is included in M. Bulgakov, *D'yavoliada*, (Moscow, 1925), 44–124 (p. 104); further references will be given after quotations in the text.

5 See V. Shklovsky, *Sentimental'noye puteshestviye – vospominaniya 1918–23gg.* (Leningrad, 1924), 35, for an account of his behaviour strikingly similar to Shpolyansky's.

6 See L. Yanovskaya, 'Vstupitel'noye slovo skazhet pisatel' t. Bulgakov', *Nauka i zhizn'*, 3 (1978), 61; and *Zapiski na manzhetakh* in *Rannjaja neizdannaja proza*, 15.

7 In *Rannjaja neizdannaja proza*, 47–61 (pp. 55–7).

8 *Moskva krasnokamennaya*, 23–7 (p. 27) and *Chasha zhizni*, 62–6 (p. 63) are both to be found in *Rannjaja neizdannaja proza*. *Pokhozhdeniya Chichikova* is included in *D'yavoliada* (Moscow, 1925), 147–60.

9 The story is to be found in *Rannjaja nesobrannaja proza* 159–61 (p. 160).

10 Unpublished letter of 24 October 1931, Pushkinsky Dom, F. 369, ed. khr. 466.

11 Unpublished letters of 20 May 1932 and 10 August 1932, *ibid*.

12 See *Bibliografiya proizvedeniy A. S. Pushkina i literatury o nyom, 1918–36* (Moscow–Leningrad, 1952), pp. 57, 88, 90, 170.

13 Unpublished letter of 12 December 1939, Pushkinsky Dom, F. 369, ed. khr. 466.

14 See M. Tsvetayeva, *Sochineniya*, vol. 1 (Moscow, 1980), note on p. 521; L. Danilevich, *D. D. Shostakovich* (Moscow, 1958), 182; and Chudakova, 'Arkhiv', 121.

15 'Stenogramma 7-go zasedaniya khudozhestvennogo soveta pri direktsii MKhAT-a', 24 October 1939, MKhAT Museum, unnumbered file.

16 Yu. Babushkin, *V. V. Veresayev (k stoletiyu so dnya rozhdeniya)* (Moscow, 1966), 3.

17 Chudakova, 'K tvorcheskoy biografii', 255.

18 A. Less, 'K istorii *Pushkina*', in *Neprochitannye stranitsy* (Moscow, 1966), 252–3.

19 Chudakova, 'Arkhiv', 51.

20 Chudakova, 'K tvorcheskoy biografii', 254.

21 Unpublished letter of 27 August 1926, Pushkinsky Dom, F. 369, ed. khr. 230.

22 Unpublished letter of 17 July 1931, *ibid*.

23 Unpublished letter of 12 August 1931, *ibid*.

24 Letter of 2 August 1933, Pushkinsky Dom, F. 369, ed. khr. 226; partially published in Milne, 'K biografii', 160–1.

25 Letters from Bulgakov of 6 March and 26 April 1934, Pushkinsky Dom, F. 369, ed. khr. 226; fragments of both are published in Milne, 'K biografii', 161 and 161–2.

26 Unpublished letter of 24 July 1934, Pushkinsky Dom, F. 369, ed. khr. 230.

27 A. Less, 'K istorii *Pushkina*', in *Neprochitannye stranitsy* (Moscow, 1966), 255.

28 'Perepiska po povodu p'esy *Pushkin (Posledniye dni)*' (hereafter 'Perepiska'), *Voprosy literatury*, 3 (1965), 151–71 (p. 151).

29 *Ibid*.

30 Letter of 18 May 1935, 'Perepiska', 152.

31 Letter of 20–21 May 1935, 'Perepiska', 155–6.

32 Letter of May 1935, 'Perepiska', 157.

33 Letter from Veresayev, 'Perepiska', 161–2.

34 Pushkin himself commented on the Tsar's favourable opinion of the work; see A. S. Pushkin, *Polnoye sobraniye sochineniy v desyati tomakh*, 4th ed. (Leningrad, 1977–9), vol. 8, *Dnevnik*, 28 and 29 (17 January and 28 February 1834). Further references to Pushkin's works will be to this edition.

35 Letter to Veresayev of 16 August 1935, 'Perepiska', 165.

36 Letter of 1 August, 'Perepiska', 163.

37 Unpublished letter of 2 August 1935, Pushkinsky Dom, F. 369, ed. khr. 226.

38 Letter of 16 August 1935, 'Perepiska', 165.

39. *Ibid*.

40 Letter of 22 August 1935, 'Perepiska', 167.

41 Unpublished letter of 19 December 1935, Pushkinsky Dom, F. 369, ed. khr. 230.

42 Unpublished letter of 11 March 1936, Pushkinsky Dom, F. 369, ed. khr. 230.

43 V. Yakovlev's article 'Pokusheniye na Pushkina', from *Sovetskoye iskusstvo*, 13 (299), 17 March 1936 is included as a cutting in M. Bulgakov, 'Al'bom postanovki *Poslednikh dney (A. S. Pushkin)*', Pushkinsky Dom, F. 369, ed. khr. 244.

44 The Vakhtangov's overtures and Bulgakov's letter of 2 October 1936 are cited in Chudakova, 'Arkhiv', 122.

45 Letter of 24 March 1937, Pushkinsky Dom, F. 369, ed. khr. 334; partially published in Milne, 'K biografii', 168.

46 Letters from Bulgakov to Veresayev of 16 January, 26 March, 4 April 1937, Pushkinsky Dom, F. 369, ed. khr. 226; the April letter is partially published in Milne, 'K biografii', 162.

47 'Vsesoyuznoye repertuarnoye soveshchaniye. Vystupleniye tov. P. M. Kerzhentseva', Sovetskoye iskusstvo, 5 February 1937 is included as a cutting in M. Bulgakov, 'Al'bom postanovki Poslednikh dney (A. S. Pushkin)', Pushkinsky Dom, F. 369, ed. khr. 224.

48 Unpublished letter of 4 October 1937, Pushkinsky Dom, F. 369, ed. khr. 230; for an account of Bulgakov's decision to abandon his adaptation of The Merry Wives of Windsor for MKhAT see Chudakova, 'Arkhiv', 122.

49 Unpublished letter of 12 December 1939, Pushkinsky Dom, F. 369, ed. khr. 466.

50 Unpublished letter of 29 January 1940, Pushkinsky Dom, F. 369, ed. khr. 230.

51 Preparatory materials for the play are to be found in Bulgakov's archive in the Lenin Library (Moscow), Otdel rukopisey, F. 562, Box 13.5.

52 The extracts have been published by E. Proffer in Russian Literature Triquarterly, 3 (Spring 1972), 431–44; and by L. Yanovskaya in Zvezda, 6 (1974), 102–4. See also Chudakova, 'Usloviye sushchestvovaniya', in V mire knig, 12 (1974), 79–81; 'Arkhiv', 116–19; and 'Biblioteka M. Bulgakova i krug ego chteniya', in Vstrechi s knigoy (Moscow, 1979), 244–300 (pp. 278–94).

53 I have used the 6th edition of Veresayev's Pushkin v zhizni (Moscow, 1936) as the basis for my comparison. Although it contains 'considerable additions' to earlier editions, there can be no doubt that all the new materials would have been made directly available to Bulgakov, who may have owned the 5th (1932) edition, by his co-author. The 6th edition was delivered to the publishers by 22 July 1935 at the latest. Bulgakov also owned Veresayev's Rodstvenniki Pushkina (Moscow, 1933).

54 P. Ye. Shchogolev, Duel' i smert' Pushkina, 3rd ed. (Moscow–Leningrad, 1928), 7.

55 See Veresayev, Pushkin v zhizni, vol. 2, pp. 464, 301, 380, 360, 378, 379, 454, and 455; see also Wright, Mikhail Bulgakov, 215.

56 Veresayev, Sputniki Pushkina, vol. 1 (Moscow, 1937), 39; see Chudakova, 'Biblioteka M. Bulgakova i krug ego chteniya', 280.

57 Sputniki Pushkina, vol. 2, 308.

58 V. V. Veresayev, Zhena Pushkina (Moscow, 1935), 34.

59 Chudakova, 'Arkhiv', 118; M. Tsvetayeva, 'Natal'ya Goncharova (Zhizn' i tvorchestvo)', in Izbrannaya proza v dvukh tomakh (New York, 1979), vol. 1, 283–341 (p. 300).

60 M. Bulgakov, *Posledniye dni* (Letchworth, 1970), 62; all further references will be given after quotations in the text.
61 *Pushkin v zhizni*, vol. 2, 398.
62 *Ibid.*, 402–29.
63 *Ibid.*, 284–5.
64 *Ibid.*, 468.
65 *Zhena Pushkina*, 32; W. N. Vickery, *Pushkin – Death of a Poet* (Indiana, 1968), 140, note 20.
66 L. Grossman, *Zapiski d'Arshiaka* (Khar'kov, 1929), 84–6.
67 *Ibid.*, 87.
68 Letter to Veresayev of 20–21 May 1935, 'Perepiska', 155.
69 E. Proffer, 'The Major Works of Mikhail Bulgakov' (unpublished Ph.D. thesis, Indiana, 1971), 288.
70 In *Russky arkhiv*, 1 (1878), 436–68 (pp. 456–7).
71 Wright, *Mikhail Bulgakov*, 215.
72 See Chudakova, 'Biblioteka M. Bulgakova i krug ego chteniya', 284–5.
73 See Pushkin's *Dnevnik* in his *Polnoye sobraniye sochineniy*, vol. 8, pp 28. (26 January 1834), 30 (8 March 1834), 42 (28 November and 5 December 1834).
74 Chudakova, 'Biblioteka M. Bulgakova i krug ego chteniya', 279, 252, 280, 294.
75 Letter of 20–21 May 1935, 'Perepiska', 155.
76 'Perepiska', 151.
77 K. Paustovsky, 'Bulgakov i teatr', in *Nayedine s osen'yu: portrety, vospominaniya, ocherki* (Moscow, 1967), 159.
78 The passage comes from *Yevgeny Onegin*, Chapter 2, XL.
79 K. Rudnitsky, *Spektakli raznykh let* (Moscow, 1974), 285.
80 The lines come from *Yevgeny Onegin*, Chapter 6, XLIV and XXXIII.
81 V. I. Nemirovich-Danchenko, 'Sokrashchonnaya stenogramma zamechaniy Vl. I. Nemirovicha-Danchenko po spektaklyu *Posledniye dni (Pushkin)*', in *Yezhegodnik MKhAT-a za 1943* (Moscow, 1945), 681–707 (p. 705).
82 'Posledniye dni – stenogramma repetitsii', 6 April 1943 (in the course of a discussion after the 'Obsuzhdeniye predstavitelyami komiteta po delam iskusstv i Glavrepertkoma general'noy repetitsii spektaklya *Pushkin*'), MKhAT Museum, ed. khr. 162 (8374).
83 'Dopolneniya i izmeneniya, sdelannye (Bulgakovoy Yelenoy Sergeyevnoy) k p'ese ego *Aleksandr Pushkin* dlya postanovki v MKhAT-e', Pushkinsky Dom, F. 369, ed. khr. 220.
84 *Pushkin v zhizni*, vol. 2, 380.
85 E. Proffer, 'The Major Works of Mikhail Bulgakov' (unpublished Ph.D. thesis, Indiana, 1971), 283.
86 Cited in Chudakova, 'Arkhiv', 119.
87 See chapter 2, note 8 above.
88 *Pushkin v zhizni*, vol. 2, 304.

89 P. Markov, 'Bulgakov', in *O teatre*, vol. 4: *Dnevnik teatral'nogo kritika 1930–76* (Moscow, 1977), 347–55 (p. 353).
90 M. Tsvetayeva, *Stikhotvoreniya i poemy* (Leningrad, 1979), 287–8.
91 M. Tsvetayeva, 'Pushkin i Pugachov', in *Izbrannaya proza v dvukh tomakh* (New York, 1979), vol. 2, 298.
92 Bulgakov to P. Popov, 7 May 1932, Pushkinsky Dom, F. 369, ed. khr. 334; mostly published in B. F. Yegorov, 'M. A. Bulgakov – "perevodchik" Gogolya (instsenirovka i kinostsenariy *Myortvykh dush*, kinostsenariy *Revizora*)', (hereafter Yegorov), *Yezhegodnik rukopisnogo otdela Pushkinskogo Doma – 1976* (Leningrad, 1978), 57–84 (pp. 68–70; the letter is incorrectly described as ed. khr. 369).
93 See M. Bulgakov, *Ivan Vasil'yevich/Myortvye dushi* (Munich, 1964), together with L. Milne, 'M. A. Bulgakov and *Dead Souls*: the Problems of Adaptation', (hereafter Milne, 'Bulgakov and *Dead Souls*'), *Slavonic and East European Review*, LII, 128 (July 1974), 420–40; M. Bulgakov and I. Pyr'yev, '*Myortvye dushi* – kinostsenariy', *Moskva*, 1 (1978), 125–64; '*Revizor* – kinostsenariy M. Bulgakova', publ. A. C. Wright, *Novy zhurnal*, 127 (June 1977), 5–45.
94 See statistics in *Moskovsky khudozhestvenny teatr v sovetskuyu epokhu* (Moscow, 1974), 543–68.
95 Cited in *Sovetskiye pisateli – Avtobiografii* (ed. B. Braynin and A. Dmitriyev), vol. 3 (Moscow, 1966), 87.
96 *Neizdanny Bulgakov*, 39.
97 V. Katayev, *Almazny moy venets* (Moscow, 1979), 67.
98 *Ibid.*, 65–7.
99 In *Rannjaja nesobrannaja proza*, 39–40 and 62–3.
100 In *Rannjaja neizdannaja proza* (Munich, 1976), 15.
101 *Ibid.*, 21.
102 Letter of 25 January–24 February 1932, Pushkinsky Dom, F. 369, ed. khr. 334; partially published in Milne, 'K biografii', 163–4.
103 V. Kaverin, 'Mikhail Bulgakov i ego Mol'yer', in *Zhizn' gospodina de Mol'yera* (Moscow, 1962), 225–32 (p. 226).
104 K. Paustovsky, *Povest' o zhizni* (Moscow, 1966), vol. 1, 221; vol. 2, 557.
105 See N. V. Gogol, *Sobraniye sochineniy v shesti tomakh*, vol. 1 (Moscow, 1950), p. 93; the word 'varenukha' is used of vodka brewed with spices.
106 See her 'M. A. Bulgakov – chitatel'', 178–85.
107 The quotations from *Nos* can be found in *Zapiski na manzhetakh* in the variants published in *Rannjaja neizdannaja proza* (Munich, 1976), 207–8.
108 *Ibid.*, 14, 203.
109 M. O. Chudakova, 'Bulgakov i Gogol'', *Russkaya rech'*, 2 (1979), 38–48; and 3 (1979), 55–9 (pp. 55–6).
110 *Ibid.*, 3 (1979), 56.
111 First published in *Nakanune*, 24 September 1922, 2–6; then in *D'yavoliada* (Moscow, 1925, reprinted Ann Arbor, 1976), 147–60

(p. 160). The last clause is a quotation from the end of Chapter 6 of *Dead Souls* (Part 1).

112 Pushkinsky Dom, F. 369, ed. khr. 533 and 394.

113 B. Thomson, *The Premature Revolution* (London, 1972), 102.

114 As note 92 above.

115 Details of the arrangements with Sakhnovsky and of the writing of the play are given in Yegorov, 58–67.

116 In the Munich edition of the text, the announcement is made by an unnamed police colonel (140).

117 Milne, 'Bulgakov and *Dead Souls*', 426–7. She provides a full account of the play's history in rehearsal, and of its reception, which I have drawn on for what follows.

118 *Ibid.*, 423–7.

119 *Ibid.*, 426; for an account of Bulgakov's views on Meyerkhol'd's *Revizor*, see *O, myod vospominaniy*, 78.

120 An account of the history of the film scenario is given in Yegorov, 71–80, from which much of the following material is drawn; it should, however, be read in conjunction with G. Fayman, 'Na polyakh issledovaniya o Bulgakove', *Voprosy literatury*, 12 (1981), 195–211 (pp. 200–8).

121 Pushkinsky Dom, F. 369, ed. khr. 334; partly published in Yegorov, 75. Lyusya was a pet name of Bulgakov's for Yelena Sergeyevna.

122 See *Myortvye dushi*, Part 1, Chapter 4.

123 As note 121 above.

124 See Yegorov, 75–9.

125 See note 120 above for the Fayman publication.

126 For the attack on Shostakovich see details in Chapter 2, note 22 above.

127 '*Myortvye dushi* – kinostsenariy', *Moskva*, 1 (1978), 127.

128 See note 93 above.

129 Pushkinsky Dom, F. 369, ed. khr. 173.

130 Bulgakov to M. V. Zagorsky, 26 November 1934, *ibid.*

131 Cited in Chudakova, 'Arkhiv', 118.

132 As note 129; Yegorov's mistake is on p. 83.

133 As note 129.

134 As note 129.

135 Fayman, 209–10.

136 Yegorov, 59.

137 Letter of 18 November 1930, Pushkinsky Dom, F. 369, ed. khr. 178, published in Yegorov, 65.

138 V. G. Sakhnovsky, *Rabota rezhissyora* (Moscow–Leningrad, 1937), 202.

139 The role of the 'chtets' has been published by Milne in 'Bulgakov and *Dead Souls*', where she traced the sources for all his speeches; these include early drafts and variants of *Myortvye dushi*, Gogol's stories *Rim* and *Nevsky prospekt*, and some of his correspondence (431–40).

140 *Ibid.*, 440.
141 See Milne's notes, *ibid.*, 440.
142 *Rannjaja neizdannaja proza*, 98–107 (p. 107).
143 K. Paustovsky, *Povest' o zhizni* (Moscow, 1966), vol. 1, 277.
144 Bulgakov's desire to go to Paris is described in *O, myod vospominaniy*, 24; references to his wish to visit Italy can be found in Veresayev's letter to him of 24 July 1934, quoted above, and in Chudakova, 'Tvorcheskaya istoriya romana', 253.
145 Letter of 30 May 1931, published in Milne, 'K biografii', 154–7 (pp. 154–5); like Milne, Chudakova in 'Arkhiv', 98, suggests that this letter, like others to Stalin, may not actually have been sent.
146 See *Sochineniya i pis'ma N. V. Gogolya*, edited by V. V. Kallash (St Petersburg, 1896), vol. 8, pp. 316–18.
147 Chudakova, 'Bulgakov i Gogol'', 38–44.
148 *Ibid.*, 44–8.
149 Letter of 2 August 1933, Pushkinsky Dom, F. 369, ed. khr. 226; partially published in Milne, 'K biografii', 160–1.
150 Chudakova, 'Bulgakov i Gogol'', 45.
151 See, for example, Pushkin's account in his *Dnevnik* (vol. 8, 19); and Bulgakov's own description of Molière burning *Corydon* in *Zhizn' gospodina de Mol'yera* (211).
152 Chudakova, 'Bulgakov i Gogol'', 48.
153 See Yanovskaya, *Tvorchesky put'*, 295–6.
154 Chudakova, 'Bulgakov i Gogol'', 59.
155 See V. Lakshin, 'Uroki Bulgakova', *Pamir*, 4 (Dushanbe, August 1972), 62.

4 THE MASTER AND MARGARITA

1 Mikhail Kreps, *Bulgakov i Pasternak kak romanisty. Analiz romanov 'Master i Margarita' i 'Doktor Zhivago'* (Ann Arbor, 1984), p. 67.
2 M. O. Chudakova, 'Opyt rekonstruktsii teksta M. A. Bulgakova', in *Pamyatniki kul'tury. Novye otkrytiya. Yezhegodnik – 1977* (Moscow, 1977), 93–106 (pp. 100–2).
3 See Chudakova, 'Tvorcheskaya istoriya romana', 235–6, 240; and Yanovskaya, *Tvorchesky put'*, 261–3.
4 Chudakova, 'Opyt rekonstruktsii', 94–6, 99.
5 Chudakova, 'Tvorcheskaya istoriya romana', 219, 224.
6 Cited *ibid.*, 248; for a fuller publication of this correspondence see 'Besedovat' s toboyu odnoyu', ed. L. Yanovskaya, in *Oktyabr'*, 1 (1984), 189–201 (p. 196).
7 A. Terts (Sinyavsky), 'Literaturny protsess v Rossii', *Kontinent*, 1 (1974), 143–90 (p. 159).
8 This passage was omitted from the first publication of the novel in *Moskva*, 11 (1966) and 1 (1967), and from the more complete Possev

edition (Frankfurt, 1969); it was reinstated for the 1973 Soviet edition in *Romany*, and is retained in subsequent editions.

9 Most recently, for example, T. Edwards, *Three Russian Writers and the Irrational: Zamyatin, Pil'nyak and Bulgakov* (Cambridge, 1982), 160. Some Soviet scholars omit discussion of it for other reasons.

10 Chudakova, 'Tvorcheskaya istoriya romana', 253.

11 E. Proffer, 'Bulgakov's *The Master and Margarita*: Genre and Motif', *Canadian Slavic Studies*, vol. 3, 4 (Winter 1969), 615–28 (p. 628, note 29).

12 V. Skobelev, 'V pyatom izmerenii', *Pod'yom*, 6 (Voronezh, 1967), 124–8 (p. 125).

13 E. Proffer, 'On *The Master and Margarita*', *Russian Literature Triquarterly*, vol. 2, 6 (Spring 1973), 533–64 (p. 562, note 31); B. Gasparov, 'Iz nablyudeniy nad motivnoy strukturoy romana M. A. Bulgakova *Master i Margarita*', *Slavica Hierosolymitana*, 3 (1978), 198–251 (pp. 234–5).

14 G. A. Lesskis, '*Master i Margarita* Bulgakova (manera povestvovaniya, zhanr, makrokompozitsiya)', *Izvestiya AN SSSR (seriya literatury i yazyka)*, vol. 38, 1 (1979), 52–9 (pp. 55ff.) and Gasparov, 215ff. are but two examples among many.

15 See B. A. Beatie and P. W. Powell, 'Story and Symbol: Notes towards a Structural Analysis of Bulgakov's *The Master and Margarita*', *Russian Literature Triquarterly*, 15 (1978), 219–51 (p. 251).

16 D. M. Bethea, 'History as Hippodrome: The Apocalyptic Horse and Rider in *The Master and Margarita*', *Russian Review*, vol. 41, 4 (1982), 373–99.

17 Gasparov, 200–3.

18 *Ibid.*, 212, 226.

19 One critic has drawn attention to the further similarities between the two cities of Bulgakov's descriptions and his birthplace, Kiev, which also has a 'Bald Mountain' (Golgotha) and is divided, like Yershalaim, into an upper and a lower part (E. Proffer, *Bulgakov*, 540).

20 Gasparov, 217ff.

21 E. Proffer, 'Bulgakov's *The Master and Margarita*: Genre and Motif', *Canadian Slavic Studies*, vol. 3, 4 (Winter 1969), 615–28 (p. 628).

22 Milne, '*The Master and Margarita*', 15.

23 A similar conclusion is reached by D. M. Fiene in 'A Comparison of the Soviet and Possev Editions of *The Master and Margarita*, with a Note on Interpretation of the Novel', *Canadian–American Slavic Studies*, XV, 2–3 (Summer–Fall 1981), 330–54 (pp. 352–3). This is, incidentally, the best study of the textological problems surrounding the novel's publication.

24 L. Skorino, 'Litsa bez karnaval'nykh masok (polemicheskiye zametki)', *Voprosy literatury*, 6 (1968), 25–42 (p. 33).

25 E. N. Mahlow, *Bulgakov's 'The Master and Margarita': The Text as a Cipher* (New York, 1975), 8, 63, 66–8.

26 D. G. B. Piper, 'An Approach to Bulgakov's *The Master and Margarita*', *Forum for Modern Language Studies*, vol. 7, 2 (1971), 134–57; and L. Rzhevsky, 'Pilatov grekh: o taynopisi v romane Bulgakova *Master i Margarita*', *Novy zhurnal*, 90 (1968), 60–80.

27 Chudakova, 'Arkhiv', 130; similar assumptions are made in Lesskis, 52–9.

28 Chudakova, 'Tvorcheskaya istoriya romana', 236.

29 Chudakova, 'Arkhiv', 130, note 187; the 'guessing' and 'writing' are evidently alternatives in the draft.

30 *The Jerusalem Bible* (London, 1966), 'Introduction to the Synoptic Gospels', 5–7.

31 R. W. F. Pope, 'Ambiguity and Meaning in *The Master and Margarita*: The Role of Afranius', *Slavic Review*, vol. 36, 1 (March, 1977), 1–24.

32 M. Hayward, 'Pushkin, Gogol and the Devil', *Times Literary Supplement*, 28 May 1976, 630–32, (p. 631).

33 See Chudakova, 'Usloviye sushchestvovaniya', 80.

34 B. A. Beatie and P. W. Powell have pointed out that Florensky's theories are scientifically absurd, if aesthetically appealing; see their 'Bulgakov, Dante and Relativity', *Canadian–American Slavic Studies*, XV, 2–3, (Summer–Fall 1981), 250–70 (p. 253).

35 Florensky, *op. cit.*, 7.

36 Yanovskaya, *Tvorchesky put'*, 241–60; I have drawn on her account for some of the survey below.

37 See El'baum and Zerkalov, *passim*.

38 Zerkalov, 213.

39 Yanovskaya, *Tvorchesky put'*, 249.

40 E. Renan, *Vie de Jésus* (Paris, 1870), 295.

41 Yanovskaya, *Tvorchesky put'*, 260.

42 El'baum, 104, 116.

43 *Ibid.*, 46.

44 F. W. Farrar, *The Life of Christ* (London, no date, although first publication was 1875), 666.

45 S. Yermolinsky, 'Mikhail Bulgakov (iz zapisok raznykh let)', published in his *Dramaticheskiye sochineniya* (Moscow, 1982), 583–700 (p. 586).

46 P. Markov, *V Khudozhestvennom Teatre – kniga zavlita* (Moscow, 1976), 231–2.

47 The story was published in *Gudok*, no. 859, 27 March 1923, p. 4, and signed Ivan Bezdomny.

48 Cited in B. Thomson, *Lot's Wife and the Venus of Milo* (Cambridge, 1978), 69.

49 The phrase originated with the cubo-futurist Osip Brik, and was elaborated by Mayakovsky in his *Kak delat' stikhi* (1926).

50 Milne, *'The Master and Margarita'*, 18.

51 *Ibid.*, 24.

52 A theory which appears to have gained a certain amount of credence is that Ryukhin is somehow based on the figure of Mayakovsky, while

Bezdomny recalls the poet Bezymensky; the evidence is tenuous, but the interested reader is referred to Gasparov, 205–6 and to L. Fleyshman, 'O gibeli Mayakovskogo kak "literaturnom fakte". Postskriptum k stat'ye B. M. Gasparova', *Slavica Hierosolymitana*, 4 (1979), 126–30.

53 See *O, myod vospominaniy*, 123; A. V. Chayanov, *Venediktov, ili dostopamyatnye sobytiya zhizni moyey* (Moscow, 1922).

54 *Faust*, line 4023, 'Make way, Voland, the devil, is coming', in the translation by Barker Fairley (Toronto, 1970), 70.

55 Yanovskaya, *Tvorchesky put'*, 224, 264 and 272.

56 A useful discussion of Bulgakov's references to *Faust* is to be found in E. Stenbock-Fermor, 'Bulgakov's *The Master and Margarita* and Goethe's *Faust*', *Slavic and East European Journal*, vol. 13, 3 (1969), 309–25. Yanovskaya has pointed out that the name Voland is considered so insignificant that it is more often than not omitted in Russian translations of *Faust* (*Tvorchesky put'*, 271–2).

57 Chudakova, 'Opyt rekonstruktsii', 99.

58 Chudakova, 'Tvorcheskaya istoriya romana', 233.

59 Chudakova's list ('Arkhiv', 72) of the articles Bulgakov took notes on does not in fact correspond to the actual titles of articles in the Encyclopaedia. A quotation she cites from the article 'Shabash ved'm' does come from there, however, and he may also have looked at the articles 'Demon' and 'Diavol'.

60 See Chudakova, 'Arkhiv', 73–6, and Orlov, *op. cit.*, 30, 32, 45.

61 Orlov, 7–8.

62 See, for example, G. Krugovoy, 'Gnostichesky roman M. Bulgakova', *Novy zhurnal*, 134 (1979), 47–81; P. Il'yinsky, 'O *Mastere i Margarite*', *Novy zhurnal*, 138 (1980), 51–65; and also M. K. Frank, 'The Mystery of the Master's Final Destination', *Canadian–American Slavic Studies*, XV, 2–3 (Summer–Fall 1981), 287–94. There are many others.

63 W. J. Leatherbarrow, 'The Devil and the Creative Visionary in Bulgakov's *The Master and Margarita*', *New Zealand Slavonic Journal*, 1 (1975), 29–45 (p. 42).

64 Milne, '*The Master and Margarita*', 19–20, 22.

65 Chudakova, 'Opyt rekonstruktsii', 102.

66 From the poem *Gamlet* in *Doktor Zhivago* (Milan, 1957), 532.

67 Chudakova, 'Tvorcheskaya istoriya romana', 244. The essential nature and function of this character in the novel appears to have been clear in Bulgakov's mind as early as 1929–31 (*ibid.*, 229–30).

68 I. F. Belza, 'Genealogiya *Mastera i Margarity*', *Kontekst 1978* (Moscow, 1978), 156–248.

69 See L. Tikos, 'Some Notes on the Significance of Gerbert Aurillac in *The Master and Margarita*', *Canadian–American Slavic Studies*, XV, 2–3 (Summer–Fall 1981), 321–9. Tikos points out that Bulgakov could well have been acquainted with the Russian expert on Aurillac, Nikolay Bubnov,.who was Professor of Mediaeval History at Kiev University from 1891.

70 Florensky, *op. cit.*, 53.
71 S. Yermolinsky, 'O Mikhaile Bulgakove', in *Teatr*, 9 (1966), 79–97 (p. 95).
72 Milne, *'The Master and Margarita'*, 23.
73 Yanovskaya, *Tvorchesky put'*, 308–10; Proffer, *Bulgakov*, 482. The notion that 'peace' represented an ideal for which Bulgakov himself yearned all his life is indicated in a letter to his sister Vera of 23 January 1923: 'I can only judge by my own feelings; after these years of difficult trials, I value peace above all things!' (Lenin Library, F. 562, Box 19.3).
74 *Faust*, lines 11936ff., in the translation by Barker Fairley (Toronto, 1970), 201.
75 See T. Ware, *The Orthodox Church* (Penguin, 1963), 259.
76 G. Gorbachov, *Sovremennaya russkaya literatura: obzor literaturno-ideologicheskikh techeniy sovremennosti i kriticheskiye portrety sovremennykh pisateley* (Leningrad, 1928), 105; Bulgakov had a copy of this book in his library.
77 See Chudakova, 'Biblioteka M. Bulgakova i krug ego chteniya', 247.
78 *Uchebnik ugolovnogo prava*, compiled by V. Spasovich, vol. 1, (Sanktpeterburg, 1863), 318.
79 Milne, *'The Master and Margarita'*, 33.
80 *...*: the 1973 edition brackets these words off as though there had been a blank here in the manuscript.

5 A ROMANTIC VISION

1 *Pamyati M. B-va*, in *Sochineniya*, vol. 2 (Inter-Language Literary Associates, 1968), 141–2 (p. 142). The poem dates from 1940.
2 In their manifesto *Poshchochina obshchestvennomu vkusu* (Moscow, 1912).
3 See B. Thomson, *Lot's Wife and the Venus of Milo* (Cambridge, 1978), 53.
4 *Ibid.*, 2.
5 M. Hayward, 'Pushkin, Gogol and the Devil', *Times Literary Supplement*, 28 May 1976, 630–2 (p. 630).
6 In M. Gor'ky, *O literature – stat'i i rechi 1928–36* (Moscow, 1937), 203.
7 F. Schiller, *On the Naive and Sentimental in Literature*, translated by H. Watanabe O'Kelly (Manchester, 1981), 42ff.
8 See A. N. Sokolov, 'K sporam o romantizme', in *Problemy romantizma – sbornik statey* (Moscow, 1967), 13.
9 See A. Fadeyev, *Za 30 let* (Moscow, 1957), 67.
10 A. I. Beletsky, *Russky romantizm – sbornik statey* (Leningrad, 1927), 14.
11 F. Kermode, *The Romantic Image* (London, 1957, reprinted 1971), 17.

12 E. A. Poe, 'The Philosophy of Composition' (1846), in *Selected Writings* (Penguin, 1967), 483.

13 In 'Neskol'ko slov o Pushkine' (1832), in *Sobraniye sochineniy*, vol. 6 (Moscow, 1950), 33–8 (p. 38).

14 P. Doyle, 'Bulgakov and Cervantes'; paper given at the British Universities Association of Slavists Soviet Literature Conference at St Edmund Hall, Oxford, 25 September 1980.

15 N. K. Cherkasov, *Chetvyorty Don Kikhot – istoriya odnoy roli* (Leningrad, 1958), 21–6.

16 M. Bulgakov, *Don Kikhot* (Letchworth, 1971, reprinted 1978), 13. Further references to this edition will be given in the text.

17 E. A. Poe, 'The Poetic Principle' (1850), in *Selected Writings* (Penguin, 1967), 505.

18 Cited by C. M. Bowra in *The Romantic Imagination* (Oxford, 1950, reprinted 1961), 3.

19 It has been argued that Bulgakov may have come to this school of thought on the nature of inspiration through the writings of philosophers such as Berdyayev, Shestov and Solov'yov, who undoubtedly influenced Symbolist thinking on the subject. Mahlow has insisted on the importance of Berdyayev's ideas for Bulgakov (*passim*); Wright maintains that Bulgakov read Solov'yov, but not Shestov (*Mikhail Bulgakov*, 171); Edwards cites Berdyayev's ideas on creativity as being relevant to Bulgakov's (*Three Russian Writers*, 157); and Glenny argues that Bulgakov would have known of Shestov in Kiev ('Existential Thought in Bulgakov's *The Master and Margarita*', *Canadian–American Slavic Studies*, XV, 2–3 (Summer–Fall, 1981), 238–49 (p. 241). While there is little concrete evidence for any of these assertions, it does seem likely that Bulgakov would have known of their work through his father's interests and connections in Kiev.

20 In his preface to H. G. Schenk, *The Mind of the European Romantics* (Oxford, 1966), xv.

21 See *E. T. A. Gofman – bibliografiya russkikh perevodov i kriticheskoy literatury*, ed. Z. V. Zhitomirskaya (Moscow, 1964), 5–26.

22 Letter of 6–7 August 1938, cited in 'Besedovat' s toboyu odnoyu', ed. L. Yanovskaya, in *Oktyabr'*, 1 (1984), 189–201 (p. 200).

23 *Ibid.*, 200; the article is to be found in *Literaturnaya uchoba*, 5 (May 1938), 63–87. For a further description of Bulgakov's annotations on his copy see Chudakova, 'Usloviye sushchestvovaniya', 80, and her 'Arkhiv', 130–1, note 188.

24 S. Yermolinsky, 'O Mikhaile Bulgakove', in *Teatr*, 9 (1966), 79–97 (p. 88).

25 Mirimsky, *op. cit.*, 66, 68.

26 See 'Besedovat' s toboyu odnoyu', *Oktyabr'*, 1 (1984), 200.

27 C. M. Bowra, *The Romantic Imagination* (Oxford, 1950, reprinted 1961), 22–3.

28 Pushkinsky Dom, F. 369, ed. khr. 325; partly published in Milne, 'K

biografiii', 168, where it is described as a letter to P. S. Popov – see note 29 below for the letter to Popov of the same date.

29 Unpublished letter, Pushkinsky Dom, F. 369, ed. khr. 334.

30 Chudakova, 'Arkhiv', 125.

31 Letters from Pushkinsky Dom, F. 369, ed. khr. 306. They have also been published in *Muzyka Rossii*, Vypusk 3 (Moscow, 1980), 213–98.

32 Letter of 4 April 1937, Pushkinsky Dom, F. 369, ed. khr. 226; partly published in Milne, 'K biografii', 162.

33 See N. Pavlovsky, 'Zoloto-krasny Bol'shoy teatr', *Teatr*, 5 (1981), 94–6 (p. 94).

34 Chudakova, 'Arkhiv', 124.

35 Cited in 'Besedovat' s toboyu odnoyu', *Oktyabr'*, 1 (1984), 196.

36 See, for instance, I. Kremlyov, *V literaturnom stroyu – vospominaniya* (Moscow, 1968), 207.

37 The play is published in *Neizdanny Bulgakov*, 137–210. For a full account of the writing of the play, see E. Proffer, *Bulgakov*, 515–23.

38 Chudakova, 'Arkhiv', 121.

39 See E. Proffer, *Bulgakov*, 479–80 and 483–86.

40 Published in Milne, 'K biografii', 159–60.

41 Edwards, *Three Russian Writers*, 146.

42 V. Katayev, *Almazny moy venets* (Moscow, 1979), 64, 65, 70.

43 S. Yermolinsky, 'O Mikhaile Bulgakove', in *Teatr*, 9 (1966), 79–97 (p. 90).

44 P. Markov, 'Bulgakov', in M. Bulgakov, *P'esy* (Moscow, 1962), 348.

45 See note 1 above.

46 Unpublished letter of 5 December 1939, Pushkinsky Dom, F. 369, ed. khr. 466.

Bibliography

Out of what is now a very large range of materials about Bulgakov I have selected for this bibliography those items which are of central significance either to the themes of this book, or to the study of Bulgakov as a whole. Particular stress has been laid on publications drawing on archival materials, correspondence, and other documentary evidence. The bibliography is arranged as follows:

Primary sources
Secondary sources:
(A) General
    Special issues of journals
    Individual studies
(B) Additional reading
    on Molière
    on Pushkin
    on Gogol
    on Romanticism

PRIMARY SOURCES

Listed below are the texts and collections of texts consulted or referred to in this study.

Adam i Eva, in *P'esy* (Paris, 1971), 5–77
Autobiographies in V. Lidin, *Avtobiografii pisateley-sovremennikov* (Moscow, 1926), 53–6, and 'M. A. Bulgakov', in *Sovetskiye pisateli – Avtobiografii*, ed. B. Braynin and A. Dmitriyev, vol. 3 (Moscow, 1966), 85–101
Bagrovy ostrov, in *P'esy* (Paris, 1971), 78–192
Batum, in *Neizdanny Bulgakov* (Ann Arbor, 1977), 137–210
Beg (Letchworth, 1970)
Belaja gvardija – P'esa v Četyrech Dejstvijach. Vtoraja Redakcija P'esy 'Dni Turbinych', ed. L. Milne (Munich, 1983)
Belaya gvardiya, in *Romany* (Moscow, 1973), 13–270
Blazhenstvo (son inzhenera Reyna), in *Grani*, 85 (1972), 3–52
'Byl may ...', publ. L. Yanovskaya in *Avrora*, 3 (1978), 67–8
Chasha zhizni, in *Rannjaja neizdannaja proza* (Munich, 1976), 62–6
Dni Turbinykh (Letchworth, 1970, reprinted 1975); see also 'An

Unpublished Scene from the Original *Dni Turbinykh'*, publ. E. Proffer in *Russian Literature Triquarterly*, 7 (1973), 475–9
Don Kikhot (Letchworth, 1971, reprinted 1978); see also 'Neizdannye stseny iz p'esy *Don Kikhot'*, publ. Ye. S. Bulgakova in *Servantes i vsemirnaya literatura*, ed. N. I. Balashov and others (Moscow, 1969), 273–7
Dramy i komedii (Moscow, 1965)
D'yavoliada, in *D'yavoliada – Rasskazy* (Moscow, 1925; reprinted Ann Arbor, 1976), 3–43
Ivan Vasil'yevich, in *Ivan Vasil'yevich/Myortvye dushi* (Munich, 1964), 1–70, and (Letchworth, 1978)
Izbrannaya proza (Moscow, 1966)
Kabala svyatosh (Mol'yer), in *P'esy* (Moscow, 1962; reprinted separately Letchworth, 1971 and 1974); see also fuller version in *Dramy i komedii* (Moscow, 1965)
'Kurs istorii SSSR (vypiski iz chernovika)', publ. A. C. Wright in *Novy zhurnal*, 143 (1981), 54–88
Master i Margarita, in *Moskva*, 11 (1966), 7–127, and 1 (1967), 56–144; (Frankfurt, Possev-Verlag, 1969: 2-e karmannoye izdaniye, 1974); and in *Romany* (Moscow, 1973), 423–812
Minin i Pozharsky (libretto), publ. A. C. Wright, *Russian Literature Triquarterly*, 15 (1978), 325–40
'Mne prisnilsya son . . .', publ. L. Yanovskaya in *Nedelya*, 43 (1974), 10–11
Moskva krasnokamennaya, in *Rannjaja neizdannaja proza* (Munich, 1976), 23–7
Myortvye dushi: stage version in *Ivan Vasil'yevich/Myortvye dushi* (Munich, 1964), 71–145; cinema version with I. Pyr'yev in *Moskva*, 1 (1978), 125–64
Neizdanny Bulgakov: teksty i materialy, ed. E. Proffer (Ann Arbor, 1977)
P'esy (Moscow, 1962)
P'esy (Paris, 1971)
'Pis'ma protesty M. Bulgakova, A. Solzhenitsyna i A. Vosnesenskogo', in *Grani*, 66 (1967), 155–61
Ploshchad' na kolyosakh, in *Rannjaja nesobrannaja proza* (Munich, 1978), 159–61
Pokhozhdeniya Chichikova, in *D'yavoliada – Rasskazy* (Moscow, 1925; reprinted Ann Arbor, 1976), 147–60
Poloumny Zhurden, in *Dramy i komedii* (Moscow, 1965); reprinted separately (Letchworth, 1978)
Posledniye dni (Letchworth, 1970)
Rannjaja neizdannaja proza, ed. V. Levin (Munich, 1976)
Rannjaja neizvestnaja proza, ed. V. Levin (Munich, 1981)
Rannjaja nesobrannaja proza, ed. V. Levin and L. V. Svetin (Munich, 1978)
Revizor: cinema version with M. Korostin, publ. A. C. Wright in *Novy zhurnal*, 127 (1977), 5–45

Rokovye yaytsa, in *D'yavoliada – Rasskazy* (Moscow, 1925; reprinted Ann Arbor, 1976), 44–124

Romany (Moscow, 1973)

Skupoy (Bulgakov's translation of Molière's *L'Avare*), in Molière, *Sobraniye sochineniy v 4-kh tomakh*, ed. A. A. Smirnov and S. S. Mokul'sky (Moscow–Leningrad, 1935–9), vol. 3, 371–497; a different version in Molière, *Izbrannye komedii*, ed. S. S. Mokul'sky (Moscow–Leningrad, 1952), 261–328

Sobach'ye serdtse, in *Student*, 9–10 (London, 1968); 3rd ed. (Paris, 1969)

Sobraniye sochineniy, ed. E. Proffer (Ann Arbor, 1982–): vol. 1, *Ranniaia proza* (1982); vol. 2, *Ranniaia proza* (1985); vol. 3, *Povesti* (1983)

'Sovetskiye pisateli o Shchedrine', in *Novy mir*, 1 (1976), 199–229 (p. 210)

Teatral'ny roman, in *Romany* (Moscow, 1973), 271–420

Voyna i mir: stage version, publ. A. C. Wright in *Canadian–American Slavic Studies*, 15, 2–3 (1981), 382–439

V'yuga, in *Zapiski yunogo vracha* (Letchworth, 1970, reprinted 1975)

'Yury Slyozkin – Siluet' (introduction to Slyozkin's *Roman baleriny*) (Riga, 1928), 7–21

Zabytoe – Rannjaja proza, ed. V. Levin (Munich, 1983)

Zapiski na manzhetakh, in *Rannjaja neizdannaja proza* (Munich, 1976); see also *Grani*, 77 (1980), 74–81; also ed. L. Loseff (New York, 1981)

Zapiski yunogo vracha (Letchworth, 1970, reprinted 1975)

Zhizn' gospodina de Mol'yera (Moscow, 1962)

Zoykina kvartira, in *P'esy* (Paris, 1971), 193–252; also ed. E. Proffer (Ann Arbor, 1971)

SECONDARY SOURCES

(A) General

Individual articles and monographs are listed below in alphabetical order by author. Articles on Bulgakov have also been published in two special issues of journals; these are listed together at the beginning.

'Bulgakov' – special issue of *Russian Literature Triquarterly*, 15 (1978), ed. C. Proffer and E. Proffer, which, together with a number of translations and publications, contains:
  P. Davidson, 'The House of the Bulgakovs and an Interview with Inna Vasilievna Konchalovskaya, with Rare and Unpublished Photographs', 99–120
  S. Schultze, 'The Epigraphs in *White Guard*', 213–18
  B. A. Beatie and P. W. Powell, 'Story and Symbol: Notes towards a Structural Analysis of Bulgakov's *The Master and Margarita*', 219–51
  D. Lowe, 'Bulgakov and Dostoyevsky: A Tale of Two Ivans', 253–62
  S. McLaughlin, 'Structure and Meaning in Bulgakov's *The Fatal Eggs*', 263–79

234 Bibliography

H. Goscilo, 'Point of View in Bulgakov's *Heart of a Dog*', 281–91
C. Rydel, 'Bulgakov and H. G. Wells', 293–311

'Mikhail Bulgakov 1891–1981' – special issue of *Canadian–American Slavic Studies*, XV, 2–3 (Summer–Fall 1981), ed. N. Natov, containing:
N. Natov, 'Mikhail Bulgakov 1891–1981: Preface', 149–50
A. C. Wright, 'Mikhail Bulgakov's Developing World View', 151–66
E. Proffer, 'Red-Bricked Moscow: 1921–23', 167–91
N. Natov, '*Theatrical Novel*: Bulgakov's Tragicomic Vision of his Theatrical Career', 192–215
H. Schmid, 'Das Verfahren des Illusionsbruchs in Bulgakovs *Bagrovyj ostrov*', 216–37
M. Glenny, 'Existential Thought in Bulgakov's *The Master and Margarita*', 238–49
B. A. Beatie and P. W. Powell, 'Bulgakov, Dante and Relativity', 250–70
V. Taranovski Johnson, 'The Thematic Function of the Narrator in *The Master and Margarita*', 271–86
M. K. Frank, 'The Mystery of the Master's Final Destination', 287–94
M. Jovanovic, '*Yevangeliye ot Matfeya* kak literaturny istochnik *Mastera i Margarity*', 295–311
D. B. Pruitt, 'St John and Bulgakov: The Model of a Parody of Christ', 312–20
L. Tikos, 'Some Notes on the Significance of Gerbert Aurillac in Bulgakov's *The Master and Margarita*', 321–9
D. M. Fiene, 'A Comparison of the Soviet and Possev Editions of *The Master and Margarita*, with a Note on Interpretation of the Novel', 330–54
A. Tamarchenko, 'Roman na stsene: *Master i Margarita* v Teatre na Tagan'ke', 355–81
'Mikhail Bulgakov's Adaptation of *War and Peace*', ed. A. C. Wright, 382–439
'A Partial Check-list of Bulgakov Materials in Soviet Archives', compiled by A. C. Wright and J. Curtis, 440–56
'A Bibliography of Works by and about Mikhail A. Bulgakov', compiled by N. Natov, 457–61

Anon., 'Vneshny blesk i fal'shivoye soderzhaniye', *Pravda*, 9 March 1936, 3
The Apocryphal New Testament, trans. and ed. M. R. James (Oxford, 1963)
Bachelis I., 'O belykh arapakh i krasnykh tuzemtsakh', *Molodaya gvardiya*, 1 (1929), 105–8
Barratt A., 'Apocalypse or Revelation? Man and History in Bulgakov's *Belaya gvardiya*', *New Zealand Slavonic Journal* (1985), 105–31
Belozerskaya-Bulgakova L. Ye., *O, myod vospominaniy* (Ann Arbor, 1979) – also available in English

Belza I. F., 'Genealogiya *Mastera i Margarity*', *Kontekst 1978* (Moscow, 1978), 156–248

Bethea D. M., 'History as Hippodrome: The Apocalyptic Horse and Rider in *The Master and Margarita*', *Russian Review*, vol. 41, 4 (1982), 373–99

Boyarsky Ya. O., *MKhAT v illyustratsiyakh i dokumentakh, 1898–1938* (Moscow, 1938)

Brokgauz–Efron (publ.), *Entsiklopedichesky slovar'*, 82+4 vols. (1890–1907), and 29 vols. of projected 48 (1911–16)

Burmistrov A. S., 'Avtograf M. A. Bulgakova', *Sovetskiye arkhivy*, 4 (1973), 101–2

Cherkasov N. K., *Chetvyorty Don Kikhot – istoriya odnoy roli* (Leningrad, 1958), 21–6

Chudakova M. O., *Masterstvo Yuriya Oleshi* (Moscow, 1972), 6–7, 88–9, 94

Chudakova M. O., 'K tvorcheskoy biografii M. A. Bulgakova 1916–23', *Voprosy literatury*, 7 (1973), 231–55

Chudakova M. O., 'Usloviye sushchestvovaniya', *V mire knig*, 12 (1974), 79–81

Chudakova M. O., 'Tvorcheskaya istoriya romana M. Bulgakova *Master i Margarita*', *Voprosy literatury*, 1 (1976), 218–53

Chudakova M. O., 'Prisutstvuyet Aleksandr Grin', *Sel'skaya molodyozh'*, 6 (1976), 61–3

Chudakova M. O., 'Arkhiv M. A. Bulgakova. Materialy dlya tvorcheskoy biografii pisatelya', *Zapiski otdela rukopisey. Biblioteka SSSR imeni Lenina*, 37 (1976), 25–151

Chudakova M. O., 'Opyt rekonstruktsii teksta M. A. Bulgakova', in *Pamyatniki kul'tury. Novye otkrytiya. Yezhegodnik – 1977* (Moscow, 1977), 93–106

Chudakova M. O., 'Biblioteka M. Bulgakova i krug ego chteniya', in *Vstrechi s knigoy* (Moscow, 1979), 244–300

Chudakova M. O., 'M. A. Bulgakov – chitatel''', in *Kniga. Issledovaniya i materialy*, XL (Moscow, 1980), 164–85

Chudakova M. O., 'Obshcheye i individual'noye, literaturnoye i biograficheskoye v tvorcheskom protsesse M. A. Bulgakova', in *Khudozhest-vennoye tvorchestvo: voprosy kompleksnogo izucheniya – 1982* (Leningrad, 1982), 133–50

Curtis J. A. E., 'Forced to Improvise' (review of first London production of *Bagrovy ostrov*), *Times Literary Supplement*, 6 March 1981, 255

Curtis J. A. E., 'Mikhail Bulgakov: Literature and the Writer (1929–40)' (unpublished D.Phil. thesis, Oxford, 1982)

Doyle P., 'M. A. Bulgakov (1891–1940). A Study of his Life and Works' (unpublished Ph.D. thesis, Manchester, 1975)

Doyle P., 'Bulgakov's Revenge on Stanislavsky: *Teatral'ny roman*', *New Zealand Slavonic Journal*, 1 (1976), 61–86

Doyle P., 'Bulgakov's Satirical View of Revolution in *Rokovye iaitsa* and *Sobach'e serdtse*', *Canadian Slavonic Papers*, vol. 20, 4 (1978), 467–82

Drews A., *Mif o Khriste*, 2 vols. (Moscow, 1924)
Edwards T. R. N., *Three Russian Writers and the Irrational – Zamyatin, Pil'nyak and Bulgakov* (Cambridge, 1982)
El'baum H., *Analiz iudeyskikh glav 'Mastera i Margarity' M. Bulgakova* (Ann Arbor, 1981)
Farrar F. W., *The Life of Christ* (London, no date); translated as *Zhizn' Iisusa Khrista* (St Petersburg, 1905)
Fleyshman L., 'O gibeli Mayakovskogo kak "literaturnom fakte". Postskriptum k stat'ye B. M. Gasparova', *Slavica Hierosolymitana*, 4 (1979), 126–30
Florensky P., *Mnimosti v geometrii* (Moscow, 1920)
Freeborn R., Donchin G., Anning N. J., *Russian Literary Attitudes from Pushkin to Solzhenitsyn* (London and Basingstoke, 1976)
Gasparov B., 'Iz nablyudeniy nad motivnoy strukturoy romana M. A. Bulgakova Master i Margarita', *Slavica Hierosolymitana*, 3 (1978), 198–251
Gireyev D. A., *Mikhail Bulgakov na beregakh Tereka* (Ordzhonikidze, 1980)
Glenny M., 'Mikhail Bulgakov', *Survey*, 65 (1967), 3–14
Goethe J. W. von, *Faust*, trans. Barker Fairley (Toronto, 1970)
Gorbachov G., *Sovremennaya russkaya literatura: obzor literaturno-ideologicheskikh techeniy sovremennosti i kriticheskiye portrety sovremennykh pisateley* (Leningrad, 1928)
Gorchakov N., *Rezhissyorskiye uroki Stanislavskogo – besedy i zapisi repetitsiy* (Moscow, 1950)
Gor'ky M., Fadeyev A., 'M. A. Bulgakov v neizdannykh pis'makh Gor'kogo i Fadeyeva', publ. Z. G. Mints, *Uchonye zapiski Tartuskogo Universiteta*, Vypusk 119, 5 (Tartu, 1962), 399–402
Gor'ky M., 'Gor'ky i sovetskiye pisateli – neizdannaya perepiska', *Literaturnoye nasledstvo*, 70 (Moscow, 1963), 30, 88–9, 139, 152, 389, 645, 647
Gudkova V., 'Pis'ma M. A. Bulgakova P. S. Popovu', *Teatr*, 5 (1981), 90–3
Gus' M., 'Goryat li rukopisi?', *Znamya*, vol. 38, 12 (1968), 213–20
Haber E. C., 'The Mythic Structure of Bulgakov's *The Master and Margarita*', *Russian Review*, vol. 34, 4 (1975), 382–409
Hamant Y., 'Bibliographie de Mikhail Bulgakov', *Cahiers du Monde Russe et Soviétique*, vol. 11, 2-e cahier (1970), 319–48
Hayward M., 'Pushkin, Gogol and the Devil', *Times Literary Supplement*, 28 May 1976, 630–2
Il'yinsky P., 'O *Mastere i Margarite*', *Novy zhurnal*, 138 (1980), 51–65
Jovanovic M., *Utopija Mihaila Bulgakova* (Belgrade, 1975)
Katayev V., *Almazny moy venets* (Moscow, 1979), 56–7, 63–72, 187–8, 218
Kaverin V. A., 'Zametki o dramaturgii Bulgakova', *Teatr*, 10 (1956), 69–74

Kaverin V. A., 'Bulgakov', in *Zdravstvuy, brat, pisat' ochen' trudno* (Moscow, 1965), 81–92

Kaverin V. A., 'Sny nayavu (Zametki o tvorchestve M. A. Bulgakova)', *Zvezda*, 12 (1976), 185–91

Kaverin V. A., 'Zametki o Bulgakove', in *Izbrannye proizvedeniya v 2-kh tomakh*, vol. 2 (Moscow, 1977), 634–47

Kejna-Sharratt B., 'The Tale of Two Cities: The Unifying Function of the Setting in M. Bulgakov's *The Master and Margarita*', *Forum for Modern Language Studies*, 16 (1980), 331–40

Kisel'gof T. (Bulgakov's first wife), 'Gody molodosti', intro. by M. O. Chudakova, *Literaturnaya gazeta*, 13 May 1981, 6.

Kremylov I., *V literaturnom stroyu – vospominaniya* (Moscow, 1968)

Kreps M., *Bulgakov i Pasternak kak romanisty – Analiz romanov 'Master i Margarita' i 'Doktor Zhivago'* (Ann Arbor, 1984)

Krugovoy G., 'Gnostichesky roman M. Bulgakova', *Novy zhurnal*, 134 (1979), 47–81

Lakshin V., 'Dve biografii', *Novy mir*, 3 (1963), 250–5

Lakshin V., 'Roman M. Bulgakova *Master i Margarita*', *Novy mir*, 6 (1968), 284–311

Lakshin V., 'Rukopisi ne goryat! (Otvet M. Gusyu)', *Novy mir*, 12 (1968), 262–6

Lakshin V., 'Uroki Bulgakova', *Pamir*, 4 (Dushanbe, Aug. 1972), 57–62

Lakshin V., 'Eskizy k tryom portretam', *Druzhba narodov*, 9 (1978), 200–20

Lakshin V., *Vtoraya vstrecha – Vospominaniya, portrety, stat'i* (Moscow, 1984)

Leatherbarrow W. J., 'The Devil and the Creative Visionary in Bulgakov's *The Master and Margarita*', *New Zealand Slavonic Journal*, 1 (1975), 29–45

Leonidov L. M., *Vospominaniya, stat'i, besedy, perepiska, zapisnye knizhki* (Moscow, 1960), 15, 172, 307, 323, 333

Lesskis G. A., '*Master i Margarita* Bulgakova (manera povestvovaniya, zhanr, makrokompozitsiya)', *Izvestiya AN SSSR – seriya literatury i yazyka*, vol. 38, 1 (1979), 52–9

Levin V., *Das Groteske in Michail Bulgakovs Prosa* (Munich, 1975)

Lyandres S., 'Russky pisatel' ne mozhet zhit' bez rodiny – materialy k biografii Bulgakova', *Voprosy literatury*, 9 (1966), 134–9

Lyubimov B., 'Mikhail Bulgakov – Dramy i komedii', *Moskva 1965*', *Teatr*, 4 (1966), 120

Mahlow E. N., *Bulgakov's 'The Master and Margarita': The Text as a Cipher* (New York, 1975)

Markov P., *V Khudozhestvennom Teatre – kniga zavlita* (Moscow, 1976)

Markov P., 'Bulgakov', in *O teatre – v 4-kh tomakh*, vol. 4, *Dnevnik teatral'nogo kritika. 1930–76* (Moscow, 1977), 347–55

Meyerkhol'd V., *Stat'i, pis'ma, rechi, besedy*, vol. 2 (Moscow, 1968), 103, 131–45, 344, 355

Milne L., 'K biografii M. A. Bulgakova', *Novy zhurnal*, 111 (1973), 151–74
Milne L., 'The Emergence of M. A. Bulgakov as a Dramatist' (unpublished Ph.D. thesis, Cambridge, 1975)
Milne L., '*The Master and Margarita' – A Comedy of Victory* (Birmingham, 1977)
Moskovsky Khudozhestvenny Teatr v sovetskuyu epokhu – materialy i dokumenty, 2nd ed. (Moscow, 1974)
Nemirovich-Danchenko V. I., *Stat'i, rechi, besedy, pis'ma* (Moscow, 1952), 328–46
Novitsky P., 'Bagrovy ostrov'. *Repertuarny byulleten' Glaviskusstva RSFSR*, 12 (1928), 9–10
Orlinsky A., 'Protiv bulgakovshchiny', *Novy zritel'*, 41 (12 October 1926), 3–4
Orlov M. A., *Istoriya snosheniy cheloveka s d'yavolom* (St Petersburg, 1904)
Paustovsky K., *Povest' o zhizni* (Moscow, 1966), vol. 1, 210–83; vol. 2, 524–36, 556–62
Paustovsky K., 'Bulgakov i teatr', in *Nayedine s osen'yu: portrety, vospominaniya, ocherki* (Moscow, 1967), 150–62
Pavlovsky N., 'Zoloto-krasny Bol'shoy teatr', *Teatr*, 5 (1981), 94–6
Petelin V., 'Vozvrashcheniye mastera. Zametki o tvorchestve Mikhaila Bulgakova', *Moskva*, 7 (1976), 193–209
Piper D. G. B., 'An Approach to Bulgakov's *The Master and Margarita'*, *Forum for Modern Language Studies*, vol. 7, 2 (1971), 134–57
Pope R. W. F., 'Ambiguity and Meaning in *The Master and Margarita*: The Role of Afranius', *Slavic Review*, vol. 36, 1 (1977), 1–24
Proffer E., 'Bulgakov's *The Master and Margarita*: Genre and Motif', *Canadian Slavic Studies*, vol. 3, 4 (1969), 615–28
Proffer E., 'The Major Works of Mikhail Bulgakov' (unpublished Ph.D. thesis, Indiana, 1971)
Proffer E., '*The Master and Margarita'*, in *Major Soviet Writers – Essays in Criticism*, ed. E. J. Brown (Oxford, 1973), 388–411
Proffer E., 'On *The Master and Margarita'*, *Russian Literature Triquarterly*, vol. 2, 6 (1973), 533–64
Proffer E., 'Yevgeny Zamyatin; Unpublished Letters to his Wife', *Russian Literature Triquarterly*, 7 (1973), 441–4
Proffer E., 'Mikhail Bulgakov – Letters and Documents for a Biography', *Russian Literature Triquarterly*, 7 (1973), 445–79
Proffer E., *An International Bibliography of Works by and about Mikhail Bulgakov* (Ann Arbor, 1976)
Proffer E., ed., *A Pictorial Biography of Mikhail Bulgakov* (Ann Arbor, 1984)
Proffer E., *Bulgakov – Life and Work* (Ann Arbor, 1984)
Renan E., *Vie de Jésus* (Paris, 1870)
Riggenbach H., *Michail Bulgakows Roman 'Master i Margarita': Stil und Gestalt* (Berne, 1979)

Rudnitsky K. L., 'Mikhail Bulgakov', *Voprosy teatra* (Moscow, 1966), 127–43
Rudnitsky K. L., 'Veshchiye sny', *Izvestiya* (20 April 1967), 4
Rudnitsky K. L., 'Bulgakov', in his *Spektakli raznykh let* (Moscow, 1974), 227–85
Rudnitsky K. L., *Teatral'nye stranitsy* (Moscow, 1979)
Rzhevsky L., 'Pilatov grekh: o taynopisi v romane Bulgakova *Master i Margarita*', *Novy zhurnal*, 90 (1968), 60–80
Sahni K., *A Mind in Ferment – Bulgakov's Prose* (New Delhi, no date, publ. Arnold Heinemann)
Sakhnovsky V. G., *Rabota rezhissyora* (Moscow–Leningrad, 1937), 201–77
Sharratt B., 'Time in the Novel: Bulgakov's *The Master and Margarita*', *Scando-Slavica*, 29 (1983), 57–67
Skobelev V., 'V pyatom izmerenii', *Pod'yom*, 6 (Voronezh, 1967), 124–8
Skorino L., 'Litsa bez karnaval'nykh masok (polemicheskiye zametki)', *Voprosy literatury*, 6 (1968), 25–42
Spasovich V., ed., *Uchebnik ugolovnogo prava*, vol. 1 (Sanktpeterburg, 1863)
Stalin I., 'Otvet Bil'-Belotserkovskomu', in his *Sobraniye sochineniy*, vol. 11 (Moscow, 1949), 326–9
Stanislavsky K. S., *Sobraniye sochineniy v 8-i tomakh*, vol. 8 (Moscow, 1961), 125, 224, 269, 270, 337, 371, 374, 406
Stenbock-Fermor E., 'Bulgakov's *The Master and Margarita* and Goethe's *Faust*', *Slavic and East European Journal*, vol. 13, 3 (1969), 309–25
Strauss D. F., *Zhizn' Iisusa*, vol. 2, *Mificheskaya istoriya Khrista*, trans. M. Sinyavsky (Moscow, 1907)
Tairov A., 'O bagrovom ostrove', *Sovremenny teatr*, 50 (11 November 1928), 803
Terts A., (Sinyavsky), 'Literaturny protsess v Rossii', *Kontinent*, 1 (1974), 143–90 (pp. 158–62)
Turkel'taub I., 'Bagrovy ostrov v Moskovskom Kamernom Teatre', *Zhizn' iskusstva*, 52 (23 December 1928), 10–11
Vega, *Apokrificheskiye skazaniya o Khriste*, vol. 1, *Kniga Nikodima*, 2nd ed. (St Petersburg, 1912)
Vilenkin V. Ya., *Vospominaniya s kommentariyami* (Moscow, 1982), 379–403
Ware T., *The Orthodox Church* (1963)
Wright A. C., 'Mikhail Bulgakov and Yury Slyozkin', *Etudes slaves et est-européennes*, 17 (1972), 85–91
Wright A. C., 'Satan in Moscow: An Approach to Bulgakov's *The Master and Margarita*', *Proceedings of the Modern Languages Association*, vol. 88, 5 (1973), 1162–72
Wright A. C., *Mikhail Bulgakov: Life and Interpretations* (Toronto, 1978)
Yanovskaya L., 'Vstupitel'noye slovo skazhet pisatel' t. Bulgakov (K biografii M. A. Bulgakova 1920gg.)', *Nauka i zhizn'*, 3 (1978), 61

Yanovskaya L., 'Kogda byla napisana *Belaya gvardiya?*', *Voprosy litera-tury*, 6 (1977), 302–7
Yanovskaya L., 'Neskol'ko dokumentov k biografii Mikhaila Bulgakova', *Voprosy literatury*, 6 (1980), 303–8
Yanovskaya L., *Tvorchesky put' Mikhaila Bulgakova* (Moscow, 1983)
Yanovskaya L., ed., 'Besedovat' s toboyu odnoyu', *Oktyabr'*, 1 (1984), 189–201
Yermolinsky S., 'O Mikhaile Bulgakove. Glava iz knigi vospominaniy', *Teatr*, 9 (1966), 79–97
Yermolinsky S., 'Mikhail Bulgakov (iz zapisok raznykh let)', in his *Dramaticheskiye sochineniya* (Moscow, 1982), 583–700
Zamyatin Ye., 'O segodnyashnem i sovremennom', *Russky sovremennik*, 2 (1924), 263–72; reprinted in his *Litsa* (New York, 1967), 211–30
Zemskaya Ye. A., 'M. A. Bulgakov: pis'ma k rodnym (1921–22g.)', *Izvestiya AN SSSR – seriya literatury i yazyka*, vol. 35, 5 (1976), 451–64
Zerkalov A., *Yevangeliye Mikhaila Bulgakova* (Ann Arbor, 1984)

(B) Additional reading

on Molière:

Barro M. V., *Mol'yer – ego zhizn' i literaturnaya deyatel'nost'* (St Peters-burg, 1891)
Chambers T., 'Bulgakov's Molieriana', *Essays in Poetics*, vol. 2, 2 (Keele, 1977), 1–26
Descaves P., *Molière en U.R.S.S.* (Paris, 1954)
Despois E., *Le Théâtre français sous Louis XIV* (Paris, 1874)
Donnay M., 'Le ménage de Molière', *L'Illustration théâtrale*, no. 212 (4 May 1912); no. 213 (11 May 1912)
Grimarest Jean Léonor Gallois, sieur de, *Vie de Monsieur de Molière* (Paris, 1705, reprinted 1930)
Ieger O., *Vseobshchaya istoriya* (5th ed., St Petersburg, no date)
Lagrange, *Registre de Lagrange (1658–1685)*, publ. Comédie française (Paris, 1876)
Mantsius K., *Mol'yer – teatry, publika, aktyory ego vremeni*, trans. from the French (Moscow, 1922)
Michaut G., *La Jeunesse de Molière* (Paris, 1922); *Les Débuts de Molière* (Paris, 1923); *Les Luttes de Molière* (Paris, 1925)
Mokul'sky S., *Mol'yer* (Moscow, 1935)
Moliere J., *Oeuvres complètes de Molière*, 3 vols (Paris, 1861)
Palmer J., *Molière* (New York, 1930, reprinted 1970)
Patouillet J., *Mol'yer v Rossii* (Berlin, 1924)
Proffer E., ed. (Documents relating to rehearsals of the Molière play), in *Neizdanny Bulgakov* (Ann Arbor, 1977), 91–135
Rigal E., *Molière*, vol. 2 (Paris, 1968)
Rudnitsky K. L., 'Mol'yer, Tartyuf i Bulgakov', *Nauka i religiya*, 1 (1972), 84–90

Sand G., *Molière*, in *Oeuvres complètes*, vol. 1 (Paris, 1877), 313–454
Savin A. N., *Vek Lyudovika XIV* (Moscow, 1913)
Sévigné Madame de, *Lettres*
Simon, A., *Molière* (Paris, 1957)
Veselovsky A., 'Zhan Poklen Mol'yer', in *Mol'yer Zh.*, ed. S. A. Vengerov, vol. 1 (St Petersburg, 1912), 447–92
Veselovsky A., *Etyudy o Mol'yere: Tartyuff* (Moscow, 1879)

on Pushkin:

Babushkin Yu., *V. V. Veresayev (k stoletiyu so dnya rozhdeniya)* (Moscow, 1966)
Bibliografiya proizvedeniy A. S. Pushkina i literatury o nyom 1918–36 (Moscow–Leningrad, 1952)
Bulgakova Ye. S., ed., 'Perepiska po povodu p'esy Pushkin *(Posledniye dni)*', *Voprosy literatury*, 3 (1965), 151–71
Grossman L., *Zapiski d'Arshiaka – Peterburgskaya khronika 1836 goda* (Khar'kov, 1929)
Lents V. V., 'Priklyucheniya liflyandtsa v Peterburge', in *Russky arkhiv*, Kniga 1 (1878), 436–68
Less A., 'K istorii *Pushkina*', in his *Neprochitannye stranitsy* (Moscow, 1966), 251–8
Nemirovich-Danchenko V. I., 'Sokrashchonnaya stenogramma zamechaniy Vl. I. Nemirovicha-Danchenko po spektaklyu *Posledniye dni (Pushkin)*', in *Yezhegodnik MKhAT-a za 1943* (Moscow, 1945), 681–707
Proffer, E., ed., 'Bulgakov's Notebooks for *Posledniye dni*', *Russian Literature Triquarterly*, 3 (1972), 431–44
Pushkin A. S., *Polnoye sobraniye sochineniy v desyati tomakh*, 4th ed. (Leningrad, 1977–9)
Shchogolev P. Ye., *Duel' i smert' Pushkina*, 3rd ed. (Moscow–Leningrad, 1928)
Veresayev V. V., *Duel' i smert' Pushkina* (Moscow, 1927)
Veresayev V. V., *Pushkin v zhizni*, originally published in 3 vols. (Moscow, 1929); 6th ed., 2 vols. (Moscow, 1936)
Veresayev V. V., *Rodstvenniki Pushkina* (Moscow, 1933)
Veresayev V. V., *Sputniki Pushkina*, 2 vols. (Moscow, 1934, reprinted 1937)
Veresayev V. V., *Zhena Pushkina* (Moscow, 1935)
Vickery W. N., *Pushkin – Death of a Poet* (Indiana, 1968)
Yanovskaya L., ed., 'Mikhail Bulgakov: iz chernovykh tetradey p'esy *Aleksandr Pushkin*', *Zvezda*, 6 (1974), 202–4

on Gogol:

Annenkov P. V., 'N. V. Gogol' v Rime letom 1841 goda', in his *Literaturnye vospominaniya* (Moscow, 1960), 47–132

Chebotareva V. A., 'O gogolevskikh traditsiyakh v proze M. Bulgakova', *Russkaya literatura*, 1 (1984), 166–76

Chudakova M. O., 'Bulgakov i Gogol'', *Russkaya rech'*, 2 (1979), 38–48; and 3 (1979), 55–9

Danilov S. S., *Gogol' i teatr* (Leningrad, 1936), 241, 267–70

Fayman G., 'Na polyakh issledovaniya o Bulgakove', *Voprosy literatury*, 12 (1981), 195–211

Gogol N. V., *Sochineniya i pis'ma N. V. Gogolya*, ed. V. V. Kallash, vol 8 (St Petersburg, 1896)

Gogol N. V., *Sobraniye sochineniy v shesti tomakh* (Moscow, 1949–50)

Milne L., 'M. A. Bulgakov and *Dead Souls*: The Problems of Adaptation', *Slavonic and East European Review*, LII, 128 (1974), 420–40

Veresayev V. V., *Gogol' v zhizni* (Moscow–Leningrad, 1933)

Yegorov B. F., 'M. A. Bulgakov – 'perevodchik' Gogolya (intsenirovka i kinostsenariy *Myortvykh dush*, kinostsenariy *Revizora*)', in *Yezhegodnik rukopisnogo otdela Pushkinskogo doma – 1976* (Leningrad, 1978), 57–84

on Romanticism:

Abrams M. H., *The Mirror and the Lamp. Romantic Theory and the Critical Tradition* (New York, 1953)

Beletsky A. I., *Russky romantizm – sbornik statey* (Leningrad, 1927)

Bowra C. M., *The Romantic Imagination* (1950, reprinted Oxford, 1961)

Fadeyev A., 'Doloy Shillera!' (1929), in *Za 30 let* (Moscow, 1957), 63–71

Goethe J. W., *Torquato Tasso*, trans. J. Prudhoe (Manchester, 1979)

Gofman (Hoffmann) E. T. A. – bibliografiya russkikh perevodov i kriticheskoy literatury, compiled by Z. V. Zhitomirskaya (Moscow, 1964)

Gor'ky M., 'O tom, kak ya uchilsya pisat'' (1928), in *O literature – stat'i i rechi 1928–36* (Moscow, 1937)

Kermode F., *The Romantic Image* (Fontana, 1957)

Levina Ya. B., 'Romantika v tvorchestve sovetskikh pisateley pervoy poloviny 20–kh godov' (Avtoreferat kandidatskoy dissertatsii, Tbilisi, 1969)

Oulanoff H., *The Serapion Brothers – Theory and Practice* (The Hague–Paris, 1966)

Neuhauser R., *The Romantic Age in Russian Literature – Poetic and Aesthetic Norms. An Anthology of Original Texts (1800–50)* (Munich, 1975)

Mayevskaya T. P., *Romanticheskiye tendentsii v russkoy proze kontsa XIX veka* (Kiev, 1978)

Mersereau J., 'Pushkin's Concept of Romanticism', *Studies in Romanticism*, vol. 3 (1963), 24–41

Mersereau J., 'Yes, Virginia, there was a Russian Romantic movement', *Russian Literature Triquarterly*, 3 (1972), 128–47

Mirimsky I., 'Sotsial'naya fantastika Gofmana', *Literaturnaya uchoba*, 5 (1938), 63–87

Poe E. A., *Selected Writings* (Penguin, 1967)

Problemy romantizma – sbornik statey, ed. U. R. Fokht (Moscow, 1967)

Proffer C. R., 'Gogol's Definition of Romanticism', *Studies in Romanticism*, 6 (1967), 120–7

Schenk H. G., *The Mind of the European Romantics* (Oxford, 1966); with a Preface by Isaiah Berlin

Schiller F., *On the Naive and Sentimental in Literature*, trans. H. Watanabe O'Kelly (Manchester, 1981)

Serapionovy Brat'ya, *Zagranichny al'manakh* (Berlin, 1922, reprinted Munich, 1973)

Shroder M. Z., *Icarus – the Image of the Artist in French Romanticism* (Harvard, 1961)

Trilling L., *Sincerity and Authenticity* (Oxford, 1974)

Wellek R., *Confrontations* (Princeton, 1965)

West J., *Russian Symbolism – A Study of Vyacheslav Ivanov and the Russian Symbolist Aesthetic* (London, 1970)

Zalesskaya L. I., *O romanticheskom techenii v sovetskoy literature* (Moscow, 1973)

Zhirmunsky V., 'O poezii klassicheskoy i romanticheskoy' (1920), in *Voprosy teorii literatury – stat'i 1916–26* (reprinted The Hague, 1962).

Addenda

Atti del Convegno 'Michail Bulgakov' (Gargnano del Garda, 1984), ed. E. Bazzarelli and J. Křesálkova (Milan, 1986).

Natov N., *Mikhail Bulgakov* (TWAS: Boston, 1985).

Index

Index

247